A Westminster Childhood

A Westminster

JOHN RAYNOR

Illustrations by Dennis Flanders

CASSELL · LONDON

Childhood

CASSELL & COMPANY LTD
35 Red Lion Square, London WC1R 4SG
Sydney, Auckland, Toronto,
Johannesburg
Copyright © Sarah Olwen Picton-Jones 1973
Illustrations by Dennis Flanders
copyright © Cassell & Co. Ltd 1973

First published 1973

ISBN 0 304 29183 8

PRINTED IN GREAT BRITAIN BY A. WHEATON & COMPANY, EXETER.

F 173

Contents

In Memoriam

Arthur Guy Sandars Raynor
Ada Shute Raynor

'We neither censure fear nor beg applause,
For these are Westminster's and Sparta's laws.'
Matthew Prior

'That voice that had always something of the
battle-cry in it.'
(From the obituary notice of A.G.S.R. in *The Elizabethan*)

Time

I

The Dawn

I was born on Saturday, 5 June, 1909, at breakfast-time. This caused my father some displeasure, as he had to leave his boiled egg, which he had just cracked, upon hearing the news; and, in any case, he never cared to be disturbed at breakfast. The scene of my birth was two long storeys above the dining-room in an eighteenth-century house, so that when my father at last got back to his egg it was quite cold, its attendant toast was flaccid, and the coffee rank and bitter. Nor was a substitute meal possible, as my father had to take his form at nine. However, both he and I survived this unfortunate beginning.

My father was Master of the King's Scholars at Westminster School, and I therefore had the good fortune to be born at Number 3, Little Dean's Yard, that inmost court of an inner court, the quietest and dreamiest place in London, where footsteps echo sharply in the silence, where the chimes of Big Ben and of the Abbey clock fall through the air like coloured stars against the hushed monotone of distant traffic, and where in the trees of the College Garden the pigeons croon a languid benediction. In holiday time, that is. During the term the Yard is alive with the voices of boys, the sound of fives-balls, the sound of rackets; or with the murmured drone from class-rooms; or the uplifted voice of the sergeant taking drill. The three houses, Rigaud's, Grant's, and Number 3, stand with solid solemnity, their large old windows looking down upon the stream of generations that passes below, the shouting boys who are replaced by other shouting boys, and by other shouting boys.

Number 3 stands at the far end of the Yard. As a child I was always delighted by its two (to a child) distinguishing features; it had double steps up to the front door, so that you could run up one side and down the other, and hide, having rung the bell half-way; and it had a plaque commemorating one Walter Titley let in above the fanlight of the front door, a plaque that gave it great distinction and grandeur and an air of haughty superiority that was very pleasing. I used to speculate a good deal about Walter Titley, and wonder whether his was one of the innumerable ghosts whose playground the house was, and I used to wish also that my name was on the plaque instead of his. Indeed, in honesty I must admit still, that nothing would give me greater pleasure in a minor way than to see another smaller, humbler plaque inset above the doorway of Number 3 with the inscription : Here was born John Raynor, the Composer.

It was a huge old rambling house of four storeys. There were cellars and basement kitchens; study, dining-room and store-cupboards (one for father and one for mother); the drawing-room and a bedroom; the nursery, two bedrooms, a dressing-room, bath-room and lavatory; and finally four attics. There was a front stair-case, and a back staircase that was useful for escape if one had been naughty, but that was so horribly haunted as to be worse than most ordinary punishments. It was an exciting house for a child, full of unexpected cupboards and dark passage-ways, dimly lit at night by rather primitive electricity; above all, a house with a personality that was a blend of smaller personalities. Every land-ing, every staircase, every room had its own smell and atmosphere —and its own ghosts. But what finally singled out Number 3 from the other masters' houses, what made it so utterly desirable to a child, was that it, and it alone, had a garden. A real garden with lime and plane trees; a garden in which could be seen the ebb and flow of the seasons, a garden where crocuses and daffodils flowered in the spring, and bonfires of dead leaves smouldered in the autumn, where in the summer one could lie on the lawn and read, and in winter make a proper snowman with pebbles for eyes and buttons; pebbles carefully collected from the little gravelled path and as carefully replaced, under pain of father's displeasure, at the first sign of a thaw.

*　　*　　*

The earliest dawning of consciousness is a difficult thing to remember. Two incidents when I was two years old, and one when I was three, remain clearly in the memory. The first took place, not in London, but at Stoke Dry, a tiny Rutlandshire village where we were spending the summer holidays of 1911. In fact each summer since I had been born had been spent there, but I have only a single memory of the place. I was just over two years old : I remember something that with great difficulty you had to lift yourself over; it was called 'step'. Beyond that was something solid and dark called 'door'. On this door were pieces of something black, not part of the door, but fixed to it. This door, with its pieces, spoke directly to me in the language that I perfectly understood, that was not words. From the door to me streamed fear; fear that gripped me in the stomach, fear that convulsed my whole small being. From object to child streamed, uninterrupted, this deadly flow of terror. If I ever found myself alone anywhere near 'door', I would scream with paralysed fear; when, holding my mother's hand, we approached 'door' together, the hair on my scalp would bristle and rise. I never forgot 'door' and I never understood it until some twenty years later, the next time I saw Stoke Dry. I had driven my father and mother over from Huntingdon to spend the day at this beloved old haunt of theirs. I remembered nothing of the place. Then my mother said. 'Let's go into the church by the side door, the way we always used to.' We walked round the church, and suddenly I was face to face with 'door'. I remembered it perfectly, and the same fear, modified and dulled by adulthood, rose in me. I knew it then for what it was. I said : 'I remember this door perfectly, Mother. I feared it then, and I don't like it now. There's something wrong with it.'

I bent to examine it closely. It was a door of about the sixteenth century, oak and nail-studded, and still nailed to it, almost a part When I turned round, my mother was looking at me curiously. of it, were a few withered strips of a black parchment-like material. 'I tried never to let you go to that door,' she said, 'but you would go there and scream. I never liked it much myself.'

'What's wrong with it, Mother?' I asked.

'Nothing's supposed to be wrong with it,' she said, with the faint and rather tired smile that with her was characteristic of a certain approach to things, 'but it's one of the few doors left in England that still has strips of human skin, malefactors' skin, nailed to it. The Abbey Chapter House, of course, is another.'

'I wonder,' I said slowly, 'if that's why, as a child, one of the words I couldn't bear was "flay"?'

'I don't know,' she said; 'but I am quite sure that no one then ever told you about the door.'

I knew, however, that the meaning of the word 'flay' had been conveyed to me in a manner that by-passed the use of words at all, at the age of two, by those tattered black strips.

Such was the first of my conscious memories, and not a very pleasant one; the other two were of a totally different nature.

It was a winter's afternoon; I was standing on the landing outside the nursery, looking out of the window down into the yard. I was about to be taken for a walk. My nurse appeared, holding my buff-coloured coat in her hand.

'You'd better wear your covert coat this afternoon, Master John,' she said; 'it's going to rain.'

As I stood there, impatiently suffering my arms to be guided into the sleeves, I suddenly knew that I was me, and no one else. My separate identity was profoundly and startlingly clear; hitherto, I had given myself no conscious thought whatsoever. Now I saw myself detachedly, standing looking out of the window, putting my coat on, filled with secret power and glee, because I was me, and nobody—no one at all—could stop me being me. The knowledge was strange, secretive, almost sly; I felt that I did not want anyone to know what I had discovered. That this moment was of profound importance in my life is clear from the vividness of the pictured scene; a scene that has never been forgotten, that will be dissolved only by death. It was as though I had stepped out of my body, was standing a little behind myself and to the right, and was watching the little boy, John Raynor, as he got ready to go out for a walk with his nurse. At the same time, I inescapably was the little boy, John Raynor. That scene, with innumerable variations, has been repeated thousands of times during my life, but I have always had the power of controlling it; I have always been able at will to slide the ghostly, watching John Raynor back into its sensuous, feeling, flesh-and-blood counterpart. This is the first essential of the true creative artist, that he should be able both to live unselfconsciously his experiences, and detach himself with equal lack of selfconsciousness from them; that he should see himself acting and not see himself acting. Here was my first glimpse of the paradox that life is.

I stood on the landing for half a minute or so, quite still, and thinking; then my nurse's sharp impatience returned me to normal life. The moment passed; though it had passed and I again was a small animal, there was a difference; consciousness of my identity had been firmly and forever established. I have never, as far as I know, had a covert coat since; I have never heard the phrase again; but from the dust of the years the words rise, I can hear still the voice of my nurse speaking them : 'You'd better wear your covert coat this afternoon, Master John; it's going to rain.'

*   *   *

And rain it did, on the occasion of the third of my early memories. Rain that I shall never forget, a pelting downpour, luminous and pearly, silver-grey, slanting strings from sky to earth. It was the following summer, we were on our way to Overstone, a village in Northamptonshire, for the holidays. At the station a cart was waiting to convey us to the Rectory. We all huddled, my father, my mother, Nurse, cook, the housemaid and myself, under the tarpaulin roof of the cart. I remember that I cried and cried as the horse jogged along the drenched roads; I could not stop crying. Why I was unhappy I have no idea. It seems to me that very small children often do not know the cause of unhappiness; it just is so, they are unhappy. I cried and screamed against the wind and rain, refusing the comfort of nurse or father. Every time I looked through the arched doorway of the cart, the grey rain was streaming down; and every time the sight renewed my tears, tears seemingly so copious that they must have substantially added to the legacy of the rain.

At last my mother in desperation cleared her lap of the luggage upon it, including cook's canary in its cage that went with us every year (as did her cat, until the fatal day that it leapt from the train window and was never seen again), and lifted me tenderly onto that warm and comforting plateau. I buried my face in mother's breast for reassurance, where I could not see, and could only just hear, the rain as it beat a tattoo upon the roof, and gradually my tears lessened. I snuggled into the safest and dearest place I knew; there flowed that contact from my mother to myself and back that was without words, that was the reversal and the antidote to the door at Stoke Dry; and at last in the warm, safe darkness I fell asleep. I awoke to find myself being lifted from the cart and carried into the open doorway of Overstone Rectory. Mother was looking down on me and smiling. I smiled back, the memory of my tears and agonized unhappiness now very dim. There passed between us that quick look of complete understanding that I have never cerebrally understood. It may be because of that look that the memory of going to Overstone in the rain is one that brims my mind with happiness. Perhaps the happiness was born from the discovery of shelter, and what it could mean, for the first time; perhaps it was the happiness of paradox. Be that as it may, this memory is the last of the very early impressions, all three of which were isolated; sharp pictures held against a background too dim for recollection. This third and last impression completed my entry into the clear and conscious world of sentient beings. Selfhood was an accepted fact. I knew *who* I was, my age and my name; *what* I was could never again be known by me with quite the same primitive sharpness of focus.

2

The Abbey

The framework of religion changes almost imperceptibly from age to age, but the heart of the matter remains constant. My father and mother were deeply religious people; the fact that outwardly, perhaps, they tended to conform to the harp-and-cloud conception is irrelevant. Nor does the fact that my father's taking of Holy orders was to some extent a matter of convenience affect his innate perception of spiritual truths. He was a reserved man, and to talk about his faith would have appeared to him a breach of good manners. The religion of my parents was of the solid good old-fashioned type. They believed in faith by works, and they read the Bible as part of life's daily round.

I was named after John the Baptist. Some months before I was born my mother consulted her Bible in the traditional manner.

It opened at St Luke, XIII, 13 : 'And thou shalt call his name John. . . .' And so it was; and Theodore was added, presumably to clinch matters. And indeed, I must have seemed like a gift of God. For ten years my mother had borne no children, and my advent was a nine days' wonder in the perhaps rather turgid waters of Abbey society. I only just scraped into life by the skin of my teeth, for my mother was forty-three when I was born. I have always been profoundly grateful that I did; and I have always tried to enjoy life, both 'the bright and the dark', from this sense of gratitude. It was, however, like being an only child; my brother and two sisters were so much older than myself that I belonged to a different generation altogether. Nevertheless, the only child who is not an only child has many adventures, especially if his is a lonely, anti-social and contemplative nature. There were children for me to play with, but often I preferred to be alone so that I could establish contact with the so-called inanimates, whose intense animism put the sluggish animism of most humans in the shade.

The largest, the most powerful and the most dominating of these inanimates was the Abbey, whose vast, grey airy bulk overshadowed all our lives. With its twin towers, its long nave and chancel, it sailed like a perfectly poised ship mysteriously arrested in motion on its grassy sea. The sun shone on fretted pinnacle and sculptured apse, on flying buttress and gilded clock-hand; the rain washed that mysterious white fabric to grey; the moon peered with silver eye into crevice and crenellation. The Abbey stood, dreaming, impervious, man's tangible monument to God, eternally pointing to the heavens. 'But where shall wisdom be found? and where is the place of understanding? Man knoweth not the price thereof; neither is it found in the land of the living. . . . It cannot be gotten for gold, neither shall silver be weighed for the price thereof . . . it is hid from the eyes of all living, and kept close from the fowls of the air. . . . God understandeth the way thereof, and he knoweth the place thereof. For he looketh to the ends of the earth, and seeth under the whole heaven; To make the weight for the winds; and he weigheth the waters by measure. When he made a decree for the rain, and a way for the lightning of the thunder : Then did he see it, and declare it, he prepared it, yea, and searched it out. And unto man he said, Behold, the fear of the Lord, that is wisdom; and to depart from evil is understanding.'

That was what the Abbey said, and went on saying, every hour of every day, week by week, month by month, year by year. Its ubiquitous presence ensured that one never wholly forgot the ascending spiritual impulse that life should be. Most holy and precious to me was the Abbey when man was not using it. In a dim unformulated way I felt that 'services' were not only unnecessary, but an obscuring shutter between God and myself. Occasionally, in the evening, when it had been closed to the public, my mother and I would wander through the great, silent building, along the aisle and transept, into St Faith's Chapel, with its rather frightening blend of windowless darkness and saintly intensity, an intensity that seemed to me sometimes to verge upon hysteria. Mother would kneel in silent prayer; I would kneel, too, pretending to myself that I knew how to pray. Then we would come out again into the south transept, and occasionally would make our way into Henry the Seventh's Chapel, with its exquisite ceiling whose only counterparts are at Windsor and King's, Cambridge. A beautiful place, but a cold place, with something faintly forbidding about it (was it the banners?) that was not really overcome by the interesting fact that there my father and mother had been married, and I christened. I was always pleased to get back to the warm, listening bulk of the building, where age and sanctity wrapped one protectively around. It would be utterly still and silent as dusk fell, the great length of the building lying relaxed, like a sleeping animal. Then from far off one might hear a clatter whose echoes mildly exploded in the distance; and the old night-watchman would come shuffling round, my mother and he would start talking, and I would slip away (but never far) to explore among the shadowy monuments.

There was an evening in the winter when I was standing still, all by myself, waiting for Mother and the watchman to stop talking, so that I could ask him to show me his mysterious clock, when from far above me something happened, like a great breathing in the dark, a breathing that vibrated in the soles of my feet and in my stomach. While I stood, undecided as to whether to wait or run, there stole out above this breathing a single pure sound, and another sound and another; and these sounds began to weave in and out among each other and form a beauty so quiet and so divine that the whole of my small being rose in ecstatic inquiry and acceptance. I had never known, and yet I had always known, that life could do this. Slowly and almost imperceptibly the sounds increased until the whole Abbey was surging and rocking with this rich and heavenly flow. Then, suddenly, the tubas flamed out, a red-gold incandescence, and it seemed that the very heart of the pain and beauty was exposed. Bursting into wild tears, half of excitement and half of fear, I stumbled back along the transept aisle to Mother. I could not explain; and the watchman, to comfort me, unlocked his clock, that tall thin clock with the odd dial, and lifted me up quite close to it. And all the time the music poured itself down from the roof, sinking now, till at last there was only the strange breathing; and that, too, died away into silence. Filled with intense excitement and rapture I trotted home with Mother, holding tight to her comforting hand, through the long gas-lit cloisters and out into the moonlight that flooded Little Dean's Yard. I was four years old, and it was the first time the Abbey had spoken to me directly, through the organ.

*　　*　　*

It was not long after this that the rather uncompromising religious views of my parents began to have effect. I was taken to Mattins and Ante-Communion in the Abbey every Sunday morning by my mother. It was a long service—two hours—and I disliked it intensely. In the hard morning light the Abbey, with its innumerable furnishings and statuary, looked fussy and uninspiring. The droning voices of the Canons as they read the lessons, the interminable prayers, and above all the endless dreary sermon (as it seemed to me then; and I am not sure that I have changed much) all weighed heavily on my youthful restlessness. Only the singing I liked; and even then there was a thing called 'Anthem', very long, that only the choir sang. I remember once asking my mother what an anthem was, and being met by the surprisingly flippant reply: 'If I said to you, "Have a piece of cake, cake, cake, a piece, a piece, a piece of cake, cake, have cake, a piece of cake, have cake, a piece of cake," that would be an anthem, darling, or that is how they are constructed, rather; for they are, of course, about God.'

'Do you like them?' I asked, puzzled.

'Sometimes,' replied Mother guardedly. I am now inclined to wonder whether even she didn't sometimes chafe under the length of the duller eighteenth-century verse-anthems. At any rate, after a time she took pity on my boredom, and, relenting a little, brought me out before the sermon.

We had our special seat in the Abbey; it was to the right of, and quite close to, the choir-stalls. It was a good place to sit. One could watch the choir-boys in their scarlet cassocks and white surplices; one could look across the packed north transept at a sea of faces; or one could lift one's eyes to the beautiful rose window; the exquisitely satisfying wheel of moving colour, rose and blue; while the one behind that one could only see by turning right round and risking a stern reprimand, was like evening; a patchwork of yellow, amber and red-gold glass. When I was tired of looking at the rose window and trying to identify its saints, I would lower my eyes again to the congregation. Sometimes there was someone I knew sitting in the transept; old Mrs Erskine, for instance, with her wrinkled ivory face, her large black velvet hat trimmed with lace, her rubber-tipped sticks, and her fat, jolly maid, Lena. Or my cousins, Elsa and Teddy, from Number 1, Little Dean's Yard, would wink across the chancel at me. Sometimes, and then I would fidget and turn white and try to look anywhere else, there was the dreadful old lady whom I and my cousins had nicknamed Mrs Cross. I never knew her real name, nor did I ever speak to her. But there were moments when her eyes would meet mine across the chancel, and I would shiver and turn cold inside. She was a very old lady indeed; her face, with a few wisps of untidy grey hair hanging round it, was like a skull in which two deep-sunk eyes blazed and silently snarled. She was tall and thin, like an old stick, and her tattered clothes, that had once been black and were now green with age, hung loosely on her shrunken frame. A rusty black hat, like an inverted soup bowl, or the cap of a black mushroom, crazily surmounted her shaking and tottering head. There was a terrible malignancy about Mrs Cross, or so it seemed to me; and when Mother found out how much I feared the old lady, she would take me to a different seat on those days when Mrs Cross was there. I was sure that Mrs Cross was a witch; and even now if in the dusk I come upon a scarecrow, its tattered draperies flapping in the wind, I am irresistibly reminded of her. Perhaps I am wrong; perhaps she was a very nice old lady indeed, with a real love for small boys; but somehow I do not think so.

*   *   *

Very occasionally I was taken to Evensong. I enjoyed this, especially in the winter, as much as I disliked Mattins. For the Abbey was full, at that time of day, with shadows and warmth and the intangible mystery of a great building dimly lit. The clustered electric light pendants cast a soft glow upon masonry and woodwork, and the roof was no more than a sketched suggestion of boss and spandrel; it seemed to be suspended in space, and sometimes I used to wonder whether it was really there at all, and half expect to see the stars shining faintly above me. Then, as the choir came in and the verger shut the gates, and the organ played softly, timelessness would descend and envelop the whole great Abbey. Light and music and prayer; and a strange, warm dusty smell, compounded of the exhalations of wood and stone and surplice and prayer-book, a smell that was a kind of spiritual incense, rising all the time, a subtle, invisible supplication to God.

And, most beautiful of all, were the candles, in their tall tulip-shaped glasses, that lit the choir-stalls, and cast a fitful light over music-desks and choristers. Sometimes, a rare and special treat, I used to be allowed to sit in my brother-in-law's stall. It was like a little Gothic room (he was Custodian and Minor Canon), and had rich, comfortable cushions, and from it one looked right down on the choir-stalls, on the grey heads of the lay-clerks, and the fair and red and dark ones of the boys, and on the white sheets of paper covered with little black dots that mysteriously told the choir how they were to sing the anthem.

One evening I especially remember, when I was five or six years old. I remember, even, the day of the month. I was taught very early to find the psalms for the day, and this was the fifteenth; the evening that has the longest psalm of all, apart from the 119th. I did not, however, mind the length, as I always enjoyed the psalms with their antiphonal verses that were like a game, the ball flung from Decani to Cantoris, from Cantoris to Decani, and back again until the Gloria. I was sitting in my brother-in-law's stall in superb lonely grandeur. The psalm started, and I stood up. The chant had a melancholy beauty that touched my imagination; there was a sudden high note in the second half that shone, through the medium of the boys' voices, like a bright silver star, pure, clear, primitive. I watched the mouths of the Cantoris boys as they expelled this beautiful sound, and finally my glance came to rest on the head boy. He stood, holding his psalter, alternately singing and silent. He was a tall boy with straight, fair hair and rosy cheeks, and the candlelight fell full on his child's face that was just beginning to be touched by adolescence; on the soft pleats of his snow-white surplice, on the sleeves of his scarlet cassock, and on the Elizabethan ruff that encircled his young neck. A kind of shy, golden purity seemed to emanate from him; his eyes remained demurely fixed on his book. He stood there, a perfect exposition of youthful beauty; the English wild rose personified; and my whole being melted in sudden response to the innate, essential loveliness that certain human beings possess. I had no desire to speak to him, to know him, I merely wanted to look at him, to absorb this beauty that was so perfect in its poise and detachment. On and on went the psalm, and I stood as in a dream, drinking in the blend of candlelit boy and a moment in time. And even now, recapturing the scene as I write, I cannot believe that that beautiful being, the very incarnation of youth, is a middle-aged man, if indeed he still lives.

*   *   *

Such was Westminster Abbey; a source of steadfast, if unconscious, inspiration to the developing sensibilities of an acutely sensitive child. Always it was with one. Every afternoon at a quarter to three the bells rang through the yard, calling the faithful to Evensong; I heard them as I impatiently endured the hateful but necessary 'rest' of a small child. Every Sunday the full twelve bells rang and clashed, clashed and rang; thrillingly and mysteriously muffled sometimes if a celebrity had died. Every Sunday morning came the walk through the cloisters to Mattins, and the much more exciting moment when, the service over, we left by the nave door to emerge into the cold, exhilarating, dusty smell of the cloisters while the organ thundered out the noble Rheinberger Sonata in E flat minor or one of the more jubilant of the Bach Chorale Preludes; and the daisies (if it was spring) shone white and tantalizing in the forbidden Garth.

As quite a small child I was, if not encouraged, certainly not discouraged from wandering round the Abbey by myself. It was my friend, and I loved it deeply and inarticulately; and only occasionally did I catch glimpses of something not good, a vague stirring of hints of evil in certain parts of the building; a dark corner here, an uneasy tomb there. Once, indeed, I knew horror. My brother-in-law took me to some part of the building that I cannot place. There was a window of clear glass, very high up; and in some of the panes there were round black obscurities, like rooks' nests; opaque against the daylight. What it was about them I do not know; but they filled me with unreasoning terror; and I have since dreamt many times of that unpleasant window. But though I have tried to find it again, I have never succeeded. And anyway, I knew that whatever was imprisoned there was powerless to disturb for long the great protective holiness that the Abbey extended to me.

* * *

And so, through the medium of the Abbey, was fostered in me a deep love for and need of religion. How well and truly the foundations were laid in me I am only now beginning to understand. There was a period in youth when I sincerely believed that I was an atheist; but even then I must have known deep in my heart that the bonds were too strong. Never now shall I escape from the knowledge gained in my childhood years; nor have I any wish whatsoever to do so.

I was beginning to learn how to 'worship the Lord in the Beauty of Holiness'; it remained for my father to show me the other side of the quotation; how to worship the Lord in the Holiness of Beauty. One winter's evening after tea which I had had (a very rare treat at the age of five) in the study, Father looked out of the window, and then said : 'Get your coat and we'll walk down the garden.' This was unusual, and excitedly I ran to get my coat. We went out of the French window of the study, down the steps, and into the cold, shadowy, rustling garden. We had had one bonfire that afternoon, and the smell still lingered faintly on the air as we walked down the gravel path. We were going to have another tomorrow, and the piled-up heaps of dead leaves whispered and fluttered in a little wind that roamed up and down the garden and through the bare branches of the trees. Father walked slowly, with his hand in mine. It was a wonderful, starlit night, and he was silent. I said nothing either, trying to match my quick short steps to his long slow ones. We came to the narrow enclosed alleyway that led to the door of the garden. Here our footsteps sounded

strange and hollow, and it was very dark. I never quite liked this
passage, and I held Father's hand tightly. We came to the back
door, father released the snib, and we stepped out into Great
College Street. It was silent and empty; the tall old houses rose
before us, their designs of cowls and chimney-pots etched against
the starry sky, here and there the orange square of a window
glowing warmly. Nothing stirred; there was no sound but the
faraway roar of traffic and the whispering of the small lost wind
about our faces. Across the street the window of the school
cobbler's shop shone uncurtained; behind the glass, a cat lay
curled in a sleeping ball. We stood still for a moment, listening
as it seemed, with expectation; my hand was firmly clasped in
Father's, and the strange racial bond, blood of one blood, flesh
of one flesh, stirred. Then, standing there in the silent, deserted
street, my father took the face of his son between his hands, and
turning it upwards to the starlit heavens held it so. He said one
word : 'Look.' Thus we stood for a few moments; then, without
speaking, we walked back up the garden and indoors again.

3

Ghosts

I inherit from my mother, Scottish, and the seventh child of a
seventh child, the profoundest psychic receptivity. As a small child
it was beyond me to question certain perceptions and knowledge;
from the beginning I accepted them as I accepted my ten pink
toes, the colour of my hair, the colour of my eyes. Indeed, I have
never been able to question them for a moment; the fact that
adult life and applied mental self-control have brought about a
lessening of fear in no way invalidates the basic perceptions. For
the benefit of myself and others, I sometimes pretend that such
perceptions are not there, or I ignore them, that is all. The ques-

tion : 'Do you believe in ghosts?' has always interested me more from the point of view of exact definition than any other. I have never seen a ghost with the physical eyes (though I am not quite sure of that statement); but with the inward eye I certainly have. On the other hand, I have undoubtedly heard a ghost with the physical ears, and smelt one with the physical nose. If, and it is a large if, 'ghost' is the right word. Sometimes only a state of intense awareness is present, spinning horrible and black; sometimes (but more rarely) its opposite, crystal-clear and holy; but equally often a 'presence' is felt, and that is the only word I can find that even begins to approximate to accuracy. As though atmosphere had gathered itself round a central column of energy, and was half-way (and sometimes very much nearer than that) to materialisation. But there is no point in trying further to define what everyone gifted with psychic awareness will already understand.

The present house of the Master of the King's Scholars was built in 1790, but undoubtedly parts of it are very much older than that; and in any case, whatever house stood there before that date stands there still from a psychic point of view. The present house, built on ancient sites, holds its ghostly predecessors within it. As a small child, running up its three long flights of front stairs, and its two back ones, I was always, especially at night, aware of different and delicate waves of feeling. I hold to this day in my mind a kind of psychic map of the house; this patch coloured red, that green, that yellow; only not in colours but in sense-perceptions. As I have hinted before, the back stairs were the most unfriendly part of the house, especially at the landing where stood the grim and heavy door that communicated with the college dormitory. The front stairs were safer; but between the drawing-room and the nursery landings at an angle in the stairs stood an alcove with two deep corner cupboards, that made one think twice before running down from the nursery to the drawing-room after nightfall. As I grew older, the fear increased rather than lessened; and when I was about eleven I would go to absurd lengths to avoid going downstairs at all. And on one occasion, I felt sure that for a second a black figure stood motionless, with folded arms, in this alcove, before the velvet depth of shadows claimed it; and after that the ordeal of passing the place gave birth to an acute species of mental torture, of which I never spoke to anyone.

There was the drawing-room, where the strangest unhappiness would fall without warning upon one; there was my sister's bedroom in which I occasionally slept, if slept is the word (the worst room, perhaps, in the house with one exception to be mentioned later), where I used to watch the filament of the electric light glow red for a second as it was turned off and think that it was devils' teeth; there was Nurse's room under the roof, that was so high up and that so pressed down on one as though it would mercilessly crush one to death if it could; and opposite, across the landing, the Blue Room.

The Blue Room was a large, square box-room full of yellow trunks and faded old newspapers; of unwanted articles of furniture, and rolls of wallpaper. Along one side of it, against the cold blue wallpaper, hung a row of bells; poised; alert; trembling on their coiled springs; ready to swing wildly and clang through the lonely, empty room at the touch of—what? From very early days the Blue Room exercised a terrible fascination over me. Laboriously I would climb the long flights of stairs, arriving breathless and defenceless at the top of the house. Then I would stand on the landing, looking out of the window, down into the yard dotted with minute human figures; the Abbey would sail through the sky opposite; a fly would buzz in the corner of the pane, the only sound in the watching breath-held stillness; and I would turn and look at the handle of the Blue Room door. I would half expect it to be turned from within; and it would be many moments before I could summon up the courage to place my own hand on the door-knob, turn it, and push. But it was something that, morbidly, I had to do; and I never went away without doing it. I would push the creaking door open at last and venture inside, never taking my eyes off the bells for fear they would suddenly begin to ring. Once right inside, I never dared shut the door, to shut myself in; I would stand, breathing the smell that was a mixture of dust, and old paper, and something else that I could not place. It was dreadfully still and forlorn in the Blue Room; I would stand, motionless, filling up with psychic tension until suddenly I could bear it no more, and would run quickly out, feeling a breath on the back of my neck, dusty hands plucking at my shoulders; run out, very near to screaming, and slam the door to behind me. Then for a fascinated moment I would watch the handle of the closed door; and shaken, but also strangely exhilarated, would make my way downstairs to where people were and the house was living again, and not dead.

* * *

I cannot now remember exactly when I first heard the sounds, but I was certainly not more than four. I was sleeping in Nurse's room at the time of the first sound, right at the top of the house. One night I was lying awake, sleepless, when a strange, quiet metallic buzzing started. I listened for a moment, and then my heart began to beat furiously, and I buried my head under the bedclothes. Still I could hear the sound, as clearly as before. I turned and twisted, trying to escape from it, but in vain. Then suddenly it stopped; and after a few moments, when I felt fairly certain that it would not start again, I fell asleep. From then onwards, night after night it would come, and I would lie awake, sometimes for hours, waiting for it, while the night-light burned steadily away in its saucer of water, and suddenly with a splutter and heave of flame would go out and plunge the room in darkness. Then the noise would start, the quiet but penetrating musical buzzing, sometimes high, sometimes low, but always constant in volume. It was filled with sadness rather than fear, and I think that I knew it was powerless to harm me, for I never felt for it unreasoning terror, only a kind of sick awe, and a devout hope that it would not start.

On my birthday I had been given a blue tin beetle with a string to drag it by. The sound was rather like the noise this beetle made when it was pulled along the stone floor of the kitchen. For a time I half-believed that what I heard in Nurse's bedroom was my beetle, moving about by itself in the dead of night. In the daytime I used to take it out of the toy cupboard and examine it with rather frightened interest. Finally, I grew afraid of it, and from being my favourite toy it became the one I never touched. I pushed it right back into a dark corner of the cupboard, and there it stayed for years. In my heart, however, I knew that the beetle was not responsible; it was the similarity of sound that tinged it with the disagreeable. It was over twenty years before I heard the real explanation, as I shall later recount.

* * *

About a year later I was promoted to my brother's bedroom, and it was there that I heard the infinitely more terrible sound. Again, I was lying sleepless in bed when it started. It shared with the other sound a quality, greatly intensified in this case, that seems best described as dimensionless. It seemed to come from far away in the street, from the foot of the bed, and from inside my own head, at one and the same time; it had in fact no focal point whatsoever. The sound itself was a terrible whirring flutter, minute but loud, the embodiment of all hatred and fear. It would rise like a little angry scream and die away to a low moan. It was completely aware of me. The first time I heard it I was paralysed with fear; I lay under the bedclothes shivering in uncontrollable spasms. It was term-time, my brother was away at Winchester, and I was all alone in the room. (In any case, being not quite five, I was always alone for many hours before he came to bed.) I tried to call out for Nurse or Mother, but the steady waves of fear that gripped my throat prevented any sound coming out. At last it stopped, but for a long time I lay awake, staring into the oppressive darkness, till at last I could fight against tiredness no longer.

The incalculability of its appearance began to play havoc with my nerves. For nights at a stretch it would be absent; sometimes for as long as a week; then suddenly, without warning, it would strike. I would be warm and drowsy, on the point of falling asleep, and suddenly that vile fluttering whine would start, from the bed, from the street, from my head, infintely far away and as near me as the pillow. After a time I managed to tell Mother about it, and she would come and sit by my bed until I fell asleep. Then, after she had gone right downstairs again, I would sometimes suddenly wake and lie still for a moment, burdened with a dreadful, inevitable knowledge; tense, shrunk within myself; and it would start. It seemed to have some kind of intelligence, for on Friday nights, when mother was unable to sit with me because of Lit. Soc. (the School Literary Society) which was held in the drawing-room and which she always attended, it never failed to put in an appearance. The very phrase : Lit. Soc. Night, has power still to stir apprehension within me.

For several months I was tormented. I grew pale and thin, and no one knew why. At that time I had no power of expression to state with sufficient clarity and intelligibility the full extent of my feelings. The climax of this little drama arrived suddenly in the early summer of 1914. Mother had suggested that the sound was probably due to one of the chimney-cowls in the yard turning in the wind on unoiled bearings. I tried my very hardest to believe this, and the knowledge that that was what Mother thought succeeded in slightly, very slightly, easing my fear.

Then, one night early in June, I woke suddenly to hear the sound very loud and clear. With a pathetic and strange courage (strange in a child of five years old), I got out of bed, shivering with fright, climbed on to the chest of drawers, drew back the curtains and looked out of the window, determined to prove to myself whether the sound had its origin in a turning cowl. It was a night of brilliant moon; the yard, the buildings of Ashburnham, and the Abbey shone spectrally cold and clear. Every cowl was visible in the flooding light. The night was absolutely still and silent, breath-held in its utter tranquillity. And no cowl was moving.

The most terrible horror I have ever known seized me; the sound rose in pitch, fluttering with shrill evil, on and on, clear, deathly and small. Crouching there on the chest of drawers, the last pretence of comfort removed, I began to scream and scream uncontrollably. The sound brought Nurse hurrying to me; she looked at me and ran to fetch Mother. Without a word I was lifted down, safe at last in Mother's comforting arms, and carried straight to her bed for the rest of the night. In the morning a doctor came and talked to me and smiled kindly down upon me. In the afternoon I was taken into the country, to spend the next six weeks at Bramley near Guildford, with my sister Edith and her infant son. Years later Mother told me that the doctor, puzzled beyond words, had insisted on this immediate change of surroundings, as I was in imminent danger, at the age of five, of a nervous breakdown. And no one understood, except, probably, my mother, the real reason.

*　　*　　*

And here I must for a few moments digress to relate a strange experience I had at Bramley. It was then a tiny country village, completely untouched by the jerry-building that makes it now little more than a suburb of Guildford. There was, however, one excessively ugly building; gaunt, angular, and dotted with small, pointed chimneys—the Tannery. One day I was playing on the common by myself, picking harebells. Suddenly on the wind was borne the smell of the Tannery. I stood, transfixed, dropping my flowers, turning green and white, gripped by the old nameless horror. A horror so primitive that it could only have been a racial memory; a horror quite outside the bounds of thought or control; something that struck deep inside my body and turned my legs to water. Across the common I could see the ugly vicious-looking building; and the smell ebbed and flowed on the wind. With my back and the base of my neck prickling, I turned and ran, not stopping until I was safely indoors. And after that nothing, to my sister's annoyance, would induce me to play on the common again. All walks had to be taken in the opposite direction to the Tannery. Once, a cart laden with new hides passed the window; I ran and hid myself, trembling in a dark cupboard under the stairs. And every time we went for a picnic in the fields or the Wonersh woods, I would make myself and everyone else miserable by unceasingly asking if the Tannery smell could reach us. Three or four times during that holiday I inevitably smelt it again with exactly the same result. For several years afterwards, whenever we went in a train, I would anxiously ask Mother if we were likely to pass a tannery. I have never been able to explain to myself satisfactorily, except, as I have said, in terms of racial memory. why the tannery smell was a psychically unbearable one. Skins— an unpleasant word; a counter, perhaps, for something else that is better nameless, even if it could be named. It is perhaps strange that I have never smelt a tannery since; I should like to do so to see what that smell, thirty years later, would evoke. The Tannery at Bramley is no longer a tannery; it has become the factory for a well-known make of ice-cream; but were the day never so hot or my thirst so intense, I should be unable to bring myself to eat an ice of that make, even though I have a rather puerile passion for ice-cream. I should inevitably remember the raw hairy hides, the glazing blood, and the little chimneys, each with its conical cap, from which flowed the smell that was like the inarticulate agony, the frenzied terror of all the animals that have ever suffered, far from dumbly, at man's intolerably callous hands.

Despite the Tannery, I returned from Bramley fit and well again in body and spirit. My first question was : 'Can I sleep somewhere else?' to find that Mother had already arranged it. Several years passed before I again slept in my brother's bedroom; when I did so, I only twice heard the sound.

*　　*　　*

If, upon entering the front door of Number 3, you turned to the left instead of the right, you came to the back stairs. Covered with brown and green oilcloth, badly lit, steeply ascending, they subtly depressed the spirit. At the top of the first flight there stood a tiny landing; in the wall of this a grim, heavy, dark door gave access to the College Dormitory.

The first thing that struck me about Wren's Dormitory was its enormous height and length. The contrast of at one moment standing on our back stairs, and the next being in this vast building, was so violent as to be queerly shocking. The long wide corridor, stretching in dusky gloom as far as a small boy's eyes could see, had the power to make the flesh creep and tingle with awe. When one spoke it echoed; the sound of footsteps was thrown back from wall and ceiling, blankly noisy; so that one spoke in whispers; and, like Agag, walked delicately. The smell was one of the strangest I have ever known anywhere; faint yet full; sweet and aromatic. Its foundation was the smell that bricks and space combine to make; and added to that was a touch of human emanations; of clothes and shoes and faint sweat; and the whole fused to a homogeneous blend by age and tradition. Over the whole long dormitory a heavy presence seemed to brood; and caught half-way between our house and the end of the building one felt unsafe and cut off, and tempted to run. Perhaps fortunately, College Dormitory was out of bounds, so that I did not often find myself alone there. It was worst in the holidays, for in term-time there were signs of life in it; clothes flung about; beds made up; and the cheerful aftermath of atmosphere left by the boys. But in the holidays it sat there, solid and brooding and alone; and if for any reason one had to make the long journey down its corridor to Matron's little house (which, like ours, had an entrance from the dormitory itself), one would suddenly feel tricked into another world; a world where one was silently watched by innumerable eyes. Sometimes, when I was happily occupied in our house, the remembrance that College Dormitory was only just round the corner would insinuate itself into my mind, like a wedge of black shadow; and the mental image of it, gloomy, silent and untenanted (by humans anyway), would flash upon the vision with uneasy clarity.

* * *

A few months before her death in 1938, my mother and I had a talk that was extraordinarily interesting and revelatory. We had somehow got on to the subject of ghosts, a subject that Mother intensely disliked. I asked her to tell me anything she knew about our house and the College.

She hesitated. 'What do you want to know?' she asked.

'What you felt,' I said.

'It was a terribly haunted house; you knew that?'

'Yes,' I said.

'I tried to make them feel happier,' she said unexpectedly, though it was a remark entirely characteristic. I waited. 'The little boy in the drawing-room was terribly unhappy. I used to talk to him but nothing seemed to make it much better. Twice in the thirty years I lived there, I saw him. He was about eleven, and he wept bitterly and silently. Then there was the girls' room. I don't know—I never felt much there. But Father told me how once, when he first became Master of the King's Scholars, before he was married, he slept there; and though he fought it, he had to get up in the middle of the night and make a bed for himself in another room.'

'Why?' I asked; 'what did he see?'

'I don't know,' Mother replied; 'he never would tell even me. It must have been bad, because you know how level-headed and in that way ordinary he was; and how courageous, too.'

Mother was silent for a moment. Then she said, with extraordinary passion : 'And College Dormitory—oh, how I hated that. The smell, and the brooding, and the other-world feeling—oh, it was hateful.' Her voice trembled a little, and I realized what she had sometimes in the past had to endure. 'There is a story about that, you know,' she said slowly. 'A boy died in College. He was about fifteen. (This was about a hundred years ago.) He was ill, and was put to bed and looked after in the room at the top of the house; you remember, Nurse's old bedroom?' I nodded. 'This poor boy played the jews' harp. He's supposed to come through from College into our house and wander about between the backstairs and Nurse's room, playing his jews' harp. He's been seen and heard. I think he must be a very harmless ghost; and the people who have seen or heard him say that he's a very sad one. I never met him myself, and I never heard him.' She stopped and looked at me.

'You're white,' she said; 'what . . . I wish you hadn't made me tell you all this.'

'I'm very glad,' I said. 'I can't think why you never told me earlier. Did you know anything about Harold's room, where I heard that terrible sound?'

'No,' she said. 'Nothing. But I didn't always care for the feeling of it; and it is supposed to be the oldest part of the house.'

'Did this boy play the jews' harp well?'

'I believe he's supposed to be a very indifferent performer,' said Mother. I smiled. Suddenly, looking closely at me, she said : 'You heard him, John! Oh, my dear boy, when?'

'When I slept in Nurse's room.'

'Did you ever see him?'

'No. I don't believe I ever can see; only hear—and smell. Why didn't you tell me all this? It would have explained so much.'

'Because,' said my mother, 'you knew far too much about such things as it was. I didn't dare tell you, because I don't think, once you had known, you could have gone on living in that house unscathed. I was right, was I not?'

'Yes, you were,' I said. I kissed her, and was surprised to feel her trembling.

The following day's sequel is so obvious that I almost hesitate to recount it. I bought a jews' harp, an instrument that I had never seen or heard, and took it to a friend to whom I had told the story, and who said he could play it. I suppose that he was right. He certainly played it better than the dead boy; but not a great deal better.

4

The Time

It was my family's proud and justified boast that I could tell the time before I was three, for one of the first of my early interests was clocks. Of all the household inanimates they seemed to me, and still seem, to have the most animism. (I do not mean because the wheels and hands move.) Clocks are full of character. The disposition, constitution, and character of even the cheapest alarm clock is not the same as that of its brother. There are happy clocks, grave clocks, sad clocks, humorous clocks, surly clocks, pompous clocks, significant clocks, sinister clocks. Only electric clocks in their complete lack of character are merely clocks. Their deadly accuracy (unless there is a power cut) is a reflection of their lack of soul. For time, as reckoned by humans, should always be sufficiently elastic to stand pulling a minute or two one way or the other without harm. I am glad that as a child I lived before the era of electric clocks.

Unfortunately, our collection of clocks was a rather meagre and indifferent one. There was the huge kitchen wall-clock with its pattering tick and moony face; there was the black wood study clock that Father had bought before his marriage and that stands beside me as I write; it has a brass handle and dial-rim that Father always polished himself, an oil-stained face, and a strangely individualistic tick that whispers still of huge coal fires, crumpets and Patum Peperium. There was the dining-room clock of black marble, like a small mausoleum, with gilt figures on a black dial, and no minute divisions so that you could not time an egg accurately by it. (Father always boiled or poached his breakfast eggs at the table; it was the main thing that could not be entrusted to servants.) In any case, in those days it was hardly ever going. It struck the hours and half-hours on a gong; and there was a thrilling story of how Uncle William, choosing it as a wedding present, had insisted that the bell on which it struck should be removed and a gong substituted; and how, despite the shopman's protests, *it had been done!* It stood on a very high mantelpiece; and my great pleasure as a little child was to cajole the page-boy into lifting me in his strong arms until my face was level with the clock's, and I could inspect at really close range what I had squinted at remotely from the floor. In the drawing-room there was a tiny eight-day clock in a pierced brass frame, not a favourite of mine; in Mother's bedroom, a travelling clock in a red leather case; and in the nursery an old Dutch wall-clock with weight and pendulum, and Nurse's little 'Bee' clock, which was interesting because the whole back revolved to wind it. A dear little clock with a charm and sweetness all its own, it was somehow more like a fly than a bee in character.

On the whole, however, ours was a dull lot of clocks : only one out of all that lot struck, and none chimed, and I had to seek outside for my greater horological thrills. I had not far to look. A quarter of a mile away, framed in the gap between the entrance to the cloisters and the wall of College, rose the great clock of Westminster, Big Ben. Every quarter of an hour the sound of his deep bells shivered the silence of the Yard, and from the upper windows of the house his milky, netted face with its thick hands and thin figures could be seen. Mother would sometimes call to me : 'Run and get the exact time, will you, darling?' and I would scamper up the flights of stairs either to the windows of Harold's bedroom or to the landing outside the Blue Room, and shout the time down; remaining to watch in superb admiration the hands of this divine clock slowly moving closer and closer to the quarter; until, after a breathless pause as the minute hand slid squarely into the three, six, nine or twelve, the bells would ring sharply out over the sea of roofs that lay between the clock-tower and me.

Then, when the last echoes had died lingeringly away I would reluctantly turn from the window and, soberly happy, the chimes still tingling in my head, make my way slowly downstairs. Most beautiful of all was this experience when a fresh, strong wind was blowing; for then the chimes would be wafted first one way, then another; a loud note, a soft; a change of timbre and tone that trembled in its changing, as though cloud and sun chased one another across the heart of the bell-noise.

Nor were the chimes of Big Ben the only ones to be heard. There was the Abbey clock with its rather meagre ting-tang chime, and its single hour-hand, so that it was difficult to tell the exact time by looking at its dial; and a little farther off the clock of St Margaret's would spin its frail quarter chimes in the spaces of silence between the other two. In fact, the whole Yard was bell-haunted. Sometimes, the three clocks chimed together; more often half-minute (or more) intervals separated them; and then, infinitely distant, if the wind was in the right quarter, one might hear the bells of St John's, Smith Square and other Westminster churches joining in.

It was by standing at one of the top windows and watching the hands of Big Ben that I learned to tell the time so early. I shall remember all my life those happy moments; a rainy, winter day, the school and Abbey buildings veiled in mist; a fine, clear, glittering summer morning, the Abbey, more like a great ship than ever, sailing sunlit and grey above the warm, creeper-covered brick of Ashburnham House, windy clouds riding the blue sky; and always the bells, now clear and hard, now diffused and mellow, sounding every day different under changing conditions of temperature and atmosphere, and perhaps at their most heavenly and ethereal when frost held the air in its still and crystalline grip. And once, when I was very small, Mother took me up to the top landing at night, so that I could see the rows of lighted windows at Ashburnham; and in the gap the twin rosy faces of Big Ben, lit from within; while from the great tower, invisible in the dark, the bells rang Handel's old tune with a gravity and solemnity that belonged only to the night.

Rare pleasures, these; pleasures, alas, that for five long years had to be forgone; for with the coming of the Great War, the chimes of Big Ben were silenced, and his faces no longer illuminated at night.

*   *   *

But besides the Great Clock, the God-Clock, Clock its very self, there were a host of lesser clocks that on my walks with Nurse I would spy out and note in my mind. There was the two-faced clock of Mooney's Irish House, that looked slyly up and down Princes Street; the minute-hand had a counterpoise painted white. A lovely smell flowed from the building to which this clock was attached; but for some reason Nurse would always hurry me past, and if I remonstrated with her, would mutter something about it not being right for the likes of little boys to hang about such places. So I would make as much of the lovely smell as I could as we walked past, and stare up at the clock which said on the dial that it was made at Catford.

There was the Horse Guards' Clock that had one white dial with black figures that faced St James's Park, and that struck the hours on a very comic and rather tinny little bell. There was the convex face on Wellington Barracks; a nasty small clock, bad-tempered, self-important, but ultimately impotent, like a blistering sergeant-major; the clock on the Army and Navy Stores that hung over the street; the pale, large milky clock on Victoria Station that looked as though it suffered from pernicious anaemia; and near it the funny little tower at the end of the Vauxhall Bridge Road with its clock with four illuminated faces.

But the best clocks were to be found on churches; and of these my favourite was on St John's, Smith Square. Each dial was framed between pillars that supported a pent roof; the gilt hands, eloquent of their period, Queen Anne, had fascinating raised knobs. I used to stand, looking up at the clock in speechless admiration, watching to see if I could actually detect the minute-hand moving. Sometimes I thought that I could; at other times I felt depressingly aware of my failure in this direction. The last time I saw this clock the hands stood at four minutes to two, a mute and pathetic declaration of that particular moment in time when the German bomb, falling, demolished half the church and abruptly halted its faithful time-recorder. There is a haunted quality in the very position of those hands; they are eloquent of an amazed and meek resignation, and one does not have to look twice to know that it was at four minutes to two in the night and not in the day that their work so suddenly ceased.

Haunted in a different way, by the hopelessness of long neglect, was the clock on St John's Church, Pimlico, a building that always made me feel sick to look at. Of simple architectural hideousness, grimed with the soot of warehouses, its unpleasant tower reared itself among the dingy buildings of the Wilton Road. Half-way up this tower, almost indistinguishable from the fabric itself, was a tragic clock-face, that had once been black, with gold figures and hands. Now it was a drab, sooty brown, the faded figures almost invisible; the tarnished hands huddled on top of one another, at eleven minutes to ten, as though for mutual protection against the callous cruelty of the world in which they found themselves. Throughout the whole of my childhood, the hands remained in that position. It was the saddest clock I knew; and I remember how, as we turned the corner into the Wilton Road, I would dart sidelong glances at it, in the forlorn hope that at last it might be going. I would do this as unostentatiously as I could, so that there should be no tiresome explanations to grown-ups—it was a little pain that I instinctively kept hidden, for I loved clocks, and was hurt by the uselessness of one that might have become a valued member of the clock-world. But no one must find out my feelings; for I hated more than anything else the way that things that appeared natural to me so often seemed targets for the insensitive ridicule of others.

*   *   *

All things considered, my family endured my passion for clocks with exemplary patience and kindness. My grown-up sisters, Muriel and Edith, spent many hours making me clock-faces of cardboard, painting figures and fixing cardboard hands with a paper-clip through their middle so that they could be turned. I was always asked what sort of figures I would like: Roman or Arabic? and I always answered: ordinary; which was what we called Arabic. My brother Harold bought me a large wooden clock-face with movable hands at the Army and Navy Stores; and for many years it was one of my favourite toys. I would spend hours with it, getting the hour-hand into exact relationship with the minute-hand. My favourite 'times' were twenty past eight, thirteen minutes past eleven, and ten to four; and I can still feel those thick wooden hands between my fingers and the sensuous thrill of turning them. Even the page-boy, Cecil Percival, co-operated. He made me two clock-dials on a large piece of cardboard, with movable hands; at the top of this piece of cardboard it said: 'Victoria Station. Times of Arrival and Departure of Trains'; and over one dial was written 'Arrival', and over the other, 'Departure'. This simple toy gave me more lasting pleasure than anything I ever possessed as a child; and I shall always remember Cecil, who was killed in the Great War, with love and gratitude, if only for this.

My brother-in-law, too, was very kind to me about clocks. He would explain just how they worked, why one hand went twelve times as slowly as the other, why some clocks had pendulums and others balance-wheels. Once he made me a lovely little clock cut out of paper, with hands shaped from ivy-leaves; it had an ephemeral life that was a perfect counterpart to its imaginative, airy fragility; though perhaps it was less fragile than one thinks, as it lives still so vividly in the memory.

The great day came when on my fifth birthday my sister Muriel gave me the plate-clock. This was a real clock; its face was made out of a plate, it had painted apples round the edges; it came from the Army and Navy Stores, and it cost five shillings. And why I am writing about it in the past tense I cannot explain, as it hangs on the wall of the room in which I am working. It has survived the years with great gallantry; apart from the fact that the plate has been stuck in three places, it is as fresh and bright as it was the day it was bought. And even that accident happened to it only a year after I had it; for, having been told that if I touched it I would be sure to drop it, I immediately touched it and dropped it, which seemed to me at the time, and still does, grossly unfair, and probably psychically engineered by the grown-ups. It still keeps excellent time; has only had two new mainsprings in thirty-two years; and is every now and then taken to pieces and tenderly cleaned by myself. I mean to keep it all my life. A good five-shillingsworth of service; and the joy it gave a small boy on his birthday years ago was beyond price.

*   *   *

Whenever I hear the name 'Parnell' I do not immediately think of the famous statesman. I think instead of the draper's shop in the Wilton Road that sold the cuckoo-clocks. In reality, they were not cuckoo-clocks at all, for there was no cuckoo mechanism. Actually, they were miniature representations of cuckoo-clocks made in the Black Forest; timepieces only. They were a quarter the size of a true cuckoo-clock; they possessed a weight and a pendulum, and carved bone hands. They kept reasonably good time and had a cheerful tick. Every now and then I would ask if we 'could go to Parnell's and buy a cuckoo-clock'. Usually I was given permission, and Nurse and I would set off for the afternoon walk. Down Victoria Street; left by the station; a hundred yards along; and there was Parnell's. Feverishly clutching my shilling I would run ahead of Nurse till I reached the window. These little clocks cost exactly elevenpence three-farthings each. The small window that housed them was beyond the dull main windows, with their uninteresting underwear and elastic. A few steps farther along, and there one was. The clocks were piled high; tumbled anyhow in a great heap; with a price ticket: 11¾d. I would stand so long trying to choose *the* one I wanted that Nurse would grow unbearably impatient, finally hauling me angrily inside the shop. There again the trouble began. This one wouldn't do because the hour-hand was set wrongly; that one had Arabic figures (though I preferred them usually, I had early a sense of fitness that told me cuckoo-clocks *must* have Roman figures); this one was too light in colour, that too dark. At last, when Nurse began to stamp her foot with impatience, a choice was made, and we would turn homewards again, I walking very carefully, holding my new treasure with the utmost gingerliness. When we got back, it would be hung upon the nursery wall, and would be safe for about six weeks, after which I would start playing about with it, 'to make it go better' (a weakness of mine which I am told caused me to destroy seventeen watches, some being mine, but most being other people's, by the time I was six); and finally, damaged beyond repair, it would be consigned to the dustbin, and another would take its place. Then, suddenly, there were no more cuckoo-clocks because of the war; and I have only rarely seen them in England since. I shall always remember them with the greatest affection; I learned from them a good deal technically about clocks, and they bravely suffered and stood up to my infant mania for destruction.

*   *   *

Every morning I used to wake about seven o'clock. I would lie in bed impatiently waiting; hearing a quarter past seven, and half past, chime from Big Ben. Then I would hear Father get up, turn on the water for his cold bath, and shut himself into his dressing-room while the water ran. I would immediately leap out of bed, run into my parents' room and jump into the warm place left by my father, beside Mother. 'Jump in, jump in, as neat as a new pin!' my mother would cry, every morning, and putting her arms round me would draw me to her to be cuddled. How I loved it! The bed was so warm and comforting, and Mother had the deliciously milky smell of all beautiful human beings. She always wore a peculiar little white nightcap, like an inverted pudding-basin, and a long white nightgown; and her hair, brushed and plaited, hung over her shoulders like a girl's. She would look at me in that way I knew so well; her eyes starry and bright in her rather tiredly beautiful face. She would kiss me good morning, and I would kiss her in return; and know how much I loved her and how much I was loved.

5

The College Garden

Even I knew, at the age of five, that Little Dean's Yard was what was called 'very pretty'. I knew for two reasons. Firstly, because the ladies who came to Mother's 'At Homes' in the drawing-room (to which I, too, was sometimes reluctantly dragged) said so; secondly, because artists arrived, set up easels and stools, and painted pictures of it.

The Yard didn't seem to me very pretty; it was just the yard, the place where I lived, nice but unexciting. The artists, on the other hand, I found most interesting. They were dressed so differently from anyone that I knew. Sometimes they were hatless, and then their hair awfully badly needed cutting; sometimes they wore huge black hats and long cloaks; and the lady artists often had funny things on their feet with holes in them so that you could see their toes peeping through, called sandals. I used to watch them at a respectful distance, fascinated far more by them than by their pictures. I asked Mother one morning if I could be an artist.

'Perhaps one day you might be, darling,' she answered vaguely.

'But I want to be an artist now,' I said. 'I want to sit in the yard and paint a picture.'

'No, I don't think you could do that,' she said.

'But, Mummy . . .' my voice turned to a wail, and the usual tears began to threaten. My mother hesitated. It was a fine spring morning; the school was on holiday.

'Well, I'll ask Daddy,' she said, relenting, and went downstairs. After a few minutes she came back. 'Daddy says you can,' she said. 'But you mustn't make a mess, and you must come in when Big Ben chimes eleven.'

I couldn't really paint a picture, I knew that, not a picture out of my head. So I selected a book of nursery rhymes, that unfortunately for itself, was uncoloured. I walked across the yard, carrying my things. I had no easel, that couldn't be helped; and I had no stool, but I could sit on the steps of Up-School, as I had once seen a real artist do.

Carefully I arranged myself on the sun-warmed stone that made my bottom deliciously hot as I sat down, spread out my materials with careless abandon; surreptitiously ruffled my hair so that it would look untidy like artist's hair, hoping that Mother wasn't watching, and began to paint. I chose a picture of a peacock, strutting with widespread tail. I thought for a long time what colour I should paint him. In the end I decided against the proper colour, because my green was nearly finished, and I knew I could never capture the iridescence of the eye-spots. So I chose a lovely bright vermilion.

I was busily painting, when I heard pattering footsteps behind me. I looked up to see a very tall lady staring at my picture. She was very bony-looking, and wore spectacles; round her neck was a curious fur boa and on her enormous feet were brown sandals. She was flat all the way down, not nice and rounded like Mother. I immediately hated her.

'Good morning, little boy,' she said, in a deep slow voice, 'and what are you doing?'

'Painting a picture,' I said, solemn and unsmiling.

'Let me look at it,' she said, not waiting for an answer.

Mutely, I suffered her to look closely. She stood back, simpering unpleasantly.

'I am an artist too,' she said. 'It's a very nice picture. But why are you painting the poor peacock *red*?'

'Because he *is* red,' I said defiantly.

'Peacocks are never *red*, little boy,' she said, in a friendly, educative voice. (As though I didn't know.)

'Mine is,' I said.

'Yes,' she said patiently; 'but he ought not to be. He ought to be green, and his eyes should be like the rainbow—subtle, passionate,' she went on, apparently to herself, 'very difficult of course, very difficult. Even Burne-Jones once said. . . . Ha, ha, ha'—she laughed with odious brightness. 'I forgot; quite forgot where I was! Little boy, you should always paint things in their proper colours. It's *wrong* not to. Now what are a peacock's proper colours?' she asked, as though I had already forgotten her lesson.

'Red,' I said.

'You naughty little boy!' she exclaimed angrily, flushing an unpleasing shade of purple. 'I shall not speak to you any more.' And giving her fur boa an irritated twitch, she pattered into the cloisters on her rubber-soled sandals.

I burst into tears and hastily collecting my painting things ran indoors to Mother who comforted me by saying she liked red peacocks more than any other sort. That was the end of my interest in artists; I knew if they were all like that one, they knew nothing at all. I played less than ever in the Yard. Instead, I would seek out what was for me Paradise itself, the College Garden. There, I knew, I should be safe from the prying curiosity of stupid grown-ups.

This beautiful secret garden has always been the centre of a feud between the Abbey and the School since Wren's Dormitory was built along its western side; and the King's Scholars are not allowed its use except for a few hours twice in the year, on Election Sunday and Monday. It is also (and wrongly) called the Abbey Gardens by the prebendaries. So that, when my sister married a Minor Canon, loyalty decreed that it should be the Abbey Gardens to her, and the College Garden to us. But in our case the feud was more theoretical than practical, and my brother-in-law with great kindness procured us our own key to the door. Before that, I had to go to the Precentor's house to borrow the key every time I wanted to go into the garden.

Of all the romantic places of my childhood, the College Garden stands at the very head. I would ask my mother for the key, and then, grasping it firmly in my hand, I would set out on a great adventure. I can feel the shape and weight of that key in my hand now. I would cross Little Dean's Yard, enter the gloomy mouth of the Dark Cloister, turn right along the damp gas-smelling entrance to the Little Cloisters with its letter-box and fire-box shining red in the dusky light, and see before me the fern-haunted fountain that splashes unendingly into the goldfish-pond in the centre of the Little Cloisters. Here all was green; the light that filtered through the leaves of the plane tree; the pellucid green of the fern-fronds, and the green-reflecting water made a square of cool brightness at the end of the black tunnel that led to it. The leaves would ripple in the wind, the fountain would spray to the glittering column upwards to fall in a shower of brilliant drops in the stone basin; the effect on a hot summer's day, with the cold air of the cloisters rushing past one, was of a pastoral refreshment beyond description. This was the foretaste of things to come. I would wander slowly round the Little Cloisters; if the gate to the fountain was unlocked I would sneak in (it was out of bounds) to see how many goldfish I could count and if the one with the pale patch on its glinting scarlet was still there; and then a window in one of the houses would be flung up and I would scuttle quickly out before I should be caught, and sedately resume my walk round the Little Cloisters. I would look at each door as I passed and the brass plate that bore the name of each Canon, and at last I would come to the door that carried no name, and through whose key-hole a torrent of cold air would be rushing. I would fit the key into the lock, turn it and push. The heavy old door would swing slowly back on groaning hinges (I can hear the sound still), and then I would stand entranced. For a few yards the grey stone tunnel of the Little Cloisters continued, to end in an open arch. And beyond this arch lay spread the garden of every child's and poet's dreams. Velvet lawns slumbered in the bright sunshine, dotted here and there with beds of gay and brilliant-hued flowers. A grey medieval wall lay along one side of it behind patches of colour; mulberry, elm, lime and plane trees cast trembling oases of shade on the green turf. The contrast between the passage that led to it and the garden itself is one of the most haunting memories I possess. It was always cold, cold and shadowy in the passage, with a smell of ancient, dusty, cold stone rising from floor and

walls and lingering around one; and beyond, the garden shimmered in baking summer heat. The door would swing to with a
clank and lock itself. Then I would slowly walk forward, step by
step, towards the mouth of the arch, and suddenly a wave of
melting liquid heat would come to meet me. Another step, and
the blazing sunshine would pounce, glorious, living, fiercely
opposed to the cool death of the old stone passage. And yet how
beautiful was that cool death, how welcoming on one's return,
when the hot sun had done its work, and one only wanted rest!
Many times I would run back and forth, out of the sun and into
the shade and out to the sun again; tasting with a joy that is
incommunicable the beauty of the contrast. And suddenly this
game would be finished, and I would run towards the daisy-
starred lawns, to play there until Big Ben, chiming a quarter to
one, called me reluctantly home again.

*   *   *

Four grey walls, and four grey towers
Overlook a space of flowers.

Thus wrote Tennyson, in that great evocative poem *The Lady
of Shalott.* All that is not said aloud in those two lines; all that by
hint and implication whispers of a serene magic behind the loud
dullness of even such quiet and interesting words as those, might
serve to convey an impression of the College Garden. It was
bathed in a cloistered peace and calm such as I have never known
anywhere else. Partly this peace derived from its secrecy; the fact
that here, in the very heart of London, lay a large and fertile
garden unseen by the eyes of all but a very few men. I could
pursue my games and explorations undisturbed. None of the things
I hated came near it; dogs and adults, indeed humans of any age,
were conspicuous by their absence. Only a few withered tabby
cats were occasionally to be seen prowling there, presumably
having climbed to the iron-spike-and-broken-bottle-guarded
high walls that surrounded it. Sometimes a Canon's wife might
stroll across the lawns, or one of the other Close children come to
play, but this happened with incredible infrequency. Or sometimes I would find and talk to the old nut-brown gardener who
might be discovered skulking in one of the greenhouses. Nearly

always, however, I would have this great Garden to myself. It was here that I learned so deeply to love the country, for the College Garden was large enough to be a true piece of country in the heart of London. In it, thrushes and blackbirds built their nests and reared their families; the caterpillars of the Lime Hawk-moth could be found, and all the common Vanessid butterflies; and many a true country wild flower, the seeds from which it sprang blown from who knows whence, had established itself at the end of the garden in its wilder part. It was here, too, that I first learned the smell of the earth, for one fine spring morning I was picking daisies to make a daisy-chain when I fell over, quite forgetting to howl in the rapture of the discovery that the earth itself smelt beautiful.

As for the 'four grey towers', how strange a feeling it is for a child to play within the range and influence of man's loftier architecture. The immense height and breadth of the Victoria Tower, especially, added immeasurably to the haunted quality of the College Garden. Though rarely consciously aware of it, one was never lost sight of by this beneficent giant that brooded so tenderly over the garden. I take it that the architecture of the Victoria Tower is open to question by the medieval pundit and the Good-Taste or Sterility Brigade. Nevertheless, it fits its surroundings; and since it was greatly loved by a small child whose *instinctive* taste was impeccable, later ages will probably whole-heartedly accept it. At any rate to me it was (as was Big Ben also) 'protector, guardian, friend'. It stood on one side of the garden; the Abbey towers and nave on the other, behind the eighteenth-century fronts of the Canons' houses; so that one was always watched by something high up against the sky wherever one went, except, perhaps in the secret places, to which sometimes, when in the mood, I penetrated. The less reputable parts of the garden, right at the far end, where the rubbish was thrown; and where from behind snail-infested forests of Japanese Knotwood I would sometimes hide, with rapidly beating heart from—but now I come to think of it, I have no idea from what I did hide. Let us say, perhaps, the less pleasing spirits of the garden, and leave it at that. In this remote corner, with its rank growths and rain-stained, moss-grown statuary, it seemed to me that something itself hid, that did not wish to be found out, and made me, in turn, hide from it. Five or ten minutes in this part of the garden was enough for me, and I would run back to the sunlit lawns and bright flower-beds with a feeling of relief and thankfulness for their open quality.

*   *   *

Before I bid farewell to the College Garden I have one more thing to say. The value of privacy, in an age of which accessibility is a keynote, cannot be overstressed. The ultimate beauty of the College Garden lay in the fact that it was hidden from the gaze of the general public. Its four walls made an enclosure, a space that, remote and unseen, distilled a rare essence. No inquisitive or prying gaze could trample its secrets under the foot of the middle-class mind. It had the power to make the few who walked there saints, or mystics or poets. Its potentiality (if that is the right word) was undisturbed. Once make a hole in any of those thick old walls, and the essential secret would bleed away until the Garden became like any other; just another London garden.

This has now been done. A door, never used (why, I have no idea), that opened straight into Little Dean's Yard and abutted on College, has, in the last few years, been removed, and a fancy wrought-iron gateway inserted, so that the College Garden is now accessible to the eyes of all and sundry who go past. One would like to know the purpose of this. Is it to rouse in the breasts of the proletariat an envy (for they may do no more than look) of the privileged seclusion of what they doubtless consider the idle rich? Is it to torment, by a locked door, the parched eyes and throats of those who have tramped London's summer pavements, and would like to sit down under trees and rest? Or is it, as I suspect, a case of false aesthetics? An addition to the glamour of Little Dean's Yard? For as I said at the beginning of this chapter, Little Dean's Yard is considered by some to be 'very pretty'. Good manners are to be set aside, then, for the sake of the picturesque? (For what could be ruder than to flaunt before people the beauty of a garden they may not enter?) Certainly I am sure this wrought-iron gate-way would have delighted the lady artist I have mentioned earlier. I think that her sandals would have creaked with rapture as she tip-toed up to the gateway to press her long nose against its bars and 'drink in' the maimed and wounded spirit of the College Garden as it fled to the farthest corners in a tragically futile attempt to escape the gaze of those all-seeing and unseeing eyes.

The Bright and the Dark

6

The Window

Every small child has a favourite window from which he can look out on life and watch the world going by. Mine was a staircase window on the third floor, near the nursery, that looked out over the Yard. The stairs, ascending beside it, made (with a cushion to relieve their hardness) a perfect seat and footrest.

It was from this window one morning when I was about five that, possessed by heaven knows what impulse, I suddenly shouted at the top of my voice: 'The boys! The boys! Daddy and the boys!' as my father crossed the Yard through a milling throng during a break. I remember clearly doing it, and being filled with an irresistible sense of power. The boys and my father looked up; there was a little subdued laughter; I shouted again, 'The boys! The boys! Daddy and the boys!' and then I was hauled away by an irate and alarmed nurse. I remember also how very angry (and rightly) my father was; he told me that I must never, never do such a thing again. I did not tell him that I had known that before I did it at all! It is possible, and I think probable, that I did it just to see how angry my father would be; I know that as I heard his slow footsteps ascending the nursery stairs after the incident I felt very frightened, and fully aware of what was coming to me. I said how sorry I was, and that I would never do it again, and he forgave me and kissed me and rubbed his cheek against my nose, which I always loved because his face smelt of shaving soap.

As soon as I could read (which happened one night, suddenly, when I was four years old; the evening before I could not read, and the next morning I could), I used to take a book, usually my great favourite, *Mr. Rutherford's Children*, and sit on the stairs for hours, alternately reading and looking out of the window across the Yard. If I heard footsteps, I would look down to see who it was, and return to my reading. Then would come break, the Yard would suddenly fill with noisy boys exchanging classrooms, and as suddenly empty again into silence and the steady sun beating down on to motionless stone and brick. Sometimes, a great and rare treat, Mother would sit on the stairs beside me, and read aloud to me while I looked out of the window.

Yet, despite the many summer mornings I spent beside it, I remember my window best as winter evening dusks fell. I would return from the afternoon walk with Nurse about four o'clock, and, directly my coat had been taken off, run to the window as the short winter day drew to its close to watch for my friend the lamplighter. I would stare at the archway to Dean's Yard, waiting, tense with expectancy, as the darkness steadily deepened. Then, suddenly, when I had almost given up hope, the interior of the archway would flush with yellow illumination, the signal that heralded the entrance of the lamplighter into Little Dean's Yard itself. I would see his dim figure, half lost in the failing light, his long pole with the tiny flickering flame at the top keeping pace with him, as he slowly crossed the Yard to Up-School. Then, in term, as he raised his pole, each gas-lamp would bloom with primrose light, and as he turned down the dark mouth of the cloisters, the long tunnel would shine, bright behind him, until at last he disappeared from view round a bend brightening in his wake. Then the Yard would be left all alone again, softly flowering with light, light that made the dying blue sky a deeper blue, so that the dark outline of the Abbey began to be lost against its background, and finally vanished into impenetrable obscurity. Then throughout the long evening the gas-lamps had it all their own way until at midnight they were extinguished but for the tiny by-pass, a faint blue point inside each lamp, and the Yard lay, anguished and primitive, in the grip of the night and the middle ages.

But now, the whole Yard basked in the soft yellow rays, and the light cast barred shadows from the grating that protected children against falling out of the window, and from the window-bars themselves, on the wall and ceiling above the staircase. This was the last safe moment. It was nearly dark, and the ghosts were gathering, thronging landing and stairs; and it was with a sense of relief that I would hear Nurse calling me in to tea.

*   *   *

And after tea I would play with my toys on the nursery floor until about half past five, when, for half an hour, there were two possibilities open to me : I could go to the study and talk to Father; or I could go to the drawing-room and sing while Mother played the piano for me. If I had a preference at that age it was for the study. It was more exciting, a tiny bit more frightening, and it had a definite sense of ritual about it, a thing that a small child always loves. Mother one knew so well, and could take liberties with, but never Father. Down the long flights of stairs, feeling very small in the huge house, I would run; quickly past the ghostly alcove, slowing up as I came to safer ground, until I reached the hall. I would stand there listening. Everything would be quiet. The closed door of the study would be before me, impenetrable, mysterious. Behind that door was warmth and light and Father; but out here in the hall it was chilly and dimly lit and comfortless. The study door seemed to say : you knock on me at your own peril. After a minute I would gather my courage and knock. There would be a pause, and then from far within I would hear Father's voice, muffled and remote, with the hint of a question in it, call : 'Come in !' I would turn the handle, and the warmth and comfort would embrace me and draw me in. I would shut the door and, blinking, run forward, safe at last in the aura of Father's strong personality.

He would be sitting at his desk, correcting Greek or Latin prose. For a while after I had entered there would be silence but for the ticking of the black wooden clock on the mantelpiece, the crackle and fall of the coals in the wide old-fashioned fireplace, and the soft slur of Father's blue pencil as, with a heavy sigh, he underlined some flagrant mistake in the work before him. Then he would lay down his pencil, push the papers aside, and turn with a tired smile towards me. He would cause his steel-rimmed pince-nez to fall from eyes to waistcoat (a black cord prevented their falling to the floor) by wrinkling his nose (a feat that I loved, and that filled me with admiration; I would make him do it again and again until I was satiated); and hold out his arms to me so that I could jump on his knee. For a time I would sit up there, playing with the things on his desk; his pipe, tobacco-pouch and ashtray. I would be allowed to turn the calendar on to the next day (a habit that surely would have caused a less clear-headed man than my father many a headache). I loved sitting there on my father's knee sniffing the delicious aroma of tobacco that hung around him.

After a few minutes, without saying anything, he would open the bottom drawer of his desk, and extract from it a long, thin book. We would turn the pages together. It consisted of a series of star-maps for the current year. Each page showed the stars for the month, a map for each fortnight. At the bottom of each map the buildings of London were spread out in panorama, black against an ink-blue sky; and above, the inverted bowl was studded with golden stars. I loved Saturn most, with his encircling milky rings; and when he was absent from a map, I would quickly turn the pages until he reappeared again. In some months the whole sky was thick with stars; in others nearly empty; but always the dark buildings, St Paul's, Big Ben, the Abbey, were strung along the bottom of the map. It is when I remember the soft blue and gold quality of the star-maps that something—whatever was the essence of Father's study—speaks still across the years. It was so golden and warm in there, and quiet, with the huge fire burning, and the wooden-shuttered windows, and the air fragrant with pipe-smoke. A sombre peace brooded over that classic room, a peace that Father had partly made, and of which he was himself a part. All that was best in the Edwardian age seemed to be summed up in the study; and my father himself, with his outward self-assurance, his serenity, his gravity, and his sternness that could melt into gentle, shy and child-like love, its guardian. No man was more reliable, trustworthy and self-reliant, and although he could be very harsh he also tried to be very fair. He was, with certain limitations, a great man; and his study reflected that greatness, the very essence of himself made, with unselfconscious artistry, tangible.

And then, after the star-maps, there was that other great treat, the Cabinet. When we had drunk our fill of the stars, Father would lift me off his knee to the floor, push back his chair and turn to the side-table on which stood the five mahogany cabinets. He would pull out a drawer, look at it, push it in again and pull out another, swiftly thrusting it before my delighted eyes. Perhaps he would choose the one that contained the Vanessid butterflies, and a riot of rich colour would flash before me; the scarlet and black livery of the Red Admirals; the tawny-brown of the Commas; the smoky-blue eye-spots of the Peacocks; the delicate yellow-flushed pink of the Painted Ladies. Or it might be the 'Blues' drawer, another great favourite, small butterflies these; the silvery greenish-blue of the Chalkhill Blue, the incredibly pure and brilliant electric blue of the Adonis Blue a perfect contrast and foil to the shining metallic red-gold of the Small Copper, and the brown purple-shot wings of the Purple Hairstreak. He would turn to another drawer and produce for my inspection the huge and frightening Death's-head Hawk-moth with its clearly discernible yellow skull and crossbones, or the gaily spotted Tiger Moths, or the beautiful soft crimson and grey of the Red Underwings. Sometimes Father would carry a favourite drawer to his desk, and we would sit down again to study the long rows of insects. Father would slide the glass of the drawer out, and at once there would be the strong, actual contact of eye and butterfly, unimpeded by the clear barrier. I would breathe heavily with excitement, and the outspread wings would flutter faintly in the stream of my breath as though life lingered still in them. Sometimes Father and I would renew the naphthaline balls wrapped in muslin that were pinned in the corner of each drawer to discourage the parasites that would make a meal of the fragile wing-substances; and the blended smell of naphthaline, cork and wood that rose from the opened drawers, elusive and subtle, has outlived the passage of the years, so that I have only to conjure it up in the mind to be sitting again on Father's knee before the long lines of shining butterflies as he lifts with his forceps a specimen to show me the contrast between under and upper side.

And all the time, the study, golden and warm, would be watching us, and lapping us round with its comfortable silence, that silence that was so deeply underlined by the ticking clock and the burning fire. The most beautiful room in the house with its corniced ceiling and Adam fireplace; the very heart and centre of the house, where work, important, mysterious and exciting work, was done. A room lined with glass-fronted bookcases, which Father would open sometimes to show me in South's *The Butterflies of the British Isles* the life-cycle of one of the insects we had been looking at. The room that held for me the most friendliness, and the most true romance, Father's study, the study of the Master of the King's Scholars, in the house known as 3, Little Dean's Yard, Westminster.

*   *   *

Our drawing-room was on the floor above the study, so that when I chose that as my evening's destination I had not so far to go. I would run down from the nursery and push open the door, without waiting to knock. Mother would be sitting on the large comfortable sofa in front of the fire, reading or knitting. The black Cramer upright would be open, with music upon it, ready for our singing. I would sit down on the end of the sofa and lay my head in Mother's lap for her to stroke my hair (sometimes rather absent-mindedly as she finished the chapter of the book she was reading). After a few minutes I would raise my head and look around me, taking in the room's atmosphere. The drawing-room was larger than the study, and very lofty. Architecturally, it was the finest room in the house. Three tall windows rose to ceiling height, the long windows common to Georgian houses; curtained and pelmeted with a brown flower-embroidered brocade. There was a carved Adam fireplace of white marble. Sofa and armchairs were covered in flowered chintz and a large, soft, Turkey carpet lay on the floor. The room smelt of stuffs; brocade and chintz and cushion-covers. At this time of day it basked in a brighter, whiter light than the study; the lamp-shades were opalescent rather than golden; the wallpaper cream instead of deep yellow, and the tall standard lamp that stood near the piano had a silk-tasselled shade that matched the chair covers; a shade upon which gay parrots and birds-of-paradise sprang to vivid life when the switch was turned on.

Yet though the drawing-room was gayer and less sombre than the study on the surface, underneath it was not. From earliest childhood I unconsciously made this comparison : that I did not mind being left alone in the study after dark, and I did mind being left alone in the drawing-room. If Mother went out to get anything I felt neither happy nor safe until she returned. It seemed to me always that the personality she had throughout the years impressed upon the room struggled against the tears of the sorrowful little boy who haunted it. Certain it was that even while we were playing and singing a watching silence would sometimes make itself felt, a silence that was far, far louder than our music, and far more eloquent; and I would wriggle my chair as close as ever I could to Mother's for comfort and reassurance.

Usually, Mother would begin by playing to me. I loved to crouch behind the piano with my ear to the plush curtain that, hanging upon a brass rod, decently draped the back of the instrument. I would press my ear as close to the soundboard as I could, and the 'Songs Without Words' (Mother's favourite pieces) would become a great torrent of roaring tingling noise, booming in my ear until I was satiated, and I had to move away and watch the piano rocking silently as Mother played. Then, the piece over, Mother would get out the songs I loved, and together we would sing them. Two books of nursery rhymes there were, and best and most-loved of all, the National Song Book. 'A Frog He Would a-Wooing Go' and 'Baa-baa Black Sheep' vied with 'Early One Morning' and 'The British Grenadiers' for popularity, until one day the grocer sent some goods wrapped up in a torn copy of 'The Marseillaise', which I found in a wastepaper basket and appropriated for my very own. And for years this absurd, torn scrap of paper ranked high in the list of my possessions as is the way of a child; and 'The Marseillaise' always began and ended the singing.

Sometimes (and always on Sundays) we had hymns, and this I really loved best. Mother chose her favourites and I chose mine alternately. 'Not For Our Sins Alone' would be followed by 'All Things Bright and Beautiful'. Hymns seemed to understand better than songs that world that I understood better than the ordinary world. Some I did not care for much; Number 570, for example : 'Every morning the red sun Rises warm and bright; But the evening cometh on, And the dark, cold night.' Yes, I knew the truth of that all too well, in that tormented old house. But there was one that, though it admitted of the existence of such things, I loved, for it was a prayer; a prayer that I used to pray with all the intensity of my small spirit. I will quote it in full.

> The day is past and over :
>   All thanks, O Lord, to Thee !
> We pray Thee now that sinless
>   The hours of dark may be.
> O Jesu ! keep us in Thy sight,
> And guard us through the coming night.
>
> The joys of day are over :
>   We lift our hearts to Thee,
> And ask Thee that offenceless
>   The hours of dark may be.

O Jesu ! keep us in Thy sight,
And guard us through the coming night.

The toils of day are over :
   We raise the hymn to Thee;
And ask that free from peril
   The hours of dark may be.
O Jesu ! keep us in Thy sight,
And guard us through the coming night.

And most important of all, the last verse :

Be Thou our soul's Preserver,
   O God, for Thou dost know
How many are the perils
   Through which we have to go;
O loving Jesu ! hear our call
And guard and save us from them all.

Yes, I completely understood what this hymn said, and why it said it. Even while we were singing it, the air would grow thin and the darkness of spiritual distress and fear hover in the room. There would come also the feeling that mocking laughter was not far away; and I would sing at the top of my voice, trying to feel secure in the knowledge that God was protecting me; and I would be aware of Mother glancing at me with anxious love. How comforting were the lines: 'O God, for Thou dost know, How many are the perils through which we have to go'; comforting but terribly lonely. I knew that *only* God knew those perils fully; and I would always substitute for the last two lines of the last verse those of the previous verses; for I *needed* to sing 'O Jesu ! keep us in Thy sight'; the other line, 'O loving Jesu ! hear our call', was not strong enough.

And if the thoughts that I have related strain the reader's credulity with regard to a child of five, I can only assure him that indeed they were so, and leave it at that. For many years 'The Day is Past and Over' was my favourite hymn; and tonight as I sit writing alone in my study I must humbly acknowledge that it still is.

*   *   *

And what have these memories to do with the window with which this chapter started? A great deal; for that window has become to me a symbol of the present through which I look out on to the past. Before the vision of the study and Father, and the drawing-room and Mother, this ghostly window stands, the glass of its panes gentle but final. I may see and I may hear, but I cannot touch; nor may I yet open it. But the scenes onto which I look live still, withdrawn behind the glass that only one event has power to remove. They live as clearly and as forcibly as they were lived thirty years ago. The study fire crackles still and the smoke of Father's pipe hangs on the air; in the drawing-room the happy sound of a piano struggles against a vast and nameless suffusion of sorrow.

The other day, looking through some old papers of my father's, ten years after his death, I came across a yellowed sheet upon which he had written three lines for translation into Latin or Greek Elegiacs :

> Man's little day in haste we spend,
> And from its merry noontide send
> No glance to meet the silent end.

When did he write them? One evening, perhaps, after I had gone to bed, and he sat alone at his desk with the star-maps and the butterflies before him, the room silent, and empty and not empty after the abrupt removal of a child's personality? Or was it perhaps years before I was born? Who now can tell?

7

The River

Anyone who studies an aerial photograph of the district will see what on the ground he could only feel, that Westminster was (and at heart still is) a riverside village. The great flowing roadway of former days serves now as a sharp dividing line between two very different parts of London. To stand in the middle of Westminster or Lambeth Bridge is to feel two opposing forces at work. The width of the river has served through the ages, as the Seine in Paris, to keep the two banks apart. The bridges are not so much a link as a foot-passage for the convenience of those who must cross from one territory to the other. Across the shining water the comfortable dignity of Westminster faces the ramshackle squalor of Lambeth whose only claim to grandeur lies in its Archbishop's Palace. In the early morning, and at dusk, it is possible to look across the river from either side, and in the eye of the imagination to see the opposite bank as it was in the Middle Ages: flat, stagnant marshland; practically unbuilt; the typical low-lying meadows of a riverside. This hallucination owes its origin to the untamable nature of a river, from whose morning and evening mists the past daily rises. For the Thames has been there since first man began to build; and there it will be long, long after man's buildings have disappeared, whether they slowly crumble away under the influence of time, or are suddenly destroyed by man himself in one of his recurring fits of madness.

I always loved the river, instinctively recognizing and applauding in it, the unconquerable. The grimy wharves and warehouses on its banks, the dirty tugs and steam-boats that trafficked on its surface, served but to emphasize its primitive invulnerability. I learned to know it in many moods; clear, glittering and calm on a bright morning of spring or summer; grey, sullen and lashed to little waves on a dark, lowering afternoon of mid-winter. We, Nurse and I, would set off down our own garden; and out of the back door we would come into Great College Street. Along this quiet, dignified, forgotten thoroughfare, with its tall old period houses and its little mews, we would walk until we came to the rush, bustle and noise of the Grosvenor Road, and finally attain the safe refuge, the quiet sanctuary, of the little riverside gardens.

There never were many people there. An occasional figure on one of the green-painted wooden seats, a stroller or two, a few children leaning over the river parapet feeding the seagulls, these made up its population. We would turn to the left, where at the end of a little secluded path is a solitary seat, hidden behind Rodin's masterpiece, 'The Burghers of Calais'. There, nine times out of ten, Nurse would settle herself with her crochet-work and a book; the tenth time the seat would be occupied, and disgruntled, we would seat ourselves somewhere else, where we could watch with unfailing attention for our favourite seat to be vacated.

I loved very deeply 'The Burghers of Calais', knowing always that when I played around it I played in the shadow of a great expression of man's spirit. The wasted figures with their anguished faces and the long, knobbly and eloquent keys they held might well have frightened a small and sensitive child. Strangely, they did not. I sensed pain, capitulation under the stress of long-continued atrocities, and a dreadfully calm and still resignation; but not the dreaded black thing. The group, though it might well have been otherwise, was *good*; that was all I knew or wanted to know. So that I played happily around it, without fear; and the stone plinth on which the Burghers stood was most excellent and right for throwing a ball against. The rebound was perfect; which would, I think, have pleased Rodin a great deal.

And in passing, I would like to praise the retiring and unobtrusive position of this great work of art. When it was finally placed there (I just remember its unveiling), a great deal of criticism was levelled at its being thus hidden away; it was said that we did not appreciate the great French sculptor, and were, indeed, insulting his work. The critics (as usual) were utterly mistaken. All good art should have to be sought for, and should not be too easy of access. In some busy thoroughfare the statue would have been lost; here, it becomes the jewel in a perfect setting, those riverside gardens that are more like Paris than London.

While Nurse was busy with her 'croasher', I would slip away and run down to the river wall. I had to pass on my left a beautiful herbaceous border, long and countrified, that in the autumn was vivid with michaelmas daisies, sunflowers and dahlias, upon the first of which Red Admiral and Tortoiseshell butterflies would sit, sunning themselves, feeding on the nectar, and lazily opening and shutting their wings. I remember with deep joy the autumn coloration of this exquisite border; it is fixed forever in my mind because I once saw a Painted Lady butterfly (rarity of rarities in London) feasting among the common Vanessids.

Arrived at the bottom of the gardens, I would lean over the wall (it was very fortunate that Nurse did not sometimes see just how far I would lean) and watch the river, staring across at the ugly buildings, made pleasant by distance, of St Thomas's hospital; at the grey pile of Lambeth Palace, sunk among its trees; at the long line of warehouses that dissolved and faded away on the distant horizon in a blue-grey smudge of faint colour. Beneath me the boats would pass, black barges laden with coal; steam-boats whose funnels were beginning to lower at the approach of Westminster Bridge; all the motley traffic, the bits and pieces of a great river. And overhead the seagulls would wheel in screaming throngs; twisting and turning, advancing and retreating, watching with sharp eyes every human for signs of bread. Sometimes I would take down a bag of crusts, and delight in watching the birds catch the pieces in mid-air, as they dived upon them with a sureness and skill that were fascinating to see. Their white wings glinted in the sun, cutting patterns against the distant background; every now and then a gull would detach itself from the throng, fold its wings and alight on the parapet, moving unostentatiously along as I edged up to it, finally taking to the air again with a hoarse scream when it could no longer stand the nervous tension of being stalked. Amusing and rather formidable birds, they were the very spirit of the estuary made tangible; they brought sea with them up the river. In bad weather they would crouch in hundreds on the grass of the gardens, rising now and then in wailing flocks, before settling again upon the ground. Into the formal and regimented artificiality of London they brought a quality of wildness and freedom that was refreshing and tonic; a breath of sea-air into the stale smoke-laden enervation of a great town. With all my heart I loved them for it, as I leaned over the wall, dreaming to the accompaniment of their harsh and mocking cries.

*   *   *

It was in these gardens that Mother once made one of her extraordinary remarks that fired my imagination for years. I had picked up a round, brown pebble and was looking at it carefully. I was about to throw it in the river, when Mother said : 'Don't do that, darling; it mightn't like it.'

'Are stones *alive*, Mummy?' I asked, half-surprised.

'Yes,' said my mother. 'They are.'

'But they don't grow,' I said, thinking hard.

'They do grow,' she said, 'but very, very slowly.'

'Would it grow if I took it home?'

Mother smiled. 'You wouldn't *see* it grow,' she said; 'it would be hundreds of years before it looked any different.'

I carefully put the stone down on the path, thrilled and mystified. I knew that Mother was right about stones being alive, yet it was not the sort of thing that grown-ups understood or admitted. It was strange—I had seen in my mother something I knew in myself; the knowledge that so-called inanimates had a life of their own. How much I owe to her for consolidating rather than weakening this knowledge! In an age where everything is rationally explained, I learned from the best person possible that fact is the lowest rung of the ladder of truth; and that innate percipience is worth a whole bagful of statistics. To have what my heart and soul told me confirmed by a grown-up was a rare experience to a child of five or six; I never forgot it, and I have never ceased to be grateful.

And again in these gardens Mother taught me another valuable lesson. I had found a penny on the gravel path, and I spent the rest of the morning with my head bent down examining the ground; not daring to look up in case I missed another penny. At last Mother said : 'Do stop looking on the ground, darling!'

'Why?' I asked.

'Because if you spend your life studying pavements and gutters for the sake of money, you'll miss all that the sky, the sun, the moon and the stars have to tell you.'

This, too, is a lesson I have never forgotten; indeed, I have followed its precepts rather too successfully.

*   *   *

After I had watched the river for a while, Nurse, getting

anxious, would leave her work, and come to find me. It seemed an immutable law of my childhood that as soon as I was really beginning to enjoy myself it was time to go home. We would walk away, collect our belongings from the Rodin seat where Nurse had trustingly left them while she came to look for me, and, with a lingering backward look on my part, leave the gardens to dream in the sunshine. We would go home a different way, along Abingdon Street, past the Victoria Tower with its flagstaff that was topped by a crown and from which the Union Jack or the flag of St George might be fluttering, past the Houses of Parliament with their bottle-green windows, past Westminster Hall and the statue of Richard Coeur de Lion, round the corner by St Margaret's Church that, standing in its little grass plot, seemed somehow to belong more to the country than to London, along Broad Sanctuary and so into Dean's Yard. Sometimes we varied this by entering the Abbey through Poets' Corner or the north transept door and coming out into the East Cloisters, when we had only to cross Little Dean's Yard to Number 3. This was especially useful if it had come on to rain. It meant that for half of the walk home we had a roof (and what a roof!) above our heads; but it was not popular with Nurse, who had all the reluctance of her class to taking liberties with large, sacred buildings.

Sometimes we would not go into the Victoria Tower Gardens at all, but would take a different, longer riverside walk. From Great College Street, down the Grosvenor Road and over Lambeth Bridge. A beautiful bridge that was so much quieter than Westminster Bridge, and between whose steel girders one could look and see the water flowing giddily beneath. And beyond, on the other side, Lambeth Palace with its grey square tower and its moon-faced clock; and to the left of it the Archbishop's Palace, indomitable; old, crouching deep among the gnarled trees of its ancient garden. Then, when we had crossed the bridge, we would immediately turn left along the path that runs, below the road level, beside the river.

I doubt if London holds a quieter place than this, or a place more charged with atmosphere. Far above runs the traffic, almost inaudible down here, where only the cries of the gulls and the infrequent hoot of a steamer break the nearly tangible silence. Rarely does one meet with anyone. Only an occasional old man goes shuffling by, eyes bent upon the ground, looking neither to left nor to right. And across the river the Houses of Parliament lie spread out, backed by the Abbey, and ending in Big Ben, their reflections rippling brokenly in the gently-flowing water. Tower and spire and battlement lying drowned, plunged point downwards into the shining river. A scene of exquisite beauty, of calm and certain peace. The very pulse of all that is truly London; the old capital city, Londinium, strangely projected through comparatively modern buildings. An utter tranquillity of spirit haunts this forgotten backwater, secluded from the hubbub and rush of the busy city. Here, for the length of time it takes to walk between two bridges, one may find the rarest kind of peace, that is a refreshment, a momentary halting and stock-taking before the re-entry into the crowded ways of thronged thoroughfares.

The final joy it offers its votaries is to lean over the parapet, alternately watching the lazy motion of the water and the face of Big Ben until the voice of one of the quarters is heard. For in the four bells (and perhaps most of all in the fifth that is struck only at the hour) when heard across the water, lies all music. The deep sombre tones ebb and flow, charged with the river's essence, as if in their passage across the liquid, shining floor, they had extracted its very heart, the secret that makes it the Thames and not the Seine. London throughout the ages, from her first beginnings until the present day, has for a few brief seconds a living voice whose eloquence is matchless in its trembling hint of the eternal music of the spheres.

And as the ripples of sound withdraw themselves slowly from the ear, sinking into the river, the point where silence again resumes the mastery cannot be captured with any certainty. A dying murmur of sound remains, backed by memory; and it is gone; the rift in the air closes up, and imperceptibly the faint lapping of the water holds sway again over the senses.

So it was on those afternoon walks. Time and time again I would make Nurse sit down on one of the regularly spaced seats, those strange seats whose arms are in the shape of swans, that always look as though no one has ever sat on them but ghosts, while I ran to the parapet to watch and to listen; aware that watch was being kept upon me by the tall lamp-standards that with their milky globes upheld by great metal dolphins seem in the strangest way to sum up this quiet sun-smitten backwater of Lambeth. For the sun here is hot, and the flies buzz around the blue-green peeling paint of the seats, and all is silence. But at night under the stars lovers walk, and on the seats down-and-outs mingle with river-wraiths, and the masts of the moored barges are crowned with small, winking lights. And all this the lamp-standards have seen; and the occasional suicides, and the terrors of the river, and the night noises that disturb its velvet silence, and the sound of wind-changing bells across the water, and the sight of the lifting of the darkness by the green-and-orange-washed skies of dawn as the white mists hover. All these things and many more are known to those mysterious and patient lamp-standards.

They know, too, perhaps, that their life is nearly over. The flowing metal scroll-work and the milky globes will give way to garish lights that will spread unease rather than rest around them. But ultimately—what will it matter? For authority cannot stop the Thames flowing. Thousands of years hence that broad and winding silver ribbon will be pushing its eternal course towards the open sea, though Westminster and London itself should be no longer even a memory in the minds of men.

8

The Holiday at Haresfield

Between 1909, when I was born, and 1921, when we left London, the years have a name as well as a date. When I want to recollect something that happened, say, in 1914 I think 'Haresfield'. The reason that the years are so named in my mind is because every summer holiday was spent in a different place. The names string out along the years: Stoke Dry, Overstone, Cottered, Haresfield, Chipperfield, Monmouth, Eridge, Latton, Didmarton, Hardwicke, Corrington; good, solid, snub-nosed, rosy-cheeked English names for the most part, each one of them charged with memories that grow fuller and deeper as the years of my childhood advance.

But it is not until I arrive at Haresfield that the memories come crowding in. For one thing, it was a most unpleasantly memorable year (though that meant little to a child of five); for another, it was a very exciting place.

I always consigned places to one of two categories; either they 'lived' and were 'real', or they were dull and meant little in any way. I still do this, but much less definitely, since adulthood inevitably means that the contact with the spirit of place is less vivid and sharply defined than it was in childhood. One has learnt too much cerebrally to put unquestioning trust in the primitive intuition and the incontrovertible knowledge that are an essential part of childhood. It is a great pity, and its sadness was borne in upon me when I visited Haresfield again in 1936 and found it a pleasant, but quite ordinary, country village. One hint only was given, and has remained, and will always remain, to haunt me. Since the experience was both indescribable and incommunicable, and since this book is essentially about such things, I will try to describe it and communicate it.

I had walked over to Haresfield from a neighbouring village, and when I found myself at the entrance to the green lane that leads to the church I realized that I was upon familiar ground. I remembered vaguely the grey tower with its tall spire shaped like a candle extinguisher. I remembered too, but without emotion, the vicarage where I had passed six weeks of my life twenty-two years before. I walked all round the church (which was locked) until I came to the tower. I stood beneath it, enjoying the hot sun, looking upwards to the weathercock that shone in the brilliant summer light. I could hear the humming of the bees' wings as they rifled the purple knapweed flowers, and the faraway crowing of a cock in some distant farmyard. And then, suddenly, I became aware of another sound; the slow and measured ticking of the clock, high up in the tower. As though I was acting in a dream I moved close up to the tower, and crouching against it, looked up at its bulk that rose sheer into the sky. Straight and smooth was its wall up half its height, and then, projecting against the sky, I saw the diamond-shaped clock-face, and the hands, pinned one above the other, black strips against the blue. And I could hear the clock ticking steadily inside the tower. Then such a sense of the past, with its power, its glory and its fear, seized me, that I was unable to move, and could only crouch there, with my back prickling, motionless, hypnotized; knowing that time and space were no more than names coined by man to protect himself from the unchanging, which he could not long look upon, and live. For I was the same small boy of five who had done the same thing so many years before; and the collapse and the annihilation of the years was terrifying in its beauty, and beautiful in its terror. In the whole of my life I have known no similar experience; have never seen eternity so nakedly revealed as in this moment. Then, slowly, it faded; and presently I was a man listening to a ticking clock, and no longer a man living being a child again. Shut out once more (and how wisely!) I crept away from the tower and back down the lane, away from my own past, feeling as I did so, strangely traitorous, as though I had left, crying all alone in the churchyard, the ghost of a forlorn little boy, who had wanted no more than to play with me a game harmless to himself, but terrible and dangerous to me. And if ever I visit Haresfield again, I shall think twice before I summon the courage needed to stand once more beneath that tower, for now there would be no longer a child only; a young man in the pride of his youth and strength would be waiting there also.

*   *   *

On 4 August, 1914, I was playing with my toys on the floor of the room that had been allotted to me as nursery in Haresfield Vicarage, when Father and Mother came in and told me that there was a war. People were going to kill each other, but it would be over by Christmas.

Something in the grave demeanour of my parents must have impressed me, for I remember the scene, and the moment of telling, without remembering any details. But shortly afterwards Father hung a large map of Europe in the hall, and every morning he stuck little coloured flags into it. Every morning, directly after breakfast, with the tapping of the barometer, before he went upstairs to the lavatory. It was an interesting ritual and I liked to watch it. If this was what wars were, how nice, I thought; why can't there always be one? My brother Harold was fifteen years old, on holiday from Winchester. Would he have to go and be a soldier? I was told, no; the war would be over long before he would be old enough. I did not believe that; I looked on him as a marked person; I felt that he would be killed. But I never said so; grown-ups did not like one saying things like that. So I kept my wagging little tongue quiet for once; and after the first excitement was over, life resumed, for me at any rate, its ordinary quiet course. Haresfield was remote, a tiny village deep in the Cotswolds; and the great surging current of war scarcely ruffled the mill-pond surface of this secluded countryside.

I had much more important matters than the war to ponder on; the mysterious plague of mice in the house, for example. They would appear everywhere; on the hall table, in the dining-room; sometimes, even, in my bedroom, or in the linen cupboard. Some of them were albinos, white with pink eyes; others were pink with white eyes. Unlike brown mice, they were good to eat, except for their tails. I used to see them when I came down to breakfast in the morning, peering at me from behind a pile of letters in the hall. They never ran away when I tried to catch them, they stayed stock-still and looked at me. It seemed unkind to eat them, but I never could resist it. I asked Father how they got to the strange places they did; but all he would ever say was that they must have gone there in the night. 'These sorts of mice,' he would say, 'can only run in the dark; directly daylight comes it catches them wherever they are, and then they can't move. If you left that one on the hall table all day it would stay there, quite still; but as soon as it was dark (long after you're in bed, John), it would run back to its hole.' I left it, to see; and sure enough, in the morning it had gone. After that, I used to seize the mice quickly and eat them, for fear that they might disappear, even though it wasn't dark. They tasted deliciously of sugar; were they cooked or uncooked? It was a difficult question to decide. One morning I came down earlier than usual, and caught Father touching one on the hall table. I was very annoyed with him; for I realized that he must have been systematically stealing what I had come to consider as 'my' mice, every morning before I was up. He looked very guilty, too; and made a movement as if to conceal the mouse with his hand. I was upset by the thought of his deceitfulness for quite a long time; I had not thought that Father would stoop to petty theft. A few mornings later I saw something moving on the hall table, and ran to examine it. I saw a brown mouse scuttling for its life round the wainscoting; and when I looked at my white mouse I saw that the brown mouse had nibbled half its head off, and had left little thin toothmarks all round its neck. I cried then bitterly, out of the tenderness of my heart, and went to find Father to tell him all about it. Watching him closely, I was surprised to see that it looked as though he was trying very hard not to laugh.

'I'll tell your mice,' he said, 'that they must *not* go near the hall table, but keep to places higher up.'

I suppose he did so; for I never found them on the table again, only on the tops of cupboards. I hoped that they might follow me back to London when the holidays were over, but they never did.

* * *

One day Mother had driven into Gloucester with the pony and trap to do some shopping. It was about four miles away, and I knew that she would be out all the morning. Before she set out she made me promise to be good, and not on any account to go near the front gate because of the traffic on the main road.

For a time I played about in the garden, feeling disgruntled. I always missed Mother when she went out without me; for I felt more at the mercy of my sister Muriel and my brother Harold, who (it seemed to me) sometimes tended to tease me a trifle mercilessly. This morning, however, they were nowhere to be seen. In fact, no one was to be seen. I looked round the deserted garden, and a great idea came to me. I would walk along the main road to meet Mother; she would see me, and give me a lift home in the trap. So, after a cautious glance all round me, I tiptoed to the gate and stepped out on to the road, to walk to Gloucester. For a time all went well. Then I came to a house that stood by the roadside, and in the garden, leaning over the gate, was a woman I very much disliked. I had been to tea with her, and she was middle-aged and fussy, with a yapping lap-dog; and she patronized me.

'Good morning, little boy,' she said. (How I hated being called that!) 'And where are you off to?'

'To Gloucester, to meet my mummy,' I said sulkily.

'Good gracious,' said the woman, 'does she know? Do they know at home that you're walking to Gloucester?'

'No,' I said, telling the truth with a great effort.

'Don't you think they ought to know?' she asked.

'No,' I said; and then decided I must trust her. 'Please don't tell them, will you?' I asked. 'It's a surprise. Promise you won't tell them.' I put on the most appealing look I could summon.

She hesitated.

'Please!' I begged. 'You *must* promise!'

'Very well,' she said. 'I promise. But you will be careful, won't you?'

' 'Course I will,' I said scornfully, and proceeded on my way. I did not know whether to trust her or not. But a promise was a sacred thing. Surely she *couldn't* break it? I thought, conveniently forgetting that I had broken mine to Mother. Nevertheless a little black cloud of anxiety hovered over my carefree world.

It was a beautiful day of late summer, warm and ripe. I sauntered along, keeping carefully to the grass verge of the road, outwardly calm but inwardly excited. It was the very first time I had really been out alone in my life. I felt very grownup and self-sufficient and self-important. The most beautiful flowers grew along the roadside; meadowsweet and purple vetch and camomile daisies; sorrel, fleabane and willow-herb. I picked a great bunch as I walked, clutching it firmly in my hot and grubby little hand. There was goose-grass, too, whose little green balls stuck to my socks and tickled as I waded through it; and one bright golden clump of yellow bedstraw. The butterflies swirled around the flower clumps. I saw that the world was uncommonly beautiful.

Slowly I plodded on, but there was no sign of Mother. And then suddenly my heart stood still. Far behind me I heard a rustling sound that grew louder; the soft sussurrus of bicycle wheels. I ran into the ditch, lying down and trying to hide. But it was too late. The bicycles slowed down; stopped; a furious Muriel and Harold confronted me. I looked desperately along the road. Oh, if only Mother would come! But there was nothing to be seen; not even Bluebeard's cloud of dust.

Soaking wet and muddy from the ditch I was hauled ignominiously out by my enraged brother and made to throw away my flowers. Then Muriel cycled back to announce that I had been found while Harold walked me home, telling me on the way exactly what he thought of me and why. I scarcely listened; I was howling too much to hear anything much except the sound of my own tears. It was a very hot day and he, poor boy, was sweating from the speed with which he had ridden along the road in the expectation of finding my car-mangled body lying in it. He had been frightened, and was very angry indeed.

At last we got home (I had walked, to everyone's surprise, well over a mile) and I was put straight to bed for the rest of the morning as a punishment. I should probably have been kept there all the afternoon too, had not Mother said I could get up again, despite general protestation. 'He was punished quite enough by being caught,' I heard her say to Father. Never again did I break that sort of promise; and never again would I go to tea with the woman who had betrayed me. Apparently, the moment my back was turned she ran straight to the Vicarage to announce that I was attempting to walk to Gloucester. Because she broke her promise to me, I learned that perhaps it hurt people if I broke my promises to them. But I also learned an even more valuable lesson; how beautiful is the natural world, and how beautiful is freedom; and how doubly beautiful is the blend of the two. I did wrong, and I was caught and punished; but I have never forgotten the loveliness of the world on that summer morning when I set out alone at the age of five, to walk to Gloucester.

*   *   *

What a refreshment the country was after London, and how different! The fields and trees that took the place of streets and buildings were playground and playthings. Cats and cows, sheep and horses were my friends. Only dogs I hated. The reason is simple. Apparently, one day, when I was two, a pug-dog attacked me in St James's Park, knocked me down and scratched my face. I can only very dimly remember the incident; but I have never liked dogs since. I dislike the way they fawn on man, their sentimental eyes, and the messes they make on pavements. Most of all I dislike the loud, stupid noise they seem never to stop making, exacerbating to the nerves, called barking.

Chickens I loved in a different way. I could not, as a small child, resist the impulse to chase them. Even the smacking that followed such chases seemed powerless to cure me. I would run among them delighting in the way they ran wildly hither and thither, cackling and squawking inanely. I loved to feel my power over them; their fluttery dismay seemed irresistibly funny. The thought of which was the best way to run never entered their poor muddled heads; they just ran. And I ran after them.

One day at Haresfield, I selected a fat, prosperous-looking Buff Orpington as my special victim. Round and round we went, the hen protesting loudly and dismally. Wilder and wilder grew the chase, and funnier and funnier became the distraught bird. Her fluffy rump jerked with comically rigid movements; her yellow legs pattered desperately about the yard. At last, spying the open door of a barn, she half ran, half flew in and, making for a corner, crouched down in it. There was a strange pause. Now that I had her in my power, I was a little frightened to touch her, for fear she would nip me with her beak. Child and chicken looked solemnly at one another. How red her comb was, and how bright her yellow, black-pupilled little eyes! I didn't know what I wanted from her. I wanted to hug and squeeze her; to tease, hurt, tickle and love her. I took a step forward. Her eyes closed, a tremor passed through her, and her head lolled limply on her neck, like a flower whose stalk had been broken. She was dead, of fright; and I had killed her.

For a few terrible seconds I tasted, as never before or since, the hateful thrill of complete power. It was orgasmic, and relaxed my limbs in melting, fluid waves of satisfaction and release. I felt weak with delicious fulfilment. I, all alone; *I* had done this; had actually made a chicken die of fright! What excitement! What power!

And then the glow faded; I grew cold and shivered. I began to realize that I had done the unspeakable, the unforgivable. I had chased to her death a creature that had never done me the least harm. I had been really cruel. I touched the poor bird's limp feathers. I wanted to weep, but I remained stony-eyed. This was beyond tears; it would never be forgiven, not by the grown-ups, but by God and by myself. For once, punishment did not matter. I knew that I couldn't even tell Mother what I had done. And I struggled painfully with the knowledge and understanding that the lustful thrill of power had been all-dominating while it lasted; and that it might happen again.

It was a very miserable and white-faced child that crept out of the barn, the frightening barn in whose dimly filtered light lay a dead chicken. Stone-dead. Nothing any more but dead feathers, dead eyes, dead comb. Its deadness filled the whole barn. I played silently the whole day. I did not want to speak or be spoken to.

I was haunted utterly by the dreadful thing I had done. At tea, my father said : "One of the chickens is dead. I found it in the barn. I suppose it must have had some disease, and died of heart-failure. It's odd, because it looks quite all right.'

My face turned scarlet, and I hung my head. Yet nobody seemed to notice or suspect me. Ah, indeed it had died of heart-failure. It had died of the kind of fright I would die of if at home something came out of the black alcove and chased me down the stairs. I knew, on that horrible day in 1914, what one means by the hunter and the quarry; and how one could be both. The haunter and the haunted. And then, the haunter haunted. The hunter hunted.

It was my especial punishment that I was not suspected, and that I could not tell about it, much as I wanted to. For days the knowledge darkened my life secretly; and then slowly it faded and a part of me forgot about it. But I never chased chickens again. The hot, burning lust would fill me with almost irresistible temp-tation; just to do it a little, so that they couldn't mind. And then I would see the crumpled, dead hen in the corner of the barn; and a horrible revulsion would fill me, and I would run blindly, any-where, to get away from the chickens.

No, I have never chased them again. All the same, I still like walking rather fast through chicken-yards; and if I have a walking-stick in my hand, so much the better; for then I can prod—oh, so gently—their fluffy behinds, and enjoy seeing them hop.

*   *   *

September arrived, and the green figs ripened on the sunny south wall, and Harold ate too many, and was ill. The picnics in Standish Woods were over; the butterflies we had collected were carefully packed for the journey home. The plate-clock was wrapped up in brown paper (for I always insisted on taking it with me for the holidays); in the garden the michaelmas daisies, the sunflowers, the red-hot pokers, and the dahlias were out. The sense of approaching autumn hung over everything; calm, silent, fulfilled. Clouds floated serenely in the clear blue sky. I went round the house saying good-bye to my favourite things.

We all bundled into the trap with our belongings. I watched the tall chimneys of Haresfield Vicarage disappearing round a bend, and waved to them; unaware that I should not see them again for twenty years. How short seemed the drive to Gloucester! All too soon we were standing on the noisy platform of the smoky station, waiting for the train. I didn't want to go home, and said so, volubly; until Father, to quieten me, went to the name-plate machine and returned with a shining strip of aluminium with my very own name, JOHN THEODORE LIVINGSTON RAYNOR on it, thereby nearly missing the train. Cook's parrot was comfortably settled in the guard's van, and her cat in a hamper at her feet. The plate-clock lay in my lap, I could hear it ticking; and in my hand was the precious name-plate. The porter locked the carriage door for us, Father tipped him, and the whistle blew. The holidays were over, and we were on our way home again.

*   *   *

When the train slid, puffing and steaming, into Paddington, the shouting porters, the friendly, smoky smell, the hazy light, the taxi-cabs and the sound of the echoing hooters under the vast roof, the roar of the traffic outside, all told me that the winter was going to start, that we were home, and that it would be a year before we went away again to the country. I was at once pleased and sorry to be home; and gradually, as familiar landmarks came into sight, more pleased than sorry. The country was lovely, but London was known and friendly. We crossed the echoing, expectant Yard that was stippled with sun and shadow and lay sombrely cool in the late afternoon light. Up the steps of Number 3, Father fumbling for his latch-key. The door opened, the hall embraced us with the old familiar smell, and we stood once again in our own home.

I ran into the dining-room, looking first out of our windows onto our garden, and then at the reflection of the garden in the huge sideboard mirror. How the trees had yellowed, and how much stiller and quieter everything seemed than the day we had gone away! The grass of the lawn was quite long, and the creeper on College was beginning to turn red. How the room and the garden were holding their breath, equivocal, mysterious and rather challenging! The house was glad to have us back, but it was watching us to see what we would do. Suddenly I wanted to see my toys; all the ordinary things I loved.

I raced upstairs, clutching the precious plate-clock firmly to my chest. I ran into the nursery, and pulled out my toys. They were all safe, just as I had left them. For a moment their strangeness and sense of novelty thrilled me; but something stronger was calling me. Without troubling to put them away I made my way slowly out on to the landing and up the stairs to the top window. It was half open. I stuck my head out. An ineffable stillness held the afternoon; all the tree-tops I could see between the roofs had turned yellow. In the country it was still summer; here it was autumn. Ashburnham's little garden looked misty and overgrown with straggly spikes of golden rod. Still the Abbey sailed the sky, unchangeable and unchanged. The Yard was quite empty and silent. In a few days, the boys would be back, and it would be full of noise and shouting again; but now it lay as in a golden dream, under the full spell of autumn. The western face of Big Ben was bright with sun, but the other, that directly faced the house, was grey and shadowed. The hands pointed to two minutes to four. In two minutes, the bells would ring out in the stillness, and I should know that I was safely, inescapably home, wrapped warmly round by the love of place of which they were both mouthpiece and guardian. I felt the old indescribable excitement mounting in me as the minute-hand crept nearer to the twelve. Another half-minute. . . . The hand was on the very centre of the figure. Now; and I unconsciously tensed my whole body. Nothing happened. The hand was definitely past the twelve; perhaps the chimes were a fraction late. And now it was quite a minute past four, and still the quietness of the Yard lay unbroken.

What had happened? Why had Big Ben not chimed the most precious hour of the whole year, the hour of homecoming? I had tensed myself to no purpose, and the disappointed slackening of my body was as though air was oozing through a small puncture and slowly deflating me. Mystified and wounded beyond words I made my way dejectedly downstairs again to ask Mother what had happened.

She was busy unpacking, and did not hear my question. I had to repeat it. 'Why didn't Big Ben chime?' I asked again, tears of disappointment choking in my voice.

'Because we're at war with Germany, darling,' my mother said.

'But why does that stop Big Ben?' I asked.

'I suppose they think it's dangerous with aeroplanes,' said Mother.

'Well, I'd rather have Big Ben than a war,' I said, 'wouldn't you, Mummy? So why can't we?'

Whether my mother heard this question or not, I don't know. At any rate, she made no reply to it, and I left the room very soberly indeed, retiring to the nursery to ponder over the incomprehensible actions of grown-ups.

9

The Bright and the Dark

In *The Woman of Andros*, that great writer, Thornton Wilder, puts into the mouth of his principal character this phrase : 'I praise all living, the bright and the dark.' All my life I have recognized what that sentence says as an ideal for which to strive. I have always realized that without the night the day would be meaningless; that man could not understand good without the evil that underlines it; that white without black is an immediate and arresting contradiction in terms. In this life, that is; for the ultimate knowledge of good in its own right, needing no foil and contrast, is a knowledge that the finite mind is incapable by its very nature of comprehending. And the same must, I suppose, be reluctantly admitted of evil. In fact, I believe profoundly in Heaven and Hell; the two watertight compartments whose ecstasy and agony spring from the same source; that in neither is there any standard of comparison. Here, on this earth, we are let down lightly; the day always contains hints of the night; and, what is much more important, the night holds eternal promise of the day. My childhood was blest, in that Westminster was never grey; it was, spiritually speaking, quite violently either white or black. So that my sense of values always remained clear and untarnished; the grey, middle course never presented itself to me in the formative years.

What were, at that time, in my early childhood, 'the bright and the dark'? There were the bright and the dark themselves, and the symbols that stood for them, and the places that housed them. The bright and the dark themselves were two points so far away, one high up, the other low down, that they could only be sensed. The symbols were many. But they are most clearly to be seen in the two daydreams in which I always indulged before I fell asleep.

They started when I was about three or four. In the daydream of the bright I saw myself, grown up, usually in shining well-polished armour, delivering a girl from evil men who were menacing her in a way I did not understand. I would hack through the group with my sharp and flashing sword, and laying about me on all sides would finally ride off with the girl on my horse. For some reason I cannot analyse the setting for this scene was usually Whitehall, near where today the Cenotaph stands. Sometimes the girl was my mother, or some kind of projection of her. After I had ridden away with her I would comfort her; and this was the most beautiful part of the daydream. In a deep, instinctive way, I knew about love-making; and the whole point of the strange ecstasy I felt lay in the fact that I did not attempt to make love to her, because I knew that she wanted tenderness rather than passion. It was my pleasure to subdue the selfish side of my nature, and to rise to heights of selflessness that were unattainable in every-day life. The old and almost lost ideal of chivalry moved and stirred my whole being; I knew, in self-denial, an ecstasy as sharp and as keen as any I have ever felt since. Happiness would flood me as I gazed with rapture on the beautiful face of the girl, and knew that it lay in my power to make her whole life happy. I would prolong to its utmost limit this stage of the daydream. And then the brightness would gently fade, like a dying picture in the fire; spark by spark it would go out, leaving a cool, misty blueness like the eastern sky when the sun has set on a summer's evening. And sleep would come as gently as dewfall.

The daydream of the dark was never as clearly defined as the other. In it, black figures moved callously, with a sensual, trampling virility. Pain was inflicted upon helpless and innocent victims. Black and unpleasant hills sometimes formed the background; at other times, the not very clearly seen movements took place in heavy, dark rooms. Always lust and cruelty were present like wreathing coils of smoke. Beauty and gentleness were trampled under by heavy-bodied feet. Yet I could never see clearly what actually happened. When I was rather older, and had read the story by the brothers Grimm of the robbers who killed a beautiful and innocent girl, cut up her body into sections, sprinkled the sections with salt and pepper and ate them, I used to add my own vision of this story to the daydream.

This dream of the dark invariably ended in a kind of infantile masturbation. I would press my body hard against the bed, tremendously enjoying the sensations that were invoked; sensations that grew sharper and sharper until something—I did not really know what—happened; and after that it was suddenly not interesting any more, and I would either fall asleep or pass to the dream of the bright. For with a curious sense of fairness I would alternate the relative positions of the dreams. At that age only the slightest of moral considerations entered; I enjoyed each dream in its own way, although I knew quite well in my heart which was the more important one, and the one to be followed up (if only I could do so) in life itself. But being full of original sin it scarcely occurred to me to question the pleasure that the dream of the dark gave me; it was as much a part of that deep, secret soul-life as was the dream of the bright. I dreamed the two daydreams of the dark and the bright until I was six or seven years old; then they were gradually received back into the world from which they had come, and lost for me both their power and their meaning under the growing pressure of such activities as going to school.

*   *   *

And as for the places that housed the bright and the dark, how can I describe them? Perhaps it is best done by contrasting the two most different atmospheres I knew; that, living in juxtaposition one with the other, never mingled their separate essences. The bright and the dark, side by side; of their brightness and of their darkness making the intangible yet permanent barrier that allowed of no fusion. White ended and black began; black ended and white began, like the beam of a lighthouse that stabs the darkness and is gone again, inevitably to return.

Ashburnham House was built in the seventeenth century; legend has it, by Inigo Jones or else by his pupil, Webb. It is the most beautiful house that the school possesses, and one of the most

beautiful in London. It faces south and its noble and gentle rooms
are saturated with sunlight on a fine summer's day. It is as though
the house possessed the power of storing the sunlight of generations.
Here the school library is situated; and often Mother would take
me with her when she went to choose a book. We would turn the
octagonal handle of the front door, and the loving spirit of the
house would rush to meet us. A warm and drowsy smell of summer
lingered always in the passages and rooms; a smell of leather
bindings and sun-blinds, and sun-warmed stone, and stone that
had cooled slowly as the sun had moved from it in his course round
the heavens; and the smell of very old polished wood, and of the
happy dead. It was the holiest place I have ever known. It has
been said of it that 'there are more gorgeous rooms in the world
. . . but none more peaceful, none more full of sweetness and light,
than those seventeenth-century rooms of which the great drawing-
room at Ashburnham House is the finest.'

And there, through many a long summer morning I would sit,
curled up on the window-ledge, while Mother browsed dreamily
among the vast library. I would hear her take out a book, and
then for a space there would be silence; and then she would put
it back and take out another; and time would slow down, and a
clear golden peace would descend, and the room would swim,
uplifted, transported, in dusty golden light. I would stare out of
the window at the dark façade of Number 3 across the Yard; and
the puffy white clouds would sail slowly, slowly, across the clear,
deep blue sky; and the sun, warm through the glass, would search
out my body, and lay gentle hands upon it. Flies and bees would
murmur on the window-panes, humming drowsily, and the eloquent, happy silence of Ashburnham, encompassing me, would
hold me in its sweet and loving spell. Never did Ashburnham turn
against one; always its arms were waiting to enfold its lovers in
the still and rapturous embrace of pure ecstasy. Never did I want
to leave that beautiful window-seat; and nor did Mother. When
she had found the book of her final choice, she would come and
sit with me, taking me upon her lap sometimes; sometimes leaving
me undisturbed. For an hour or more we would sit there, drenched
in golden peace, until the bells, heard dimly through the glass,
whispered that outside time was measuring its inexorable course.
And only then, and often very reluctantly, would we gather up
our books, and slowly leave this beautiful house, saying, I know,

many private farewells in our hearts to the gracious ghosts that were its only inhabitants.

I have known well in my life only two human beings of consummate beauty; my mother and one other; beings about whom one must remain silent, since what is known of them may not be said in words; and both those beings remind me of Ashburnham House; and when I think of Ashburnham House I inevitably think of them. For the two beings and the house have in common the rarest quality that is known to man : the unshakable, rock-like strength and love that, springing from holiness, are at the same time its first-fruits. Ashburnham House came as near as any place can come in this finite and imperfect world to housing the bright, and only the bright.

*   *   *

And as for the dark; my sister Edith, after her marriage, lived at the far end of the Cloisters. Sometimes on a winter's evening I would go round to her house to talk to my brother-in-law in his study, or to take a message for Mother. I could either go right round through Dean's Yard and into the fringe only of the Cloisters, or I could make the journey through the Cloisters themselves. Nearly always I took the latter course. Courage forbade the other way. I had to face what was there to be faced. I would shut the front door of Number 3 behind me, and stand in the Yard, by Up-School, summoning all my resources, all my reserves of courage, before plunging into the long tunnel of the Dark Cloister. Never was a name more apt. Ill-lit, damp and musty-smelling, it combined the qualities of an underground passage and a tomb. To the right, the dark lane that led to the bubbling fountain gaped open-mouthed, and the sound of the water plashing into the basin in the darkness was the first of the eerie horrors. The walls seemed to close around me as I was sucked into the tube of stale, cold air. I would stand sometimes, listening, the hair pricking on my scalp. What was that? And that? And the black shadow that had seemed to be lurking in the passage to the Inner Cloisters. Was it anything : did it move? Was it more than shadow? And where had it gone? Certainly there was nothing there now. But had there ever been? Far away at the other end of the cloisters I could hear the policeman patrolling; the sound of his boots squeaking in the distance accentuated the lonely horror that welled around me. If I called, he would not hear me. No living person would hear me, though the sound of my voice would echo mockingly around the suffocating thickness of the old stone walls, and return to me in a series of threatening echoes that would wake something that I hoped was sleeping, even though it had one eye and one ear open.

I would force myself to walk on, with halting steps, wanting to run, but knowing that if I did so I should lose all control of myself. And now came the worst thing of all, the Pulteney Memorial, at the angle where the Dark Cloister turned left into the South Cloister. The figure of Daniel Pulteney is represented at full length, reading a book, and his eyes seemed to follow me and bore into me at that terribly defenceless moment when, turning the right-angle, my back was presented directly to his gaze. I have since learnt that this unpleasing monument has the reputation of being haunted; for at midnight Daniel Pulteney is supposed to turn the page of his book. It is not a difficult story to believe, for there hovers a kind of feverish sub-vitality around his monument that is the opposite of calm resignation to death.

The South Cloister was better lit than the Dark Cloister; it had a kind of false, airy brightness that was deceptive. One could keep one's eyes steadily fixed on the tomb-stones let into the floor. There was 'Murio Clementi, called the Father of the Pianoforte', and 'Susanna, Ursula and Samuel, infant children of Samuel Wesley' and many others to walk over in the uneasy knowledge that beneath one's feet lay their bones, time-whitened and sardonic, the fleshless grin upon their dry faces, and the hollow eye-sockets staring blindly at one as one passed. I used to try not to see out of the corners of my eyes the stone effigies of the Norman abbots that lay under the seat of the wall, in case they moved slightly.

At last I would come to the door of my sister's house and knock upon it, listening to the rapid beating of my heart as I waited on the doorstep for the old servant to let me in. And then there was warmth and light again and safe sanctuary for an hour, until the time came with ghastly inevitability for the dreaded return.

For some reason it was always worse than the outgoing journey. It was as though the Cloisters, having seen me pass and knowing that I had to return, had in the interim been marshalling all their forces in a final endeavour to terrorize. By the Refectory door I would fancy that a hairy, cowled and hooded figure was waiting to slip out and join me. Half-way along the South Cloister they clustered round me, threatening, muttering, their chilly breath stirring the hair on my neck; dozens of them, all the uneasy, wrestling denizens of these haunted corridors, whose bodily remains lay in varying attitudes beneath the crumbling flagstones. And as I passed the Pulteney Memorial, my whole body covered with gooseflesh, I would fancy that an eighteenth-century, lace-fringed hand fell from the stone book and reached towards my collar. But no; I was safe; and there remained only the Dark Cloister. *Only* the Dark Cloister! I would clench my teeth and my hands until the knuckles showed white through the skin; I would place each foot carefully before the other; and I would propel my reluctant body forward by the force of nervous energy. I must not look at the high-up semi-circular black windows that were like eyelids. I must not look at the door to the Undercroft. I must not look down the passage to the Little Cloisters, and I must put my fingers in my ears to shut out the gradually increasing sound of the dripping fountain. Ahead of me lay the end of the tunnel, the archway that led into the comparative safety of Little Dean's Yard. I would get there and I could get there; God would help me to. Even though, because my fingers were in my ears, I should have to smell the dank stream of fusty air that told me I was opposite the passage to the Little Cloister. And now I could see the lamp on Up-School; a few steps more and I should be safe. But those last few steps were the worst of all, for behind them lay the full force of the Cloisters and their final chance to catch and keep me. A desperate heave of my body, and I stood, trembling and sweating, with the clean and starlit vault of heaven above my head. I was bruised but unhurt, and I could afford to look down the long gaslit shaft, and laugh defiance at it.

And suddenly I would think of Ashburnham, and see its outline only a few steps away, and imagine its sweet and silent rooms lying patiently in the arms of the rising moon, and I would be absolved of all fear, and know that 'though terror endureth for a night, joy cometh in the morning'. My eyes would fill with tears of relief as I thought of that beautiful house and of my mother and of all the pure and holy things that had been given, at the last, by the grace of God, dominion over the powers of darkness.

10

The Nursery

When I started having 'visions' my parents came to the conclusion that it was time I went to school. I can scarcely blame them. Mother had been reading to me stories about the Irish saints; and the tale of one, St Columba, had deeply impressed me. It seems that he was constantly having visions, which fired my competitive spirit; if a saint had visions, why shouldn't I? So I did.

One morning, when for some reason I was sleeping in my mother's bed, I woke her at half-past five.

'Mummy!' I cried; 'I've had a vision!'

'Oh have you, darling?' she muttered drowsily; 'Well, go to sleep again now.'

I was very disappointed, but her tone of voice did not seem to me to admit of remonstrance. I had to wait until later on to tell her. When she was properly awake, I began again.

'You know that sparrow's skeleton I found in the Yard on the gravel yesterday? Well, I saw the sparrow in a vision sitting before the throne of God. It was in the middle of the night I saw it. It was all bright, and its feathers were back on it, and God had made it sit bang opposite to him, in front of all the angels, and it was singing, and—and . . .' but here my invention petered out.

Mother very kindly did not laugh. She merely looked at me rather curiously. Had I left the matter there, all would have been well. Unfortunately, with the instinct of the artist, I wanted to tell my story to everyone. In a bad moment I chose Harold and Muriel as fit receptacles for the great news that I had had a vision.

Their reception of the tale was catastrophic. They laughed and laughed until tears were running down their cheeks and they could scarcely stand. In a tremendous huff, I drew haughtily away from them, protecting my lofty and superior spirit in an icy enclosure of silence. But, alas, I was not allowed to maintain it there. Every time I met Harold, for days and days afterwards, he would say: 'Tell me, John, have you had another vision yet?' in the tone of one who says: 'Tell me, John, have you been to the lavatory yet?'

I would say 'No' sulkily, though once I was so intrepid as to say 'Yes'. But the screams of laughter that followed the attempt to extract from me details depressed me so much that I blabbed to Mother about the teasing; and she forbade Muriel and Harold to mention visions again. Nevertheless, my brother would look at me with eyes full of laughter, and noiselessly form with his lips the words: 'Have you had another vision yet?' It was weeks and weeks and weeks before the matter was finally allowed to drop; and it was almost with a sense of pleasure and relief that I saw Harold, my hero, return to Winchester for the term. With the removal of this obstacle, my imagination began to run riot once more; and when I again told Mother that I had seen the throne of God, and that round it were sitting Grannie and Auntie Elizabeth and Auntie Jessie and cook's tabby-cat that had died, and Auntie Mary and Uncle William and the spaniel Mother had had as a girl, called Mac, she told me, sharply for her, to make quite sure of my facts on another occasion. It seemed that one, at least, of that company was still enjoying in a hale and hearty manner the land of the living; while I gathered by implication that another member was scarcely likely to be ensconced in so exalted a position as that occupied by the said person in my 'vision'. After this I gave up 'visions' and contented myself with my plasticine and my transfers.

For hours I would lie on the nursery floor with the blue, the green, the red balls of plasticine, kneading them into strange shapes that were for me the symbols of human beings, of cats, of clocks, of telegraph poles. I remember now the delicious smell of plasticine, and the good earthy satisfaction of having something mouldable in one's hands. I learned not to roll the colours together into a single ball because you couldn't separate them again; I knew all the joy of being a sculptor. But even more than plasticine did I love transfers, and it was one of the real and sad losses of my young life when the war put an end to them.

Nurse and I would go to the Army and Navy Stores to buy a three-halfpenny packet. They were in a long, thin yellow envelope, the very sight of which would fill me with joy. When we got home I would get out my scrapbook, put it on the table with a bowl of hot water, and set to work. A varied collection of transfers lay in the envelope; there were about half a dozen large ones of postcard size and an infinity of smaller ones. Some of the large ones were incredibly ambitious and extremely beautiful. Once there was a complete reproduction in sepia of Sir Joshua Reynolds's 'Angel Faces'; sometimes (which I think was very Germanic) one picture on the face of the transfer concealed the real picture. I remember one that looked as if it was a balloon sailing through the sky against a fiery sunset; but when it 'came off' it turned out to be St Paul's Cathedral by moon and starlight.

Doing the transfers was an art in itself. If the transfer was held in the water a second too long, the picture floated off its base into the bowl and was lost for ever. If it was held a second too short, it came off on the paper in bits. Equally, the exact temperature of the water was a vital factor. I remember still the sense of triumph, of having produced a perfect work of art, when one 'did' the transfer successfully. The colours of the wet picture had for a few moments a divine freshness and purity that were like the colours of living nature. This delicious toy did a great deal towards stimulating and confirming both my sense of beauty and my love of perfect craftsmanship. It was not easy to do the transfer completely flawlessly; but after a time I had the exact technique at my finger-tips.

Then, with the coming of the war, they stopped, for like most other good things of that nature, they had been made in Germany. Rather later, they were replaced by British sheets that roused my utter contempt; the pictures were of silly and vulgar comics; and they never 'came off' properly. And besides that, they cost at least four times as much as the German ones, and were in every way, and especially in colouring, inferior. After the war, the German ones, much smaller and humbler, returned; but by then I was too old to care. I have often wondered since whether the glorious, the almost mythical transfers of my early childhood, in the long yellow envelopes, ever returned. Somehow, I do not believe that they did; for they were extraordinarily representative of a period whose death-knell was forever sounded on 4 August, 1914.

Though there were no more transfers, I could always console myself with soap bubbles. Except that they were so messy that Nurse usually kicked up a terrible fuss before she finally gave way under the pressure of my single-minded aim. But at last I would cajole out of her the bowl of water with the piece of carbolic soap at the bottom, and the clay pipe. Then I would be happy for hours. First I would blow what I called 'A Crystal Palace', by inserting the pipe under the surface of the soapy water and blowing hard, which produced a glittering edifice of small joined bubbles that rose high in the basin, till pipe, lips and face were entangled in it. Sometimes, a little masochistically, I would deliberately suck through the pipe instead of blowing, shuddering and spitting as the raw, soapy fluid filled my mouth. Infuriated by the horrid taste, I would throw the pipe angrily on the floor, which meant going round to the little shop in Marsham Street and purchasing, for the sum of a halfpenny, another. I would try to find one that had the design of a windjammer embossed on its bowl, but I was not always successful. Sometimes, if I was rich, I bought two for a penny. And when we got home, red sealing wax had to be plastered round the mouthpiece; for the touch of the raw clay was supposed to be damaging to little lips. After that, the new pipe was ready. Then, through long use, inch by inch would break off the stem, until finally that pipe, too, had to be discarded and another bought.

When, through the medium of repeated Crystal Palaces, the soap and water solution had attained the exactly right density (which was tested by holding the pipe, bowl downwards, high up, and if a shining film sealed the mouth of the bowl it was all right; and if a dribbly spurt of soapy water fell on the tablecloth or in my upturned eyes, it wasn't), I would blow the first bubble. Would it be one of those big, but rather watery and colourless ones? Would it be small but very brilliant, and quickly burst in a sound-less splash? Or, would it be both large and well-coloured? And, finally, would it perhaps be the best bubble I had ever blown?

I would blow, very, very gently until the bubble was as big as I dared make it. I would hold the pipe high above my head, with the shiny globe dangling and quivering from it. How beautiful it was, with the soft, iridescent colours going round in it, and the convex reflection of the nursery window-pane with the row of geraniums on the ledge, diminutive but clear! A gentle shake of the pipe, a soft breath from underneath, and the bubble would sail round the room, miraculously avoiding for a time the sharp point of the electric light bulb, the handle of the toy-cupboard, or Nurse's inconvenient ironing-board at the other end of the room. Alas, only for a time! Suddenly, there would be a faint hiss, a tiny bright explosion that was like an exclamation of surprise, a muted splattery sound; and somewhere a few grey wet beads of soap lay, the poor earthly remains of my beautiful bubble. (Usually, somewhere unfortunate, such as Nurse's head, or in the jampot.)

If it was summer, and the window open, I would guide the bubble past the sharp glassy points of the tinkling Japanese Wind-bells, and out into the free air of the garden. I would lean out, watching the glittering sphere sailing in the sun, gradually sinking, down and down, smaller and smaller, until at last it made a wet blob far away on the study steps. One had to be very careful to make sure that Father was not walking below, thinking out the more ticklish parts of an exam paper, otherwise there might be grave trouble if the wet bubble was so misguided as to burst upon his grey head.

One day, my brother-in-law, Francis, whom I adored, strolled into the nursery smoking his bulldog pipe. When he saw me blowing bubbles, he said: 'I'll show you quite a new sort of bubble.' Filling his mouth with tobacco-smoke, he picked up my soap-bubble pipe, and blew. What a miracle emerged! Not the usual clear bubble, but a beautiful soft grey one, opaquely shining, inside which furry wreaths of smoke gently revolved. He sent it into the air. Breathlessly I watched it. It hit the electric-light bulb, and exploded. And there, where it had been, was a lovely patch of sweet-smelling smoke! I could not believe it. I made Francis do this trick again and again, pressing my nose (which was never a small one) forward so that the bubble burst on its tip, and deluged my nostrils with smoke. Which is probably why to this day I cannot smell Waverley Mixture without being nostalgically assailed by the past. After this experience I made poor Mother's life a misery by trying to make her smoke a cigarette (which she hated) in order to blow me smoke-bubbles. About twice I succeeded; for my mother was always extraordinarily ready to sacrifice her own feelings for the sake of giving pleasure to someone she loved.

* * *

At this time of my life my other great nursery interest was the blackboard and chalks. Coloured chalks, that is; not the dull white ones. For some reason, like so many things one wanted badly, they were very hard to come by. I used to go to the little toyshop in Marsham Street, where the pipes came from, to buy a packet of chalks. When the proprietor saw my expectant face he would solemnly shake his head. 'Only white ones today,' he would gloomily remark, 'there ain't no call for colours, see?' Why, oh why, I used to wonder, was there no call for colours? Only this deathly white? Very occasionally, I would return, radiant, with a glorious packet that was not white; that contained rose pink, sky blue, and lime green sticks of beautiful length and treacherous fragility; and sometimes, purple, yellow or chocolate. Then I would settle down for the rest of the day to emulate the pavement artists whose work along the Embankment or Birdcage Walk I so admired. I would try faithfully to reproduce the figure-of-eight loaf with its touching caption : 'Easy to Draw, but Hard to Get', or the blushing cut of salmon on its snowy plate; or even 'His Majesty the King, God Bless Him', which was, alas, far beyond my infant powers. I would also draw a cat sitting on a brick wall with its back to the spectator. Auntie Ruth had shown me how to do this, and I was very proud of it. Its great advantage was that there was no face. And should it go wrong, I could easily change it into the figure-of-eight loaf. I also drew the usual rather dreary current-bun representations of human beings indulged in by all children, with thin, sticking-out arms and legs. Aware that the outline left much to be desired, I would do my best to redeem it by the liberal application of colour. The finished result, if crude, was at least original. I was particularly fond of purple ringlets of hair for my women; thereby anticipating by some twenty years the fashion of dyeing the hair to match the ensemble. Purple was my favourite and most precious colour, because there was only one purple chalk (if that) in a box; and so it automatically became the king of the chalks.

And then . . .

'Now then, Master John, your dinner's ready. Rub them pictures off the board, come on now, do. 'Urry up, put them chalks away in the top-cupboard—come along now. Just look at your 'ands, all over colours. 'Ow you do get in such a mess, I don't know, I'm sure. Come 'ere, while I get the flannel. . . .'

Resentfully, I would glower over my dinner, eating as fast as I dared, so that I could quickly get back to the blackboard. And yet, when at last I was allowed to return to the toy-cupboard, I would find that I had mysteriously lost interest in the chalks, and wanted to play with other toys. I could never understand what made the change inside me; was it that food altered one's angle of vision? Whatever the reason, chalks were now dull and meaningless, while the toys shone with a new desirability.

What should it be? The old grey battered Noah's Ark; the plasticine; the top? The top! It was a bulky old top, shaped like a soup tureen; you spun it by pressing a sort of cotton-reel affair on the handle; and suddenly it was tracing patterns on the floor, humming with a deep-throated organ chord. A skilful smack with the palm of the hand, and the chord changed to a higher one; another smack, and it changed to a higher one still. Then, fainter and fainter would grow the humming; one would watch the top breathlessly; and suddenly, with a sort of wobbly choking noise, it would heel over and come to an abrupt stop on its side on the linoleum. A final spasmodic kick, and it would be dead, waiting to be spun to life again.

On the whole, I held a strangely superior and adult attitude towards toys. Even in very early days I was only fairly fond of teddy-bears; and I always hated golliwogs because they were so ugly and silly, such a clownish distortion of human beauty, which even then I realized was a matter of the deepest moment, and never to be made fun of. If God made man in His own image, in whose image were golliwogs made, and why? I didn't know, and I didn't care; I preferred my beautiful white cat that mewed when her tummy was pressed. I still have this toy; it is so lifelike and well made that it has on several occasions been mistaken for a real kitten, stuffed. That, and a doll called Peter Benvenisti, are all that have survived from the welter of childish toys. Peter Benvenisti has a little cape of red-edged rough towelling which ties round his shoulder for the purpose of draping decently his naked form; only, when you take the cape off it, it is immediately apparent that there is nothing, really, to conceal; even his navel is conspicuous by its absence. On this account I was always hopefully inclined to believe that he was an angel, since angels, I had been told, were neither male nor female; but this belief was dashed by the fact that he had no wings either. Nevertheless, despite the fact that he was in some ways a little lacking, I was extremely fond of Peter B. and used to take him to bed with me when I was about four. How he avoided being squashed flat, since he is made of celluloid, I have no idea; it is sufficient that somehow he did, and lives still to tell the tale.

Not so, alas, my celluloid ducks; they always in time got trodden on the nursery floor. Nor is it fair to call them ducks; they were undoubtedly drakes, with their bright plumage and little curly tails. They enjoyed my bath with me every night till I was a real schoolboy and too big for such childish pastimes. At this time, when I was five or so, there were always one or two of them lying about in states of varying damage on the shelves of the toy-cupboard.

And now I am impelled to describe the toy-cupboard itself. It stood, some three feet high, against the nursery wall; it was painted a pale green and the paint had long ago lost both its glossiness and its true colour. It had a white china handle on its door; and inside were three shelves. I never knew whether I loved or hated it. It was nice to feel that my toys were safe from prying grown-ups inside it; but it was nasty—exceedingly so—to be made to tidy it, as periodically happened. One day the white china handle broke off, and was replaced by a black china handle. It at once became a different toy-cupboard; and I had completely to relearn its animism. It was slightly more threatening with its black handle; less easy-going and lovable; more likely to take frowning offence if its shelves were left untidy. What I should have felt about it had the grown-ups taken it into their silly heads to repaint it, I tremble to think. Like all small children, I hated having to make a new adjustment towards a familiar object. Gradually the adult grows away from this passionate object-sensitivity of the child; the link between person and thing withers and finally snaps, until it means less than nothing. Which is why pepper-pots can be made of red plastic and get away with it.

And now let us look inside the cupboard, and see what we can find. Right at the back of the top shelf is the sinister blue beetle mentioned earlier, and next to it, my messy paintbox, with the palette uncleaned and the brushes unwashed. There are a few of an old alarm-clock with the main-springs protruding, on the second shelf, and the old red and green fort with a few lead soldiers lying flat on its floor; and beside that, the Noah's Ark transfers in an envelope, and the plasticine. There are the bowels with its painted windows like those of an eighteenth-century chapel. And the dolls'-house, hardly ever touched, with some broken-legged gilt furniture in it, and grubby lace curtains sweeping down across the windows at an angle of forty-five degrees, half-concealing a tiny plaster aspidistra. And beside the dolls'-house, the planisphere, which showed the stars, and was illuminated by a candle. A favourite toy while it lasted, which was not for very long, for the candle dropped wax on the revolving paper disc, creating a false Milky Way; and the next time it was used this milky way caught fire, and I hastily dropped the blazing toy on the floor where it was equally hastily stamped out by Nurse, with many grumbles. I was not very sorry; for the stars were printed white against a black background; whereas every self-respecting child knows that stars are a blend of gold and silver against a sky of velvet sapphire-blue. The fact that it revolved was interesting; but it could never compete with Father's star-maps for beauty.

And what else lay upon the shelves of that legendary cupboard of so long ago? There was the large wooden clock-face with movable hands given me by Harold, and the cardboard ones made by my sisters, that I have mentioned before. And, of course, there was the set of telegraph-poles that I had been given for Christmas, black metal representations about a foot high, with real white insulators. And a reel of fine wire had been enclosed, so that they could be properly strung, and then spread out on the nursery floor to edge an imaginary highway that vanished over the top of the hill into infinity. Then, when the day's march was over, the wire could be unwound, and the poles packed neatly away (but not by me, if possible) in a cardboard box. A beautiful toy, this, because it demanded of one a certain constructive ingenuity to assemble. It, in turn, reminds me of my wooden bricks, that were square and of a natural colour, but for some rose-red and grass-green corner pieces with curved and triangular tops that were like lovely cakes to look at and always crowned the evanescent edifice of the moment. And the interlocking cards, with which one could build a tremendously tall house that a single puff of breath could in a second demolish; and many other simple toys of the same nature that were inextricably mixed up with stale alphabet biscuits that I had taken from the tea-table when no one was looking, and with which I would write little sentences until greed overcame me and I ate what I had written. So that the threat, 'I'll make you eat your words', was no idle one to me. About an inch high, each biscuit was beautifully made in the shape of a letter (or a numeral); it had a crinkly edge and the little air-holes that biscuits have, and tasted deliciously dry. Its counterpart and companion was the picture-biscuit, whereon in white relief against chocolate or pink sugar, some simple scene was represented; it was beautiful to bite away the donkey's head, or pollard a willow-tree with a single snap of the jaws; and I have often wondered since whether alphabet and picture biscuits have returned, to give pleasure to other generations of children.

There were the books; few but much loved and well worn. The first book of all, with red and black pictures, 'Bess and Jess had a rab-bit. It was black'; a copy of *The Child's Guide to Knowledge*, *Mr. Rutherford's Children*, a book called *The First Book*, but really about the tenth; and nearly all of the Peter Rabbit series, without question the best books ever written for children. Effortlessly still the titles return to mind : *The Tale of the Flopsy Bunnies*; *Mr. Jeremy Fisher*; *Tom Kitten*; *Mrs Tittlemouse*; *The Tale of Pigling Bland*, and (because of its pictures) my favourite, *The Tailor of Gloucester*. Books that in size and content are the natural complement to a child's mind. The Andrew Lang Fairy Books were there too; the Blue, the Green, the Violet, the Orange, the Olive; and the tales of the Brothers Grimm (was ever a name more apt?) and of Hans Andersen. But we shall hear more of these in a later chapter.

*   *   *

'Now then, Master John, put all that rubbish away, do; 'urry up now, or the water'll get cold.'

And, still struggling, I would be hauled ignominiously off to the bathroom, feverishly clutching a celluloid duck in one hand and a grey Dreadnought in the other, determined that if I had to have a bath I would have something to sail, at least, on its heaving waters.

Our bathroom was long and narrow, and very gloomy. The bath stood like a white coffin against the bead-spangled walls, and a hard unshaded electric light bulb glared nakedly around the tunnel-like room. Nevertheless, the preliminaries over, I loved my bath. The Vinolia soap smelt so delicious, and Nurse's hands, as she soaped me, were tender as well as firm. Only the infernal scratch of the loofah I hated, and tried to wriggle away from it, with the inevitable result that a soapy flannel found its way into my eyes, on purpose or accidentally—who shall say? But once that was over, that hateful scraping of my back, I was free to play with my duck or my ship, to gaze admiringly at my pink little body, to make (within reason) what I was pleased to call 'waves'; and to listen to Nurse singing in her sweet, rusty voice that was like an old violin, either 'My Bonnie', or an even sadder song about a girl who, finding her lover unfaithful, did away with herself in the fifth verse to the accompaniment of details so melancholy that I was sometimes hard put to it not to cry.

Dear old Nan! I see her still, bending over me, with her sharply handsome, slightly masculine face (she was the daughter of a sea-captain and a Spanish girl) singing in that cross, sweet voice of hers; bidding me hurry up, the kindness belying the irritation, so that I could be wrapped in the warm towel and rather roughly dried. The very best type of old servant, who had done the same by every one of my parents' children; her stern exterior scarcely concealing an undying loyalty and faithfulness to 'the master' and 'the mistress' and their offspring; a type that one may now seek in vain. Whose whole life was a labour of love, untroubled by self or any other kind of questioning; who was loved in return and whose heart it would have broken to leave us.

Steaming and fragrant from the bath, I would be bundled into bed with Peter Benvenisti for company; and after the ritual of the two dreams I would fall asleep, to dream of my toys and the following day's adventures. But (and I had almost forgotten) first I would kneel at my mother's knee, to ask God's blessing, and forgiveness for my sins.

And so the day ended; and still I am no nearer to the school that was threatened in the very first sentence of this chapter. And if the reader cannot wait any longer to hear about it, he had better skip the next chapter too; for something of much greater importance and interest than school is under way.

I I

The Garden

I have before me on my desk a half-sheet of notepaper in my father's handwriting. At the top of it is written : 'A List of Lepidoptera taken in the garden of 3, Little Dean's Yard, Westminster', and there follow the names of over thirty species of butterflies and moths.

*   *   *

This garden was long and narrowish, bounded on three sides by high walls; and this in itself gave its three great lime trees a feeling of infinite height. I think of them as I used to see them on a day of midsummer; tall and green and full of quivering light; the broad, translucent leaves throwing back the gold of the sun high overhead. It was then that they flowered, and scented the whole garden and the rooms of the house, and were noisy with the murmur of bees. Birds flew and alighted restlessly in their high branches, darting to the Virginia creeper that draped the house and back again to the trees. They had a companion, a magnificent plane whose blotched and speckled trunk rose from a cool and graceful bed of ferns. Beneath them lay the long strip of lawn, dappled with hot sun and cool shadow that flickered as the branches above stirred in a gentle breeze. They were backed by the tall, smoke-encrusted black wall that concealed the play-yard of Grant's. Occasionally a high-thrown rubber ball would be seen mysteriously sailing over the wall to bounce on our lawn once or twice before subsiding into stillness. Then there would be a shout, 'Ball, please!' which would sometimes, and sometimes not, be responded to. When I wanted something to do I would wander about the garden collecting all the old balls I could find, and fling them over the wall, whereupon an unseen voice would cry 'Thank you!' and the game next door would continue with renewed vigour. I would sit down in a deck-chair, or lie on the grass of the lawn, staring up into the forest of lime leaves bright against the sky, hypnotized by their gentle unceasing movement. Then I would look towards the house and see it standing very tall and still, clothed from head to foot in its green mantle of Virginia creeper, and flanked by the little wood, the most beautiful thing in the garden.

The wood had come into being thus. The garden was on the level of the first storey of the house; the lawn swept down to the basement by means of a steep bank, on whose arid slopes little would grow. Father had years ago conceived the idea of turning the bank into a little wood, a wood of real country trees. And so every year, a wild sapling had been brought back from the summer holiday and planted on the bank. Father knew the history of every tree, the date of its planting and from where he had dug it; the wood formed a living memorial to the summer holidays of the past. By the time of which I am writing, when I was five or six, many of the trees had grown to a height of twenty or thirty feet. There were two oaks, one much taller and stronger than the other, but both putting forth sturdy yellow-green leaves in the spring; there was a strong young ash (so that even there, in the heart of London, we could tell whether the oak was out before the ash, or vice versa), there were two tall and graceful mountain ashes, one of which occasionally produced drooping clusters of red-gold berries; there was a beech, which though it was not happy and did not grow much, never failed to unfold leaves of magical silken delicacy year by year; a small and rather stunted elm; and a most noble birch that grew as tall and as strong as if it had still been in its native haunts. And probably there were one or two other trees that I have forgotten.

This wood was the child of my father's imagination and artistry. A countryman born and bred, and never altogether happy in London, he succeeded in creating, in his wood, a tiny piece of pure country. In the spring, bluebells flowered beneath the trees; one could lie, dreaming, on the sloping bank, and fancy oneself deep in the heart of the countryside; and with half a dozen steps could be outside it and back again in London. A place of great magic, and adored by each child in turn. It served a double purpose, for besides providing one of the great joys of our lives, it supplied also provender for the caterpillars we brought back each September, and which needed feeding on birch, oak or beech leaves, a diet hard to come by in a great town. But perhaps the wood was most beautiful viewed from the windows of the dining-room or drawing-room, for one looked out upon forest green. Level with the eye from the dining-room, only the birch and the rowans soared to the level of the drawing-room; so that up there one looked down upon a roof of glowing sun-shot verdure pierced by the silvery trunk of the birch and its delicate, pyramidal top, whose leaves, even on the stillest summer day were never quite still, but shivered and twinkled against the blue sky.

Slowly and steadily the wood grew. Father had allowed for that in the skilful spacing of the trees; as he had ensured that the trees were not near enough to the house to darken its windows. It began to become a blended unity of varying greens; it began to cast shade, and to lie, dark and mysterious, under the moon. It began to assume the quality of a grove, dryad-haunted and remote; somewhere near its heart there should have been a tiny classic temple. It was twenty years old when we left London; one of the rarest things, surely, in the whole city; truly sylvan and truly pastoral. The old woodland gods began to haunt and bless it. It was a memorial to the gentle spirit of the man who had made it. Its existence had no ulterior motive; its sole aim was to surround men with leafy beauty and remind them that somewhere, far from the bricks and mortar, the smells and noises of urbanization, was the holy quiet of the undisturbed heart of the countryside.

*　　*　　*

The tops of the trees of the little wood, tenderly green in spring, serely yellow in autumn, reflected in the great sideboard mirror in the dining-room, constitute one of the most atmospherically-charged memories of the garden that I possess. And hard on the heels of the autumnal memory follows another, of the strange little roofless brick enclosure into which we swept the rich brown leaves in great heaps with the aid of the birch broom, to lie fallow until they had matured to leaf-mould for the flowerbeds. Here, too, the daffodils that had flowered in bowls, their long leaves tied in knots, were heeled in to ripen for their next flowering. It was a sad little structure; melancholy and nostalgic as autumn itself; rich with the breath of natural decay. Through its glassless window one had

a good view of the garden as it stretched its length to the house.
And how, in autumn, the walls of the house and of College
flamed! The long tassels of the Virginia creeper hung, scarlet as
blood, the delicate, five-fingered leaves shading through yellow to
palest rose-pink to deepest crimson. For weeks, the red would
remain, exquisitely static, waiting for the first roaring wind of
winter. And one morning one would wake to the sound of a gale,
and, running down the garden, would tread on a soft carpet of
countless fallen leaves, a bright-coloured carpet that hid the
crunching gravel; and turning, one would see the house and
College, sombre and dark, wintrily naked, standing in their brick
strength to face howling gust and driving rain. The long winter
lay before us; and yet, indoors, already the Paper White Narcissi
and the Roman Hyacinths were driving the green spears of spring
through their fibre-filled bowls. The snow would fall silently in
the night, Christmas would come and go, and so soon, to a child,
it would be spring again, and the ferns unfolding their crozier-like
fronds, and the Solomon's Seal that grew in the darkest corners
where nothing else would, hanging its stem of creamy, waxen bells
shyly against the wall. Slowly the garden would wake up; the
crocuses flare into patches of gold, lilac, purple and white; the
daffodils sprinkle the grass with lemon-coloured fire, and the gay
diminutive Duc van Tol tulips crouch, vermilion against the black
soil.

And then, suddenly, the bulb-flowers would be over, and the
long flowerbed, that divided the lawn from the path and was the
pride of our garden, cleared in readiness for its summer occupants.

Sometimes, I was allowed to help Father clear it. He would
call to the nursery window from the study steps. I would hurry
down to join him. Since it was the Easter holidays he would be
wearing his ancient striped grey flannel trousers supported by the
gold and sea-blue old Reptonian tie, and a cream-coloured flannel
shirt, open at the neck. He would wrinkle his nose, and the pince-
nez would fall on their black cord. He would smile at me and
say : 'Pick up a kneeler, and you can have that old trowel and
dig up the daffodil bulbs. But be careful you don't slice them.'
Then we would start at opposite ends, each on a kneeling-pad to
prevent the gravel of the path bruising our knees, gradually working towards the middle. Even when I was a very small boy Father
trusted me to do this simple job well; and soon it was very rarely

that I cut by mistake into the heart of a bulb. After a time, Mother would call 'Tea, my dears. It's a quarter past eleven', and I would have the delicious experience of sipping real tea from a grown-up cup with Father and Mother in the study. Father's face would be rosy from his exertions, his silver-grey hair and moustache would shine; his shirt would look so creamily clean, and the clouds of smoke from his pipe would seem to smell even more fragrant than usual. I never loved Father more than when I was gardening with him; the cares and troubles of the schoolmaster seemed to fall utterly from him; and though he must have been past the age of fifty, a kind of unquenchable, boyish enthusiasm would suffuse his whole being and make me feel that life was a most jolly thing. Like giants refreshed, after the tea we would hurry back to the garden bed, and by lunch-time it would be empty and smoothly raked, prepared for the summer bedding-out plants. And in the afternoon, under the hot spring sun, we would heel-in the bulbs we had removed in the rich mould of the little roofless potting-shed. Father would do the planting, and I would collect the bulbs from the edge of the lawn where we had piled them, in the little wheelbarrow. Then Father would stand in the open doorway of the little brick building, waiting with open arms and smiling face to receive the barrowload of bulbs. Or perhaps, as I am now inclined to think, waiting to receive me.

*   *   *

After the long flowerbed had been prepared and the window-boxes sown with nasturtium and sweet-pea seeds, a period of excited anticipation would ensue. When would the bedding-plants arrive? That depended upon Father; and Father would never tell. But one morning, unknown to anyone but Mother, he would get up at half past four, and bicycle through the quiet streets to Covent Garden market; and there he would choose the boxes of plants. Then, still before I had got up, they would be delivered. I like now to think of my father, cycling all alone through London, secretly free of school and family for an hour or so, to buy our summer flowers. This yearly adventure was a little ritual, of great importance and gravity; and as he pedalled home through half-empty streets that were flushed to brightness by the rising sun, his mind filled with the colours of the dewy flowers he had seen,

I am sure that he was vividly aware of the paradox of the flux and the stability of life. Year by year he had done this same thing; and still it was the same thing; still Big Ben rang his chimes through the cool morning air, and the river sparkled in the early golden light; and the cart-horses clattered noisily along the emptily-echoing streets. Still the children—though now there was only John—would be entranced by the flowers he had chosen; and if his hair was now grey where once it had been black, and perhaps the bicycle was a trifle harder to push, what matter? Nothing was changed. And yet, and yet . . . the years *were* passing, and nothing could stop them. And, of course, sometime there would come a year when. . . . And after steadily looking that year in the face for a moment, I think that my father would smile, and turn his mind to the steaming cup of coffee that Ada would have ready for him, and to the joy of bedding out his plants.

*   *   *

Every morning I would run to look out of Mother's bedroom window. Father would tease me. 'Do you think it's worth my going to Covent Garden this year, John? Perhaps if we sowed a few seeds it would do just as well.' Even Mother could not be got round; she would put me off with mysterious smiles if I asked any really pertinent questions. So the only thing to do was to look out of the window every morning when I woke.

I remember one year, when I was about six, being doomed to disappointment, morning after morning. I had almost made up my mind that no flowers would come. Day after day I had turned to the window on waking, to look up at a cloudless sky and down at the empty garden. Again and again, only the yellow gravel stared up at me. And then one morning, a few days before my birthday, below me on the path was box after box of flowers, whose colours shone and sang in the still, pure morning light. I drew in my breath with rapture. There were the geraniums, a splash of vivid scarlet; the azure-blue lobelias; the golden bubbly-flowered calceolarias; the white marguerites. And the petunias, whose soft trumpets were some of them white, some of them purple, some of them white streaked with purple, some of them purple streaked with white. I could see the tender green of the young tobacco plants; the darker green of the marigolds, starred here and there by a striped red and gold blossom. And all the boxes arranged side by side to make a great oblong of blazing, indiscriminate colour. And there was a small box filled with the yellow-green leaves of the pyrethrum plants that edged the bed and that smelt so deliciously pungent and that were never allowed to flower.

I stood at the window, and stared and stared, drinking in the riot of colour, until my whole being was filled with it, and uplifted to heaven by it. I didn't want, yet, to go downstairs and examine more closely; I was content to view comprehensively and from afar off. I stood, as in a trance, subconsciously hearing the sparrows twittering in the creeper that framed the window, the feeling and not the thinking part of me aware that it was a glorious summer morning. And still that rainbow clot of gayest colour vivid against the drab, sedate gravel and the dark old wall of College illumines my soul; and the years fall away and memory is reality. I must leave the window, and I must leave the garden and return to the bleak facts of everyday adult life. But for one moment more I will stay there, and no one shall pull me roughly away.

The french windows of the study are opening, and Father is coming out. He doesn't know I'm watching him. Tenderly he bends over the petunias; I can see him straightening a leaf that has got caught up. The box of blue lobelias is dry; and he picks up the watering-can, and I see the shower of silver drops descending. He is wearing his old grey trousers and Repton scarf; his grey hair is outlined against the scarlet geraniums. He rises, straightens himself, turns round, and catches sight of me. Shading his eyes with one hand, screwing them up against the sun, with the other hand he waves to me, smiling. Thus for a moment he stands. The sun burns downs. The flowers blaze. The little wood is in tender leaf. Thus for a moment and forever he stands; the creator among his creations.

The Old Order

12

'The Class'

We have reached Chapter Twelve with scarce a mention of other children. Which, if you care to read it as such, is a pointer. But there *were* friends, with whom I played sometimes, and went to tea. There were Daphne and Audrey Radcliffe, for example, who lived in Dean's Yard, and had a governess called Miss Snipe, who broke the pendulum off their cuckoo-clock one day and then pretended that she hadn't. There was Michael Adeane, the son of one of his Majesty's Equerries; there were Bobby and Rosemary Brittain, the children of Sir Harry Brittain, who had a great big revolving globe in his study, and a grandfather clock that chimed on eight tubular bells; there were Charlie and Howard and Margaret Nixon, the Precentor's children; and my cousins, Elsa and Teddy Fox. But I cannot pretend that I remember much about any of them with the possible exception of Michael Adeane. He had a very holy-looking Norland nurse, and she and my nurse used to take the afternoon walk together, with Michael and myself in tow. Michael and I spent most of the time quarrelling and trying to impress one another. Only one memory stands out clearly.

One evening in our nursery I had seen something that was to me purely innocent, but that with the strangest deep instinct I knew the grown-ups would think naughty. I decided to try it out on Michael, and see the effect on the two nurses. So in the middle of the walk I suddenly said loudly : 'My sister's got black hair under her arms,' and waited for the general reaction. It surpassed even my expectations. Michael giggled; the Norland nurse stopped dead in her tracks, hand to heart, as though she had been shot, and Nan turned on me, and spanked me soundly, there and then.

'You naughty little boy,' she said; 'I'm ashamed at you, Master John, saying such naughty, dirty things in front of Michael and his nanny, too! Whatever next! Don't you dare say anything like that again!' And though I yelled as usual I was secretly very thrilled, and satisfied with my experiment. It was wonderful to have been able to upset the grown-ups so! When I stopped crying, I said, 'But it's true!' and Nan replied: 'Never you mind that! Maybe it's true, but it's not for a little gentleman like you to say', whereupon Michael and I went off into a fit of subdued giggles, which earned me further black looks from the two nurses. I pondered for quite a long time over the incident, wondering how I had known they would think it naughty; for it was the truth, and the truth couldn't be naughty, surely? I decided that I would ask Mother; but if I ever did I have completely forgotten her reply.

*   *   *

It was soon after this that I was sent to The Class. My first school was run by two maiden ladies of indeterminate age and rather terrifying aspect; the Misses Josephine and Carr Richardson. I did not care for either of them very much; they were in turn soapy and bad-tempered. Miss Josephine was the senior and more important one. We were all encouraged to take her daffodils and things, and when she was pleased with our gifts she would kiss us, which I hated.

I was soon the top boy in my class, for at the age of six my reading and spelling were exceptional. But in other ways I was perhaps backward; and one incident in which I was involved with Miss Josephine I have never forgotten or, to be truthful, forgiven. It was a very small matter indeed; but she made out of it an emotional tension that mortified and humiliated me more than anything had so far done.

It happened when I first went to the Class. Like all the other children I sometimes asked to go to the lavatory; and when I had emptied my bladder I could not do my buttons up, and so Mother told me to ask Miss Richardson to help me. One day, about the third time this had happened, she attacked me in one of the mild rages to which she was subject.

'It's simply ridiculous,' she said, 'that you, a big boy of six, can't do your own buttons up. You ought to be ashamed of yourself. I shall tell your dear mother that you *must* learn, and at once.'

I said nothing, but grew red-faced and hot with shame. It was bad enough to have her standing over me, watching what I hated to have watched. Did she think I couldn't do my buttons up on purpose? But somehow, subtly, or so it seemed to me, there was more in it than that; I felt that she was casting aspersions upon my malehood. I never forgave her; and I suffered agonies holding my water rather than ask for help. And in the end of course I learnt. But it made some mark on me which perhaps I have never quite got rid of; for at home no one made just that kind of fuss. I was teased about such things, perhaps; but kindly. And indeed I was slow to learn the small practical things; I never learned to tie my shoelaces until I was seven; and later, when I was a wolf cub, I never could tie even a reef-knot with any certainty, nor can I today.

Perhaps my mental work (as long as mathematics were not involved) was a compensation. I had an unusually good memory, and soon after I went to the Class I learned Poe's 'The Bells' by heart, and solemnly recited it quite flawlessly to an admiring collection of parents at the end of term. I remember now being surprised and very pleased at the exclamations of astonishment that greeted what to me was an easy feat; and I still remember parts of the poem; for in the learning of it, the noise it made got right into my brain : 'the bells, bells, bells, bells, bells, bells, bells; the tintinnabulation of the bells'. And who knew better than I, living under the shadow of the Abbey, what that meant?

The Class was held in one of the tall old houses of Great College Street, the only one into whose Restoration fastnesses I ever penetrated; so I had not far to go. And soon after I went there, my sister Muriel was taken on as a mistress, and we used to set out together. It was very strange to find her, five minutes later, stern and aloof, rebuking me for some slip in my dictation. On the other hand, however, she was always perfectly willing to do up my buttons for me.

There were other mistresses; dear Miss Hilda Morse, whom I loved, a rugged old spinster with the kindest heart; Miss de Valda, who was excitable, wore pince-nez and a fringe, and taught French; and a very strange couple who were devoted to one another. Miss Sackville was petite, sadly beautiful and rather helpless; her friend, Miss Croft, was an enormous woman with a baritone voice, brown brogues, a collar and tie, and a tweed suit. She adored Miss Sackville, looked after her, and was never seen apart from her except in form. I nicknamed her privately The Man-

Woman. I liked her very much, and did not mind her being a man-woman, and I knew that she was wise to adore Miss Sackville who was a very sweet and gentle person. I did hope, however, that there was no such thing as a woman-man; a man-woman was just bearable, but its reverse would be quite intolerable. I do not think that on this point I have changed much in thirty years.

As for the children, most of them were pleasant, but I made no especial friend. John and Chippy Bradshaw were nice rough-and-tumble boys; Christine Illingworth and Betty Mellon were my girl-friends. I adored them both, especially perhaps Christine, whose birthday was the same as mine. She died from, I think, pneumonia, when she was about seven. I missed her presence greatly, but death was at that age such a monstrous unreality that I never grieved. It was, and perhaps is, exactly as though she had gone away for a long, long time.

I have a photograph of the children of the Class, myself amongst them. I look such an awful little weed that I have every sympathy with those children who bullied me. I should like to do it myself. I look timid, introspective and sloppy. Probably I was all of those things, but fortunately, somewhere deep down I felt strong in myself, which gave me a certain self-confidence. Nor was I always good. I remember leading a raid of the boys on the girls. We pulled their little pigtails and made them cry. We got excited. What we might have done had not Miss Josephine appeared on the scene I scarcely like to think. She gave us a long and excitable lecture, in which she compared us unfavourably with the Germans (it was about 1916). I am sorry to say that her words had singularly little effect; it was not long before another girl-raid was in progress.

Miss Josephine was a large, unwieldy, hippopotamic woman, with a bird's-nest of dull white hair; and a face like a dried fig, across which generally flickered a haze of assumed directionless amiability. Her sister, Miss Carr Richardson, was angry and red-looking, with protuberant, bloodshot eyes. She taught me drawing from nature. Coloured flowers were painted on white paper, white flowers were painted on brown paper. If I was slow or stupid she would rap me on the knuckles. I was secretly terrified of her harsh temper, and it was left to her subordinate, Miss Morse, to encourage in me what Mother had already instilled : a love of poetry. Miss Morse would read to us from a fat book with a cobalt-blue cover called, I think, *English Poetry for the Young.* I remember a poem which began : 'Up the airy mountain, down the rushy glen', and another one about two boys (one called Billy) who went nutting and trout-tickling, if I remember rightly. There were two horrid poems, one called 'We are Seven' (but they weren't); and the other, 'Lucy'. (She dwelt either among the untrodden ways or beside a mossy stone, I am not sure which, and I cannot bother to get out my Wordsworth, as I don't really care which she dwelt among or beside.) Which is no reflection upon my love of Wordsworth; it is merely that 'Lucy' seems, of all that great poet's work, the most meretricious and dull. The poem that most fired my imagination was Blake's 'Nurse's Song'; I dimly felt that all the melancholy of evening and hills was strangely caught in it.

One afternoon in the nursery I was fired by the idea of writing some more great poems, as there seemed to be rather a dearth of them. So I did so; and I still have the results before me, carefully put away and treasured by Mother and found by me after her death. Here they are :

English Poetry for the Young

The Plant.
   No. 1.
      There lived a plant upon a hill.
      It found a tiny little bill.
      It threw it away on a fine summer day.
                              John T. L. Raynor.

The Dockplant.
   No. 2.
      There was a lock inside a clock.
      It struck so loud that there came a great crowd.
                              J.T.L.R.

The Boat.
   No. 3.
      There was a boat, it went afloat,
         On the river Wye.
      It sailed away at break of day
         Which made a little child cry.

                              J.T.L.R.

The Pencil.
No. 4.
     There was a pencil,
     It wrote on a stencil.

                              John Raynor.

After that one session with the muse, my inspiration flagged, my interest fled, and it was twelve years before I again committed to paper, in a poem called 'A Bonfire in the Woods', those poetic yearnings that have dogged me all my life in one form or another.

*   *   *

One day (and it was the sort of extraordinary thing I was always doing) I made myself a ring from the bark of our plane tree, and stuck on it a paper representation of a sapphire cut from an illustrated catalogue. I wore this on my little finger when I went to the Class, where it excited the admiration of all the other little boys and girls. After a few days it broke, and I worried Mother until she let me rummage through her jewel-case, where I found a very small gold ring that had been set with garnets, two of which were lost; not, unfortunately, the two side ones, but the large middle one and one of the others, which gave it a rather lopsided air. Nevertheless, I was very pleased with it, and proudly set off for the Class wearing it. The triumph I scored was spectacular. All the children crowded round me, gaping with admiration; one boy offered me his penknife for it (an offer hastily rejected when I saw that its blades were broken), and the little girls were nearly mad with envy. For ten minutes I was the centre of admiration, until Miss Josephine saw the ring. Puffing slightly, she pattered up to me. I watched her face. It was cold and hard.

'I can't have you wearing that here, dear,' she said. 'Only little girls wear rings, not little boys. It isn't *manly*. You must take it off at once and tell your dear mother that I do not encourage boys to wear jewellery.' There was a pause. I waited. Then she went on : 'I had already noticed you wearing that silly thing made out of a bit of bark. I don't like it, you understand, and I will not have it.'

Red-faced and sulky, I sat at my little desk. 'Silly things made out of a bit of bark,' indeed! Didn't she realize that my rings were magic rings, like the ones that kings wore in fairy-books, that they protected me from harm and brought me good fortune? Why couldn't grown-ups understand? Not only had I been insulted, but my beautiful ring as well. And I had been made to feel that I was girlish.

All the morning I wouldn't cry. I sat, red-faced and solemn, holding back bitter tears. But when I left the Class and set out for home I could restrain them no longer. The pent-up floods burst uncontrollably forth. For a long time I wept and wept, and Mother could get no coherent account from me of what had happened. When at length I had made her understand, she was indignant and said I could wear the ring whenever I liked, and that it was nothing to do with Miss Richardson. But I only wept the harder. My beautiful gold ring with the red fiery-hearted jewel was spoilt for ever. I never wore it again, and I never forgot this, my first deep hurt from the outside world. It made me wary and cautious, where before I had been open and trusting, as I was at home.

13

The Fireside

All my life I have loved fire; all kinds of fire. The beautiful bon-fires we used to make in the garden on cool autumn afternoons, for instance, when the column of blue smoke wavered here and there, and the hot air above it trembled, and the mournful bitter-sweet smell stole forth, and the gnats danced beneath the yellow-ing limes, and one waited for the royal red-gold flame to pierce the mound of brown leaves and spire heavenwards, so that one could damp it down with more leaves on the end of a rake, and wait for it to burst forth again. Or the brazier of the roast-chestnut man who used to open shop so to speak at the base of the Crimean Memorial on freezing winter evenings. How beautiful it was to stand warming one's hands over the shining red-hot coke with its tiny blue flickering flames, as the chestnut man deftly plied his trade; to see from far off the glowing holes of the brazier on its tripod-stand as one returned from a walk down Victoria Street. And like it, and yet different, were the pierced bucket-fires of the road-menders, that as one passed suddenly enveloped one in quivering heat and a faint sulphurous stench, and that glowed brighter and brighter outside the night-watchman's shelter as darkness fell.

I have known many beautiful fireplaces in my life, from the great beam-supported chimney corners of our country forefathers in which one sits and watches the stars overhead and the sparks and smoke flying up the great encrusted chimney-stack, and is warm as nowhere else in life, and happy as nowhere else in life; to the daintiest, most graceful coal-burning grates of eighteenth-century drawing-rooms. But I have never loved any fireplace more than that of my childhood's nursery.

The grate, with its wide hobs and tulip-shaped firebox, dated from 1790, when the house was rebuilt. Wreathed urns decorated it, which shone in bright relief when Nurse had applied the black lead and polished the metalwork. It was a fireplace of atmosphere, beauty and distinction. Yet my first awareness of the nursery fire and of fire in general is not a happy one.

It occurred when I was four years old. Mother had been making toffee; she had just lifted the shallow tin from the fire to the table when someone called her urgently away. She said to me : 'I shall only be a moment, darling. You are not to touch the toffee, you understand; it is boiling, and would burn you if you did.'

She left the room. What, I wondered, was this burning people talked about? I would find out. So I plunged my right hand into the boiling, glutinous mass. I screamed with pain, and struggled desperately to free my hand, but it stuck fast in the toffee. So there I remained, screaming, until Mother, her face very white, came screaming back. She freed my hand, and I was put to bed, and the doctor sent for. Every vestige of skin was burnt off my hand, and I learned years later that I had been in danger of losing it. But I only remember the fiendish, unending pain that lasted for days and days. Thus I learned, once and for all, not to take liberties with flame, but to regard it with deepest respect.

When I was rather older, and could read, I used to pull up the little chair that had served in turn Muriel, Edith, Harold and myself, and get out the fairy-books. I would read of Little King Lok; of the girl who went, via a well, into another world, and had to fill a sieve with water and take her choice of magnificent caskets that were filled with jewels; of Hans Andersen's little mermaid who lost her tail for love and walked as on sharp knives, of the icy Snow Queen, and the dreadful tales of the Brothers Grimm, who had apparently understood what I knew about our house, especially in a story called 'The Man who could not shudder'. To my young mind at that time I can fitly apply a quotation from one of my favourite stories. 'No one would ever have guessed that that little black box could have held such a quantity of beautiful things. Rings, crowns, girdles, necklaces—all made of wonderful stones; and they shone with such brilliance that all the people came running to see if the house was on fire.'

Bemused, my brain dazzled with light and beauty, with princesses, fairy princes, witches, dwarfs, gnomes, kings, queens, and talking animals who were really handsome young men in disguise, I would look up from my book to see the steady, peaceful flames of the nursery fire flickering in their ascent from the bed of red-hot coals in whose heart I could discern the turreted castles, the embattled drawbridges of which I had been reading. Which was the real world? The fairy-tales or the everyday life of the nursery? I never was sure; nor am I to this day. Even though I knew, when I asked Mother for a magic wand as a fifth birthday present, that I should not get it, at any rate in tangible form.

*   *   *

In the story of the girl and the caskets, it was the big, opulent, gay caskets that had only flames inside them; the one that held so dazzling a display of jewels was small, shabby and black. I was always reminded of the truth of this when Mother got out her jewel-case for me to play with. No one, indeed, certainly not I, would have 'guessed that that little black box could have held such a quantity of beautiful things'. It was square, covered with leather and securely locked. On Nurse's evening out, when Mother had bathed me, she would place it on the nursery table, and with considerable ceremony unlock it and raise the lid. A strange and beautiful smell of silk lining and russian leather would rise from it, heady in the silent old nursery, under the white-shaded electric light whose rays were mellowed by the flickering fire. Another, inner, lid to be raised; and the glory of the jewels would flash out, winking and multi-coloured, dazzling with divine beauty my appreciative and eager eyes. Together, we would draw them out in handfuls and lay them gently on the table. One by one I would hold them and turn them over in my hands, loving them with tender caress. There was the dress-buckle made entirely of garnets, that burned like the pure heart of fire; there was a butterfly of filigree work, incredibly fine and delicate, that nevertheless slightly roused my scorn because it resembled no known species; there was the heavy malachite brooch in a chased gold setting; the old cameo that had been Granny's and that was semi-transparent if you held it up to the light; there were necklaces of tonquin beads that smelt aromatic, of pink coral, of grey and yellow beads that had come all the way from Jerusalem. There was the tie-pin in the shape of a scimitar whose hilt was set with a sapphire, a ruby and a diamond; and there were all Mother's rings, the very thin gold one that flashed with brilliants, the thick one set with seed-pearls arranged like a cross, and that beautiful ring which spelt, by means of jewels, the word '*Regard*'; R for ruby, E for emerald, G for garnet, A for aquamarine, R for ruby again, and D for diamond. I was never tired of spelling out the word, slowly and sensuously fingering out each letter as I did so. Then there was grandfather's tiny gold propelling pencil with a large flat amethyst set in the top, a pencil so fragile that it seemed better adapted to fairy, rather than human, fingers. There was the pendant set with opals, perhaps the precious stone I loved best; certainly the one that fascinated me most because of the gleam of imprisoned fire that flashed in its depths.

There were other things in the box too, that were not in themselves of much value, but were valued by Mother as keepsakes. There was the lizard brooch fashioned of green and yellow metal. There was the hank of spun glass that was not like glass at all, but white hair; there was the battered old silver locket that concealed in its depths a fragile curl from the head of each of Mother's children. Oh, and many, many things more, whose memory time has dimmed. Very much, especially, did I love a certain mosaic brooch, in the shape of a daisy, and with a tiny pink-tipped daisy inset. The vision of it hovers before me still, so blue, rose, green and white in spirit, so shining and delicate, with a long silver pin.

Sometimes I would load my patient and long-suffering mother with her jewels, till she sparkled and glittered all over, her mild protest, 'But I shouldn't ever wear all of these *at once*, darling', quite overridden in the excitement of the moment. My only aim was to make Mother shine from head to foot. The bangle with the little gold hunting-horn on one wrist, her diamond bracelet on the other, and her bosom and fingers glittering with amethyst, ruby, sapphire, diamond, emerald, opal, turquoise and pearl, her neck hung with the tonquin, jerusalem and coral beads, I would at last be satisfied, and having examined her critically from head to foot would allow her to sit down, jingling and tinkling with every movement and breath, in the armchair by the fire.

And then it would be bedtime, and the jewels would be poured back into the jewel-case. A last look, and the lid would snap to, the key be turned in the lock, and suddenly I was back in the dingy old nursery, looking at a dull black box. Where had all that flashing, sparkling fire gone to? Deep inside the box, in total darkness, the jewels lay hidden, at rest; waiting for the next lifting of the lid.

A suddenly sleepy child would kneel at his mother's knee in the glowing firelight to say his prayers. In his drowsy mind the jewels were still wheeling and scintillating in rainbow glory. So much so, that one night, instead of beginning, 'Please God, take care of Mummy and Daddy and all we love,' he said : 'One, two, three, four, five, six, seven, eight,' to his own and his mother's surprise. And when, a little shamefacedly, he confessed that he had still been thinking of the garnet buckle that burned like red fire, she only smiled and said : 'Never mind, darling, all beautiful things are the gift of God; and I'm sure He'll forgive your inattention because He knows you didn't mean it.' It was at that moment, I think, that I first consciously understood something of the meaning of those two most mysterious words 'love' and 'goodness'. It is also conceivable that I knew, for the fraction of a second, before the vision faded, why of all Mother's beautiful rings that one which spelt the word 'Regard' lay nearest to my heart.

*   *   *

It is strange how people will almost wantonly demolish an object of beauty and dignity, that has long staunchly withstood the test of time, such as the fireplace in our nursery. Is it because they resent the beauty of the past and want to impress their own personality on a house? I knew that the nursery fireplace was so homely, so friendly, so truly heart-warming because it had become tried and trusty in its hundred and twenty years of use. I knew that I was not the only child who had sat before it watching the smoke rise, listening to the kettle boiling, and dreaming of what I saw in the flames; and I gained immeasurably from the knowledge. Why is it that nowadays, more than ever before, the venerable quality of things is disregarded? That the time-honoured country phrase : 'What was good enough for my father is good enough for me' is today utterly discountenanced. Once you have cut down a hundred-year-old tree; once you have demolished a hundred-year-old fireplace, you cannot replace either for exactly a hundred years, even though you were to grow a tree of the same variety, or get a blacksmith to make a replica of the fireplace you had destroyed. We should do well to think twice before destroying what has for so many long years been the casket of the holy element of fire.

Certainly, sometimes, as I sat in my little chair on a winter's evening, I would become strangely aware of the continuity of the old fireplace. The soot-encrusted back, the broad, shining hobs, the convex firebars, all spoke eloquently of an age wherein generous comfort counted for something. And as the ancient pot-bellied black kettle began to hiss and sing, it made the sweetest, most consoling music, until the point was reached where the lid began to lift and rattle, and steam mingled with ascending smoke was suddenly sucked sharply back. Then Nurse would hurry in and return the kettle to the hob on which the teapot was already warming. How many, many times that must have happened before those brief years in which I watched it ! And that knowledge gave it a ritual air, and I would suddenly feel incredibly happy and far away from the noise and trouble of the outside world. The peace that the old house could sometimes so wholeheartedly give would descend, wrapping all the chimneyside in a silent calm. Then Nurse would make the tea and remove the tall old fireguard that was made of criss-cross wire and had a brassbound top and had got a bit battered through generations of children kicking it and falling against it, and I would be comforted by the calm, glowing open fire that spread its delicious warmth through my body on a frosty, spear-sharp winter's evening, with no tiresome barrier to impede our intercourse.

*   *   *

It was exactly the right sort of grate for children. Potatoes could be roasted in the ashes beneath, chestnuts carefully arranged along the wide firebars, and all kinds of childish messes, from flour-paste to home-made chocolate, could be stood on the hobs to keep warm. Sometimes, if there was to be a big dinner party downstairs, we prepared the salted almonds for it over the nursery fire. It was done as follows, with never the slightest deviation from ritual. First we split the almond-shells with nutcrackers (or teeth, if no one was looking), extracted the kernels, and plunged them into a saucepan of boiling water for a few moments while olive oil was poured into the round enamel frying-pan which in turn was stood on the hob to heat. Soon, under the influence of the hot water, the brown outer skin of the almond would soften. I remember still the deeply sensuous pleasure given to fingers and eyes as the softened skin, wrinkled between finger and thumb, split, and slid away to reveal the ivory-white kernel, virginal and fresh, within; a pleasure only slightly lessened by the difficulty of extracting the almond from the boiling water. Then, when they were all skinned, the pan of olive oil was set on the fire and when it bubbled the kernels were dropped in and turned about until they were a rich golden brown, and the room was full of the exquisitely appetizing smell given off by roasting nut and sizzling oil. Finally, still hot, they were rolled in a saucer of salt as thoroughly as possible, and left to cool on a sheet of kitchen paper. I regret to have to add that, strangely, not nearly so many finished salted almonds went downstairs as had come up in their unprepared state. Indeed, a good salted almond is an unbearable thing to see lying about; it has an air of loneliness that makes one, for the poor thing's own sake, pop it in one's mouth as quickly as possible.

*   *   *

Another thing I used to do with the fire, that Father had taught me, though Mother thought it 'dangerous' (that mysterious word of grown-ups!) was to make coal-gas in it. I had early noticed that sometimes a lump of coal bubbled fascinatingly, and suddenly lit with a long, pale flame. Father told me that it was gas in the coal. He took one of my old bubble-blowing clay pipes, filled the bowl with coal-dust, covered it over with a thick layer of damp earth from a flower pot, and placed the bowl between the bars of the grate, among the red-hot coals, so that only the stem of the pipe struck out into the room. He waited a moment, then struck a match and held it to the end of the stem. To my surprise and delight, it lit and burned steadily with a pure, bluish-white flame about an inch long, very like the flame of the gas-jets of the geyser in Edith's bedroom. That, Father told me, was roughly how gas was made. After that, all my bubble-pipes got turned into retorts for the manufacture of coal-gas; I even dreamed of schemes for lighting the whole nursery all the evening by means of home-made gas made in a gargantuan clay pipe and conveyed to appropriate positions through long tubes. These dreams came to an abrupt end when one of my pipes burst in the fire with a horrible report and scattered the fender with bits of clay and coal, scaring me out of my wits, and drawing from Nurse the inevitable 'I told you so'.

*   *   *

Nurse had every Sunday evening off, so that she could attend Evensong in St Margaret's Church. It was my favourite evening in the week, for then I was free to enjoy wholeheartedly Mother's company, and to establish and strengthen the deeply felt and psychic link between us. Sometimes, as I have already related, we had hymns in the drawing-room; but I think that my favourite Sunday evenings were those spent around the nursery fireside. Mother would give me tea (and how different, somehow, were those teas from Nurse's), and then, after a pause for clearing-up and making the nursery tidy, we would be ready to settle down for the evening.

'What shall we do?' Mother would ask, smiling at me. Occasionally, I would plump for some game, or to turn over the pages together of the two great volumes of *The Bible in Art*; but nearly always I said: 'Let's have the light off, and sit in the dark and tell stories.'

'We'll make the fire up first, shall we?' Mother would say. And there we would be in the dark, in the firelight. Immediately, the nursery assumed a different personality. Familiar objects—tables, pictures, chairs—loomed larger but unimportant, on the extreme edge of the fire's radius. The fire became the focal point of the whole room. The flames, leaping and eating round the mound of new coal, threw soft and fitful rays of dancing light in the dark old mouth of the chimney, and on the nearer walls and objects. And beyond, the room stretched, shadowy, illimitable, insubstantial. The fire-irons and the fender shone red in the glow from the red heart of the fire. And the listening, watching ghosts crept a little nearer as Mother sat down in the comfortable, bulgy old chair, and took me on her knee. It had begun. The long journey into the farthest realms of the imagination lay before us. A journey that lasted perhaps in actual fact for an hour, but that encompassed eternity, and from which one never knew whether one would come back.

First there would be unfolded, either from Mother's own mind or the depths of her knowledge, a tale of magic castles and sunlit turrets, of handsome princes and beautiful princesses; or of happy birds and gay butterflies, or red foxes and of sombre moths. Or of Odin and Thor and Wotan and Baldur the Beautiful, and Bifröst, the magic rainbow bridge, and Yg-drasil, the tree of life and death, and Aurora Borealis, the flashing Northern Lights. Hercules and Zeus, Juno and Persephone and her mother Demeter, goddess of the ripening wheat. And Pluto, and his three-headed watchdog, Cerberus. Into the hushed, firelit room the words would softly fall, spun of the frail material of eternity, and I would listen, spellbound with their beauty and wonder. And then, after another space of silence, Mother would tell the old, old Bible stories; of Samson and Delilah and the pillars of the temple; of Adam and Eve wandering through the Garden of Eden; of how the ruddy, golden-haired youth, David, slew the uncouth giant, Goliath; and of his deeply loved friend, Jonathan; and of those three wise men who, following a star that led them, found a babe lying in a manger.

From the dark corners of the room the poor lost ghosts would stream, crowding round us in the firelight, to hear of the Saviour of Mankind, slipping again into the shadows as the fire reddened and sank, redeemed and peaceful. Nothing disturbed the tranquillity of the happy, flame-and-shadow-lit nursery. I would turn, as Mother's tales died into silence, and stare into the very heart of the living, glowing coals. There was the magic bridge; and so tall a castle with a window high up; and there was a witch in a peaked hat; and beyond, the landscape of the Garden of Eden. And as a spark flickered up the chimney I saw that it was indeed the Epiphany star.

14

The Old Order

We did our shopping in two different worlds; two milieux wide apart yet not antithetical. One pole was represented by the Army and Navy Stores in Victoria Street; the other, by what was known to us vaguely as 'The Back', which consisted mainly of Marsham Street with occasional divergences to the Horseferry Road. I loved being taken to either; and the contrast was so intense that I never in any way connected them. The Army and Navy Stores was golden and warm, and haunted always by an air of cosy luxury; of ladies in furs and gentlemen in top-hats. The smells it housed were joy indeed to my keen nose as I trotted along holding Mother's hand and sniffing the aroma of each department. The smell of the glazed meats and hams, of bread, of poultry, of fish, of flowers, of drugs, of ironmongery, of clothes, of groceries, mingled in a glorious jumble of sensation in my mind. I had my friends there too. There was an assistant who always gave me a chocolate biscuit shaped like a cigar; I loved him very much, and was for weeks inconsolable when he joined up. I felt that he had played a dirty trick on me, and should, for the sake of our chocolate biscuit association, have remained at his post behind the counter. Then there was the man in the fruit department who was so kind when I disgraced my mother by stealing a cherry and gave me another. (Both he and Mother thought that I really did think that things were there to be taken; if they had only guessed the truth, that I had long planned the theft, I should not have escaped so lightly.) Nan's nephew, too, Bertie Uncle, was an assistant at the Stores and would sometimes come and talk to me. The overwhelming impression the A and N (as we called it) left upon me was of great civility, courtesy and willingness. Everything was very tidy, clean, and beautifully arranged. There were revolving doors too, an unending joy to a child; and just outside one of them a gas-flame burned always so that you could light a cigarette or a cigar on leaving the Stores; for no smoking was allowed inside it. The age of manners was still with us. There was a bridge, too, to the Auxiliary Stores, thickly carpeted, so that one's feet made no sound as one crossed it and looked out of the windows on to the busy street below. The Army and Navy Stores was a world of light and movement and delicious scents; but a world conditioned always by propriety and decorum. There was no misbehaving there; and I was aware that a certain beautiful crude reality was lacking, that was to be found in abundance round 'The Back', in the shops of Marsham Street.

The contrast was sharp indeed. Marsham Street had a vitality, a sordid gaiety that has practically left the uniformly dreary prefabricated grey world in which we now live. It was dirty and poverty-stricken; yet its inhabitants were often gay, dancing in rings round the barrel-organ, flamboyantly drunk on Saturday nights, expressing themselves in cheap bright clothes and tawdry finery. I used to look with awed eyes at the pubs and gin-palaces on the street corners of that district, hoping that the doors would open to disgorge masses of rolling people, though they never did, probably because I was never there at the right time of day or night. Here were the true Cockneys, feather-hatted and be-buttoned, with loud cheery words of greeting, and indefinable but strong sex-appeal. The women would look saucily at the men, their eyes rolling and flashing above their mountainous breasts. The men would wink with portentous mock solemnity, and strike a what-a-fine-fellow-am-I attitude. All this I would excitedly observe, as I demurely held Mother's hand and waited for the interminable conversation with Mrs Smith, the greengrocer's wife, to end.

Mother was deeply loved in Marsham Street. 'A real lidy if

ever there was one' was the unanimous verdict; and she would
stop for a long time in each shop, sympathetically listening to the
troubles of her who was about to have her thirteenth; or her who
had told her husband exactly what she thought of him when he
had threatened her with the poker on Saturday night. It was
understood that I was not supposed to listen to such conversations;
it was equally understood and tacitly accepted that I did. Thus
I learned a great deal about life that I might otherwise never have
guessed at.

Smith's was my favourite shop. Mr Smith, a little man with
immense mustachios and a battered straw hat always on his head,
morosely picked over and arranged the wilting vegetables while
Mrs Smith engaged us in conversation. She was an enormous
woman, blowsy and Rabelaisian, and somehow suggested one of
her own monstrous cauliflowers. Her iron-grey hair was screwed
tightly back, and the humorous wrinkled old face would peer
shrewdly at me as she pressed an apple into my expectant hand.

'And how's our little gentleman today?' she would say; 'a little
love, that 'e is, with 'is curls and 'is face that solemn 'e might be
in church 'stead of old Smithy's shop. Bless 'is little 'eart; there;
bless 'is little 'eart. 'Ow 'e do grow, m'm. Ah I 'spect 'e'd like a
disy, too,' she would add, and stick a beautiful crimson pyrethrum
into my hand.

I loved Mrs Smith, I adored her. It was so interesting and
funny the way when she leant against the counter hard, the fat
would rise up in a mound almost to her chin. She had brought up
fifteen children, about seven of whom were always hanging round
the shop, getting in her way, edging off when, exasperated beyond
control, she screamed at them. A very large, vital, vulgar old
woman was Mrs Smith, with a sentimentality always ready to
overflow through her eyes, a loyalty both broad and honest and,
I am now inclined to believe, a penchant for gin.

*   *   *

After we had taken tender farewells of Mrs Smith we would
proceed on our way to Tillott's the chemist's or Gillett's the hard-
ware shop. You could easily get lost in Gillett's, among the pails
and kettles and galvanized baths that cluttered its long single
corridor. The prices were painted on the larger objects with 'blue-

bag'; I used surreptitiously to lick my finger and rub the powdery figures off while Mother was busy at the counter. From Gillett's we would pass to the toy-shop, that magic little shop of my childhood, whose clay pipes and coloured chalks I have already mentioned. Empty-handed, I would go in, beseeching Mother, tugging at her arm; usually emerging triumphantly with a new hoop (which would immediately get in the way of everyone's legs), or a brightly coloured rubber ball that smelt deliciously of new paint, a smell that got stronger as the ball, clutched firmly in my hand, got warmer and stickier. On into the Horseferry Road we would go, to Mr Smellie the locksmith, or sometimes—and this was best of all—to old Mr Barrett, the clock and watch repairer.

Here was Paradise indeed! As we pushed open the door into the warm, fuggy little shop, we were greeted by a conglomerate pandemonium of ticking. There they were, the beauties, dozens of them; marble clocks, brass clocks, wooden clocks, carriage clocks, alarm clocks, china clocks—all ticking with such vociferation that it was difficult to hear what old Mr Barrett was saying. In this shop, with all the clocks hurryingly, racingly muttering, time at last stood still. Here was heaven itself. If only Mother would keep on talking until the hour! Looking at the forest of clock faces I perceived that it was between ten and three minutes to the hour. Would she? Yes, she had got on to the subject of Mr Barrett's married son. That was good for five minutes, surely? In a fever of anxiety I watched the hands creep so slowly up to the hour. Mother was getting ready to take her departure. Oh God, let them go on talking, please. They were, they were— Mr Barrett had begun again. Then suddenly: Bong! Ting! Cuckoo, pung; cuckoo, pung; cuckoo, pung! Ting-tang, ting-tang! Peel-peel, peel! Drumf, drumf, drumf. Cuckoo! Dang, dang, dang. And the little shop would shiver again into ticking silence, but for one belated old grandfather who from his corner suddenly said: 'Urr-urr-urr-Bing! Urr-urr-urr-Bing! Urr-urr-urr-Bing!'

'Good gracious!' Mother would exclaim, 'is that three o'clock?' (As though there could have been any doubt about it.) 'I'd no idea it was so late! Come along, darling.' And moving unwillingly to the door, I would take a last look at the only begetter of this wonderful place, old Mr Barrett, with his bull-like head, his gold spectacles, his magnificent grey beard, and his kindly, twinkling eyes and smile. As he turned away from us and sat down again at his bench with the magnifying glass in his eye, I thought that he must be the happiest man in the world. With a sigh of pure happiness I would adjust my legs to the homeward walk, while my thoughts dwelt still on the clock-filled shelves of the little shop, and my head echoed and rang with the gongs, the rods, the bells and the cuckoos that were the voices of the personalities of my horological friends and lovers. Then I had an idea. When the term was over I would get Mother into that shop at five minutes to *twelve*! Pondering the problem of how best to do this, I noticed nothing more until, suddenly, I found myself standing on the steps of Number 3 while Mother fumbled in her bag for the latch-key.

*   *   *

Sometimes we went up the Strand, past the Horseguards and Charing Cross Station where the trains blew and puffed and clanked, past the Civil Service Stores to Maynard's, the shop that sold the most delicious sweets even I have ever eaten in my life. We called them 'the flowery sweets'. They were round, white and clear and in the centre was printed a flower—a forget-me-not, daisy or pink. They tasted both sweet and sharp and entirely individual. Then, soon after the coming of the war they stopped, and have never returned; and I know in my bones that they will never return, unless St Peter has a bag of them in his left hand to offer me, as with his right hand he unlocks the golden gate.

Sometimes we went over Westminster Bridge and along the Embankment. At the corner of the bridge stood the old man with the brass-mounted telescope focused on Big Ben. For the modest sum of one penny, he would let one look through it, first at the great hands, and then at some details of the statuary. After which, he would thrust into one's eager palm a dog-eared postcard of the great clock with a profound description of its works printed on the back. He was only there on certain days, so that it was with a great sense of triumph that I would espy him from afar off.

'W'at's the *'urry*?' Nurse would say, as I strained at the leash, ''e won't run away.' Fool that she was! How did she know? Nothing seemed more likely to me. The old man was so tottery and his beard so white that I think I instinctively feared he might drop down dead before I could get there.

The telescope joy behind me, we would turn down the Embankment, along beside the river, where you could hear the trams rattling along above, among the leafy plane trees. Here were seagulls, ragged children and pavement artists. It was a breathless joy, this examination of each artist's work. Some favoured pink and blue pictures; some green and yellow, and a few (poor things) drew only white ones. My favourite was a very old man who sat with crossed legs, his cap filled with coloured chalk stubs on one side of him, on the other his tin cup over which a ragged mongrel kept guard. The old man wore a boot on one foot and a velvet slipper on the other; his creased, stubbly and rather angry old face peering irritably at the passers-by used to make me clutch Nurse's hand a little tighter. Occasionally I was allowed to drop a penny into his ringing tin cup, and he would growl sourly : 'Thank-'ee, kind sir.' I used to marvel at the energy and faith he showed in drawing his bright pictures afresh every day; he was not one of the modern, slack pavement artists who carry their pictures about on boards, and just lay them down in the morning and pick them up in the evening. Every day they were drawn afresh; and if on our walk it started to drizzle I used to scowl angrily at the cold-hearted rain that had the power to make a muddy puddle of all his labours in a few moments. My favourite picture was called 'Eventide'; it portrayed a very peculiar church rising from a green meadow encircled by a blue river, with a crimson sun setting behind the nave and shining through the windows. There followed the Prince of Wales, the salmon, and the figure-of-eight loaf that I have already mentioned with its pathetic caption : 'Easy to Draw; But Hard to Get.'

"Ard to get ! 'Im !' Nurse would say, tossing her head; "e makes a good enough living, I'll be bound ! And 'oo wants a loaf like that, anyway; let alone the butter !' With which cryptic remark she would urge me onwards in the direction of Cleopatra's Needle, while the thronging seagulls screamed and wheeled overhead, and the dirty and beautiful barge-haunted Thames flowed smoothly along beside me.

*   *   *

To go for a walk with Father was an event so rare, so solemn, that I fear I shall quite fail to do its memory justice. Occasionally, at the beginning of the Christmas holidays, it would happen. Father would do an afternoon's shopping, buying presents, crackers and special sweets for the Christmas dinner-table, and offer to take me with him. We never went to the same places as Mother and Nurse. The walk usually began by a bus-ride to a very strange place called Soho, where one saw men in earrings, and had coffee in a place called Pinoli's that was not in the least like Lyons or Fuller's. I always felt very proud when Father took me out; he looked so grand in his black overcoat and shiny top-hat. We would board an L.G.O.C. (known as a 'General') or a Thomas Tilling bus, and go upstairs to the front seat if it was unoccupied; and the crisp, wintry air and sun would refresh one's face (all buses had open tops in those days); and the scenery and the people would slide past in a glorious panorama, and all too soon we would reach our destination. And then Father would buy bottles of wine in dark little shops, and rich-smelling cigars and boxes of tangerines, and hurry us on to buses again, and off again at the Haymarket Stores, until I was quite breathless. There he would buy fondants, and crystallized fruits and liqueur chocolates and hams. And when he had finished he would say 'Let's walk home through the park,' and we would descend the Duke of York's steps and turn into the wintry quietness of St James's Park. Father would tell me the names of the ducks on the water there, and point out the pelicans as they stalked along, gobbling ridiculously; and the hurrying would drop from us, and we would walk along together, soberly happy, looking at the trees and the lake and the clustered buildings of Whitehall, until we came to Birdcage Walk, and turned down Prince's Street, and crossed Broad Sanctuary and so arrived home. And Father would say to me, as one conspirator to another: 'Well, John dear, I trust you not to tell your mother what we bought this afternoon, for it must be a Christmas surprise, you understand.' And I would nod solemnly, laying finger to lip, and help Father off with his coat and top-hat in the hall; and I would smell the white Roman Hyacinths that were coming out in bowls in the dining-room, and see a star or two in the clear blue darkening sky; and the sudden frosty feeling of approaching Christmas would grip me by the throat, and I would stand for a moment by the window, spellbound, until the smell of toast and Patum Peperium stealing from the study would remind me of the empty state of my stomach, and

I would race upstairs to the nursery with the dusk-filled windows flashing past me, one by one, as I went—and the knowledge of the birth of Christ tugging at my heart.

*   *   *

In those days, in any quiet street, one might hear round the corner of the next street, the throbbing, plangent strains of the most magically haunted sound that London knew; the full, sad blom-blom-blom of a barrel-organ. From afar my ears would pick it out from a multiplicity of other sounds; then, far along the street I would espy it, resting (how briefly!) against the pavement. As we came up to it, something always brought a lump to my throat, I never knew exactly what. There was a quality to barrel-organs that was hard to define; they seemed to struggle so bravely against indifferent ears; the odds were against them; and yet they poured out so blithely their cheerful music that was the most melancholy I had ever heard. My eyes would fill with unshed tears as I stood, like a little ghost, watching the red-brown organ on its trolley, its sides and front adorned with pieces of looking-glass and faded photographs of flag-framed Royalty. Below would be chalked : 'I have seven children to support, and no other means of earning a living'. Steadily the old man would turn the handle; and sometimes a small, serious-looking mnkey on a chain, wearing a red fez, would hold out a battered enamel cup to passers-by as he crouched on the top of the instrument. And on and on the divine, painful music would pour into the empty street, eloquently beseeching the deaf ears and hard hearts of those who passed. Even when a ring of children danced round the organ the inner mournfulness was not dispersed. And the tunes . . . 'Daisy, Daisy'; 'In the twi-twi-twilight'; 'Love's Old Sweet Song'; 'Soldiers of the Queen'; and the tune that of all barrel-organ tunes lacerated something inside me so deeply that I could no longer hold back tears: 'Lily of Laguna'. To hear that trembling its way into a silent street on a misty afternoon, the wavering notes mingling with the feathery smoke against a background of chimney-pots and yellowing plane trees was to be caught up in something quite outside the sordid world. And as the penultimate phrase, 'She is my Lily of Laguna', soared, hovering, before closing its wings and gently falling to earth, it seemed that my whole being, exposed, extended itself in trembling ecstasy towards whatever was the real source of the music. I would be led away, weeping my heart out, to Nurse's intense annoyance. And I must admit that if I ever hear a barrel-organ now (the last one I heard was in 1943, near Euston Station; it played 'I Know Why' and 'Chattanooga Choo-Choo'), exactly the same effect is produced on me, and I am unable to hold back my tears.

*   *   *

One more picture of the old London that even then was passing, and that no one realized mattered until it had passed; and that only a few realize even now. Very often the afternoon walk led us down Victoria Street, past The Old Times Furnishing Company, and the Singer Sewing Machine Shop, where ladies sat in the window and sewed, and the photographer's where I had been taken in my page's clothes at Edith's wedding, to the Station, or the Wilton Road, and back again up the other side of the street. And at practically every side-turning off Victoria Street in the shelter of the wall angle sat one of the old flower-sellers, with her fragrant basket beside her. I knew them all, and they were, in varying degrees, friends, and would often give me a cornflower or a sweet-pea to take home. But my special friend, and Nurse's, had her pitch outside the Victoria Palace Theatre. She was very old; a nut-brown wrinkled face, crowned by a black straw hat secured by long black-headed hatpins, peered and shook above a soot-coloured woollen shawl. The rest of her was swathed in a patched and shapeless assortment of indeterminate garments, that billowed voluminously around her, and were in general of a musty shade of black. When she saw us coming along the pavement, the old eyes would brighten, and a smile form on the trembling lips.

'Dearie, dearie, it's good to see you, dearie,' she would croon to Nurse, 'and the young gentleman too. Here's a nice bunch o' stocks for 'im.' And she would press into my hand a sweetly-smelling mound of pink, firmly refusing the attempted payment. 'No, I likes 'em as appreciates 'em to 'ave 'em. There's nothing like a bit o' flower, I say. Reminds me of the country where I was born and bred. Yes . . .' and the old head would nod in smiling memory. Her great ambition was to return there, if only for a day, before she died.

One day, we found her simmering with excitement. 'I'm goin' !'
she proclaimed. 'I'm goin' ! On a day's outin' with some other old
'uns, w'at the passon's got up. You won't know me when I come
back.'

The day after the outing we went that way specially to find out
how she had enjoyed it. She sat there in a state of tranquil con-
tentment.

'It was grand !' she kept saying; 'it was grand ! Reminded me
of me girl'ood, it did. To see all them fields and trees again, it was
grand, it was !' Then she looked at me, almost shyly. 'I didn't
forget me young gentleman,' she said; 'I got a fern for you—dug
it up meself, I did. There lovey, you take that 'ome and pop it in
yer garding, and it'll remind you of old Annie. . . .' She placed a
brown clump of fern-root in my hand. A few green crozier fronds
were beginning to unfurl from it. I was speechless with pleasure
and excitement. 'Aren't you goin' to thank 'er?' Nurse said
sharply. Still I could say nothing. 'Don't you worry 'im, dearie,'
the old woman said. 'I don't want no thanks. You only gotter look
at 'is fice.'

We said goodbye. Hardly daring to breathe lest I should drop
it, I carried the fern home. It was ceremoniously planted beneath
the plane tree. Every spring it sent up its pale, feathery fronds.
Every spring it beat the other ferns in the vernal race. It remained
always 'my' fern, and it was still flourishing when we left London.
At its roots, as a great honour, were buried such white mice of
mine as had reached their earthly span. Very few presents during
the whole of my life have given me so much pleasure as old Annie's
fern; and I believe that she knew that, for she always asked me
how it was getting on, looking searchingly at my face as she did so.

One afternoon she was not there. She had 'took a fit' and died.
I feel sure that, though she left the useless old black straw hat with
its pins, and the soot-coloured shawl and all the accoutrements of
the tired old body behind, her spirit took wing to the fields, woods
and pastures that she so dearly loved and so rarely saw.

15

Lepidoptera

This morning, when I entered my study to write, I saw, sitting on the window-curtains, a newly-emerged female Eyed Hawk-moth. Its chocolate-brown forewings were folded over the rosy, peacock-hued hind wings; it looked rather like a crinkly dead leaf. It had broken from a chrysalis kept by me since last summer, when I collected its fat, green, rough, horned caterpillar, with several others, from the apple trees in the garden.

To such an extent does my father's training live in me, I no longer collect butterflies and moths, for I have grown to feel that it is wrong to kill them; but I still bring home any caterpillar I may see and keep it until its final metamorphosis. And if I had a son, I should repress my humanitarian feelings towards lepidoptera, for I know of no other hobby so fascinating, so illuminative, so instructive without ever being dull, as the collecting of butterflies and moths. Just as my beautiful Eyed Hawk conceals beneath her brown upper wings the most exquisite smoky sunset tints of pink and blue, unknown save to the initiated; so does the pursuit of entomology bring the unsuspecting acolyte face to face with the thrones (not *always* unoccupied) of the oldest gods of all.

Bug-hunting (as I believe it is vulgarly called) runs in the family. My father and his four brothers were keen collectors, as was his father. The family living of Hazeleigh, Essex, provided a good hunting-ground. The eldest of the five boys, my Uncle Gilbert (the most eccentric man I have ever been privileged to know) became, in his day, one of the leading entomological authorities; and after his retirement from the rectory at Hazeleigh made a modest living out of the common Currant Moth, from which he had various aberrant strains that fetched large sums from collectors, and are named after him to this day. He also achieved fame in the pages of South's *The Butterflies of the British Isles*, where, on page 175, during a description of the Holly Blue Butterfly, the following passage occurs: 'The Rev. Gilbert Raynor, on May 18, 1901, observed a female deposit an egg on an unopened flower-bud of rhododendron in his garden; and he also mentions that he beat a number of the caterpillars of all sizes from holly during the first week of July in the same year.'

That is good as far as it goes; but it does not go far enough. I am tempted to supplement it. I see my uncle, tall, thin, exactly like an emaciated parrot (he bred those, too), in his alpaca clergyman's jacket, his high collar, his egg-stained waistcoat, and his old cloth cap, poking about among the wild Hazeleigh garden until he unearthed this wretched Holly Blue, which he probably chivvied with the ferrule of his umbrella, until at last it crouched on a rhododendron bush and laid its immortalized egg in self-defence (rhododendron is not an accepted *pabulum*), or possibly in pure fright, before my uncle allowed it to seek its more natural pasture of holly while he rushed indoors (almost certainly falling over the garden-seat in the porch, to the vociferous delight of his parrots) to fetch his notebook. But I must resist the temptation to digress about Uncle Bertie, who needs a whole book to himself, and will, I hope, one day get it, if I live long enough.

Himself the youngest, my father often unwillingly and rather irritably bowed to the superior entomological knowledge of Bertie, the oldest. In which, I feel, he showed a becoming but unnecessary modesty; for I have never met any man who knew, from a practical point of view, more about butterflies and moths than my father.

I have already written of the cabinet; the winter evening delights of going over it. Now I shall describe a few of the processes whereby it came to be filled. But first I must record my two earliest encounters with butterflies, one of them with deep shame.

The first was in the garden at home in London. A small white butterfly came flickering over the study steps and settled. I managed to catch it in a box. I asked Father if I could kill it, and set it. He did not much want me to; he said that it would be kinder to leave it in peace as we had no need for it. However, I prevailed on him to put it in his killing-bottle, and when it was dead, I pinned it rather crookedly, and spread out its wings on one of my father's old setting-boards. Father was impressed with how well I had done it (I was only five) and soon after, he gave me an old butterfly-net. This was my first real introduction to collecting.

The other incident, a strange and unhappy memory, occurred about the same time, in the summer holidays. I was standing beside a long herbaceous border, filled with early autumn flowers. At its edge grew a fine clump of rose-pink phlox; the sun blazed silently down. It was morning; I had just pushed my nose into the dewy centres of the phlox flowers and inhaled the heady scent with deep satisfaction, and that yearning pain that the smell of certain flowers has always given me, when a small blue butterfly hovered and settled on the pink phloxes, opening and shutting its azure wings in the warm brilliance. What followed, I have never really understood. It was too beautiful to bear, or so it seemed to me, this clear blue living thing against the soft pink scented flowers. It did something to me that I wouldn't face, and scarcely dared to acknowledge; it was life itself, unattainable life; and it was too nearly perfect to be admissible. That is all I can really say. On a sudden impulse I took the butterfly between finger and thumb and fiercely rubbed it to nothing. When I looked, there was a tiny grey ball of damp matter on my thumb; all that was left of a small, vivid and perfect life.

The pink phloxes stood there in the clear morning light, but no blue butterfly flickered above them. They alone had seen my swift, secretive action. I was seized with craven panic fear and self-disgust. 'It was only a butterfly,' I said to myself; 'there are hundreds of them.' But not that one, said the phloxes. It was borne in upon me as I stood there, trembling and horror-stricken, that I had *wantonly* destroyed; I was not innocent, as I had been a few moments before. And yet I knew that I was never really innocent; I was always fighting something; whereas the butterfly, of its nature, was truly innocent. I know that in that strange moment, I felt, though I was so young, the full burden of what is perhaps rather loosely called 'original sin'. I knew that I belonged to mankind, that I was not an innocent species of being. I knew that I *had* to destroy that butterfly, to learn something of myself; and that I would never again wantonly do such a thing, remove beauty just because it was beauty. Instead, I would always, after this experience, be on beauty's side; and would take up the cudgels in its defence against man, who had so deep and strong an impulse to destroy what he himself could never quite attain to, from certain motives that were as violent as they were mysterious. A deep-seated envy of natural innocence? Rather, I now feel, and dimly felt then, a base and perverted act of love. So beautiful was the butterfly on the flowers that I really wanted to bare my chest, open it, and take the beauty forever within me. I couldn't do that, and so, I destroyed. In a vain attempt to ease the pain and ecstasy, I became a murderer. If I couldn't have the butterfly, it shouldn't have itself. In a vain attempt, I say—because I somehow saw that by murdering the butterfly I had tried to murder myself. I stood there for a long time, very shocked and unhappy; anxiously watching the phloxes in the hope that another blue butterfly would arrive, so that I could look at it steadily, clear blue against soft pink, and love it, and bear the pain for the sake of life. But life, loving me, sternly refused the anodyne of the little sacrifice I wanted to make. I must be punished; and rightly. No butterfly came near the phloxes. And after a time I wandered disconsolately away, unshed tears trembling on my eyelashes, waiting to fall at the slightest provocation.

At the edge of the lawn, I stopped. I looked up at the old creeper-covered house. A great magnolia, crucified against its warm brick, had opened four or five large creamy flowers. They smelt of lemon, I knew. I stood there, I looked at it, and I burst into tears.

$$* \quad * \quad *$$

The life-cycle of a butterfly or moth consists of four stages : the ovum, or egg; the larva, or caterpillar; the pupa, or chrysallis; and the imago, or perfect insect. The perfect state of the insect is rightly so named; growth is finished, it *is* the perfect state. Nor do eggs or chrysalids grow, at any rate as far as flies or lepidoptera are concerned; the only growing stage is the eating stage, that of the grub or caterpillar. During the caterpillar period the size of the imago is irrevocably determined; the chrysalis stage is a time of rest and change, not of growth. Inside its hard shell, the organs it possessed as a caterpillar are dissolved into a fluid that is re-formed into the completely different organs of the perfect insect. How this miracle happens we do not know, any more than we know why a thrush lays blue, black-spotted eggs, or what 'life' is. It is important, for the sake of what follows, to hold these four stages in the mind. In this order : egg that hatches into caterpillar; caterpillar that changes into chrysalis; chrysalis from which emerges the perfect insect that, having been fertilized, lays eggs and starts the cycle again. A cycle that may take a fortnight to complete, or many years. (A cycle that started—where? How strange it is that the mayfly, for example, spends over two years in the indeterminate stages to live for one day only as a perfect insect. Are those twenty-four hours slowed down, sharpened unbelievably, extended in time, to compensate for the weary two years of preparation for so brief a perfection? I cannot tell.)

It will be seen, then, that a butterfly or moth may be found in any of its stages, and kept until the perfect insect emerges; and for collecting purposes it is better bred in captivity, for then it will be undamaged in any way by contact with leaves and other objects that would rub the scales from its wings; or the sharp beaks of predatory birds that often tear out small pieces of the wing itself. It is difficult, and not much fun, to search for the eggs of lepidoptera; it is when we get to the larval stage that the hunt is really up. Large caterpillars may be spotted on trees, shrubs, and low-growing plants; smaller ones may be 'beaten' into an open umbrella. Chrysalids may be found on palings, fences, old barns; they may be dug for with a trowel at the roots of trees. Butterflies may be netted on the wing; or taken at rest towards sunset; moths may be caught with a powerful light, or at sugar patches, or hovering at dusk over their favourite flowers.

Every fine morning of the summer holidays, Father and I would set out, our knapsacks filled with glass-topped boxes for butterflies and tins for caterpillars. Each of us would carry a white butterfly-net (Father did not care for the green ones), and one of us would carry an old umbrella. As far as possible we would predetermine whether it was to be a larval or an imaginal morning, for on that would largely depend the direction we took. If we were after caterpillars we would make for hedges or woods; if butterflies, for flowery pastures and pieces of thistled wasteland.

'Let's go beating this morning, shall we?' Father would say, and we would set out, while the dew was still on the long field grasses, in the quiet, motionless air of morning. Along the side of ripening wheat-fields we would pass, where the red poppies stood like drops of blood among the green-gold ears, and rabbits and field-mice rustled deep in the forest of stems. It was always so still and expectant in the morning, and the dewdrops would flash silently in a mist of prismatic colour. We would stop by the edge of the wood, near an old gate, where oak-trees haphazardly lined a grassy glade, and the sun, shining on their leaves, seemed silently

to sing, and the strong scent of wild peppermint rose in the growing heat of morning. The earth would begin to quiver in the
shimmering summer loneliness. What did we feel then? I know
that I, for one, was an unconscious inhabitant of a world that has
since puberty cast me out.

Father would open the umbrella and, detaching the handle of
his butterfly-net, would hand me the net itself to hold by the brass
Y-piece. Then, holding the umbrella upside down beneath the oak
branches, he would gently thrash leaves and twigs with the stick.
The branches would shake and sway, and down from them would
descend a multitude of things; small caterpillars on silken threads,
spiders, earwigs, bits of dead twig, tiny moths, spinning and falling
in the still sunshine. He would place the umbrella on the ground
and together we would examine its contents. Its black bowl now
held a small world. A pea-green spider with white legs and ruby
eyes scampered about; the larvae of various flies lay greenly trans-
parent and unpleasantly twitching, a somnolent wasp crawled
over one of the ribs, and a host of small geometer caterpillars,
some brown, some green, took long loping strides in comic haste
across the strange, dark plateau on which they so unaccountably
found themselves, arching their backs into the shape of a horse-
shoe, extending themselves flat and repeating the process. What
was this, half-concealed under a leaf? Yes, it was—it really was
the fat, beautiful, pale bluish-green caterpillar of Camelina, the
Coxcomb Prominent. That, though not scarce, was a good omen
for the success of our beating. (And when, later on, we beat the
extraordinary brown, humped larva of Fagi, the Lobster Moth,
a true rarity, my joy knew no bounds.) Father would turn the
umbrella right way up, having carefully removed and placed in a
tin any caterpillars we wanted to keep. A little dusty shower of
leaves, twigs, spiders and other insects would cascade to the ground,
hastened by a gentle tap of the stick on the top of the umbrella.
We would move along, deeper into the wood, where the beeches
formed a high green canopy overhead, and there were waves of
bracken stippled with broken sunlight, and a deep, soft bed of
brown leaves to walk on. Woods that were like the natural aisle
of a great cathedral; or short, hot stumpy oak-woods. Both kinds
I remember; and how I would sometimes chase after a silver-
washed Fritillary that was sunning its hot brown wings on a pink-
flowered bramble spray; chase it far into the depths of the forest.

It would rise, high in the air at last on strong agitated pinions, and I would know that it had escaped me. And suddenly I would listen, and far away I would hear the beating of Father's stick on the branches, and I would realize that I had run a good way and was, perhaps, lost. And the watching, silent, friendly forest would close me in, and high in the branches a wood-pigeon would coo; and for a few moments I would enjoy, half-frightened, the strong, glancing pressure of the spirit of place, and the vivid, strawberry smell of the hot bracken that the sun was silently drawing out, and all the strange evanescent wood-smells; the rustlings and cracklings, and what the tall, grey beech-trunks said in their own language, and the spongy green mosses in theirs. And then the need for human company would powerfully overwhelm me; and crying, 'Daddy! Daddy! Where are you?' I would run, stumbling over tree-roots in my haste, in the direction of the sound of the distant beating. And there in a clearing I would find my warm, human father; who, when he saw me, would produce biscuits and lemonade from his knapsack; and we would sit side by side on a fallen tree-trunk, eating and drinking and examining our caterpillars. And the dearest tribute I can pay to my father is that he never went away and left me alone in those moments. For he, of all men, understood the heartbreaking loneliness of spirit that walks the deepest woods; and he did not intend that it should wholly encompass me, while he was there to prevent its doing so.

On our way home I would espy, across the other side of the wheat-field, a clump of sallow-wands rising above the hedge. (By the time I was six I could distinguish any ordinary tree at a distance, even though I had never lived in the country.) That, with luck, meant one thing; the magnificent caterpillars of Ocellatus, the Eyed Hawk, or of Populi, the Poplar Hawk. Arrived by the sallows we would look to see if there was any stripping; that is to say, if the lateral and terminal leaves had been eaten away, leaving nothing but bare stalk. Yes, here it was; but it looked rather old; for where the leaf had been bitten from the stem the wound had turned brown. Here was some fresher stripping. And here was the culprit! At the top of the bare twig, outlined against the sky, looking deceptively like a leaf, a large green caterpillar, some three inches long, sat at rest, its head thrown back; its hind-claspers firmly attached to the twig. As I touched it, it swayed the top part of its body threateningly from side to side. Its suction grip on the twig was so firm that to have pulled it off would have damaged it; so Father cut off the whole twig with his pocket knife. At once we saw another, rather smaller. And then, to my delight, I saw one of a different colour, the beautiful, rare glaucous form. Again Father cut the sallow-wand. That seemed to be all, and it was nearly lunch-time, so we set off home, I carrying the long twigs, each with its caterpillar.

It is a scene that I shall always remember. Three caterpillars of the Eyed Hawk-moth; the two in my left hand a beautiful bright apple green; the one in my right a soft blue-grey, all of them with blue-tinged horns, rose-ringed spiracles and powdered all over with rough white dots. Exquisitely beautiful creatures; a gift to me from the gods themselves. I was divinely happy that morning as I trotted home beside Father, along the edge of the wheatfield with its scarlet poppies blazing now under the scorching sun of noon. It was very hot and my back was damp with sweat. Over the farther hedges the heat-haze shimmered, so that the bushes and twigs looked as though they were seen through wavery, melting glass. Father had a caterpillar of Fagi; I had three beautiful Eyed Hawks. I was happy. I was tired. I was a king. The earth lay, happy in the heat of a summer's morning, before me. I had no care in the world as I kicked my way along, holding my caterpillars, at my feet the little pink bindweed flowers common to the paths of cornfields. Beyond, waited lunch, and long glasses of lemonade. . . .

And now, even as I write this, it is full summer, and out of the window I can see an oak tree and a blue, burning sky. A few fields away is a wheatfield, greenly hot in the sun, and the poppies are just beginning to open their drops of blood. I admit that my eyes are filled with tears. I can go to the wheatfield, and I can walk in it, but I can no longer become of it. I am forever doomed to see it and to write of it from the outside; never again to be a participant in its joys. Why? Is it that those three lines of A. E. Housman hold the answer: 'My father and my mother/They had a likely son,/And I have none.'?

*   *   *

Such was a larval expedition. An imaginal one was perhaps even more exciting. Butterflies like the sun, the hotter the better, so that most of the time we would be on bright open land, away from all shade. Sometimes, having first got the owner's permission, we would haunt a field of red clover, or of lucerne, in the hope of catching Clouded Yellow, either Edusa, the ordinary one, or the much rarer Hyale, the Pale Clouded Yellow. Neither of these butterflies was common, though certain years (since they are immigrants) were more favourable than others. To see this rich, golden-yellow butterfly come zig-zagging over the deep crimson of the clover flowers is an unforgettable experience; it was always tinged with agony if the butterfly refused to venture near the edge of the field, as one was never allowed to chase it among the growing crop. More often we would make our way to some sheltered quarry or piece of rough pasture land where thistles grew; for butterflies love thistles, especially the sort that has small, lilac-coloured tasselly flowers.

It is strange how impossible it is to dissociate butterflies from blossom. Richard South in his preface to *The Butterflies of the British Isles*, with a sudden flash of poetry calls them 'these aërial flowers', a description that is beautifully apt. One cannot, in fact, study butterflies without, in the process, getting to know a great deal about wild flowers also. Sometimes a flower seems almost incomplete without its complementary butterfly. Anyone who has seen a Red Admiral alight on the dull pink flowerhead of Hemp Agrimony, flashing its scarlet, black and white wings open and shut as it probes for honey, will realize the truth of this. The flower seems transformed, as though this was the purpose for which it was created, as indeed may well be the case. Away flies the butterfly and the swaying, quivering flowerhead resumes its meek pink dullness.

In the shelter of the quarry on the hills it would be blisteringly hot and still on a fine August morning. We would sling off our knapsacks, and sit down on an outcrop of chalk, where we could watch the thistle-clumps. The grasshoppers would keep up an endless chirruping, cut across now and again by the swift zoom of a bumble-bee, and accentuated by a myriad of small insect sounds—the indefinite, indefinable hum of a summer's day that is so much quieter than silence itself. From far away would come the tinkle of sheep-bells. Father would take a large, clean white handkerchief from his pocket and arrange it under his speckled straw hat, so that it hung down around his sweating face and kept the flies off a bit. I would idly swish my butterfly net around my head, until it resounded with the angry buzzing of a quarter of a pound or so of flies that made a black ball like a small swarm of bees at the bottom of the muslin. (A habit that was not approved by Father; for how could I catch a butterfly if my net was full of flies?) And over the pale thistle flowers, the small Coppers, glistening as if they were wet, and the common Blues, soft, feathery and azure, would dance and flutter, dart away and return. A worn old Marbled White would visit the thistles, the last of its brood; a newly emerged Gatekeeper, slick and smart as paint; the Whites, flickering hither and thither; and the bold, beautiful and inevitable Vanessids, disturbing the little butterflies as they grandly arrived and took possession; the magnificent Red Admirals, the calm, rich Peacocks with their beautiful pale lilac eye-spots, the busy, fussy Small Tortoiseshells. The Vanessids would arrive, suck, dart away again, gliding with motionless outspread wings over the short turf and the chalk before resuming flight for a moment, only to glide in superb arrogance once more till they were lost to sight over a shoulder of the down.

These were the commoners. And now, here comes what we were waiting for; a freshly-emerged Painted Lady, resplendent in delicate tints of salmon pink and black, the underside marvellously ringed and mottled. A quick swoop of the net, and she could be seen, a faint ghostly shape through the muslin, fluttering in amazed surprise. Father would draw a round glass-bottomed box from his pocket, and inserting his hand into the net would skilfully box her. Into his pocket she went, into the darkness that would soothe her and stop her from fluttering; and we would wait for the next capture.

For some minutes nothing of any interest would arrive, and lying on the ground I would study the tiny life around me. Then I looked up, adjusting the focus of my eyes. The distant hills were half lost in heat-haze; over the brow of the quarry the fertile valleys stretched out, a remote chequerboard of colour, yellow of mustard, red of poppies, green of wheat. A long way below. Could I jump, and land among them?

'Quick, John!' Father cried. I looked. On the thistles a Comma butterfly sat, fanning its indented wings; I could clearly see the white comma mark. I struck at it with my net; missed; it was gone. Why was I so bad at catching butterflies? I could always catch the ones I didn't want. I must have looked disconsolate, for Father pulled out of his pocket the little red box of seedless raisins that he always carried on these expeditions and poured some into my immediately outstretched palm. 'Day-dreaming, you silly-billy,' he said, smiling kindly. Then he added, 'We must go back soon.'

I didn't want to go back. I lay down again, relaxed in heavenly laziness, chewing the raisins. How pretty the downland flowers were! The wiry-stemmed scabious, the fragrant cushions of green and mauve thyme, the delicate harebells with their pleated purple buds, the golden rock roses, the blue and pink and white milkwort, and the salad-burnet that you could chew and that tasted of cucumber. How the insects hummed and murmured, and how lovely the hot sun felt on bare legs and arms. The hills, the summer hills. . . .

The Comma had come back! Father had disappeared for a moment behind a wayfaring tree. I mustn't miss it this time. I crept up to the butterfly, aimed, swung my net. I had got it! I called loudly to Father to come and box it. 'Well done,' he said, 'I'll set it for you and you shall have it for your own collection.'

My happiness was complete. The morning was fulfilled in me. It was time to go. I looked with love at the pale thistles, over which little orange beetles never stopped trickling; the thistles on which I had caught my Comma. The silence and the beauty and the dignity of the hills filled my being; the pure air and the haze and the murmur; and the rapturous loveliness of being alive on a sunny summer morning. I felt that my body must burst to let out something inside me. The moment, the divine moment, was stamped forever upon my memory. I turned to my father. 'Please, Daddy, can I have some more raisins?' I asked.

*   *   *

One beautiful and calm evening of late August, just before sunset, Father called to me. 'I'm going to take you for a little stroll,' he said. 'I want to show you something. Your mother says I may,' he added, looking at her with the mocking smile that was peculiarly his own.

We went through a great wheatfield, between the aisles of stacked sheaves, the harsh stubble pricking my feet through my thin plimsolls. In the distance mists were beginning to wreathe and coil in vaporous white levels. We came to a gate that led into a pasture field of longish grasses.

'I thought you would like to see where the butterflies sleep,' said Father.

We climbed the gate and wandered into the long grass. It was wet with dew and in a moment my plimsolls were sopping, which made me very happy. For I was never allowed to get them wet alone.

'Look,' Father said, pointing to the grass. I bent down, and saw that each grass stem was clasped by one or two Common Blues, that slept, their wings closely folded together, so that only the grey, orange-spotted undersides were showing. Hundreds and hundreds of blues, male and female, were there, dotting the grass, all fast asleep.

'Even if you touch them,' Father said, 'they won't wake. They're fast asleep for the night '

Gently I touched one of them. It opened its wings sleepily, revealing the clear blue of the male, then shut them again.

'I found them last night,' said Father, 'and I thought that you would like to see them.'

I was beginning now to feel sleepy myself. We set off back through the thickening dusk. Honeysuckle smelt strongly now; moths blundered through the soft air. I nearly fell down in the cornfield through sleepiness. Father picked me up and carried me in his arms. I nestled against his shoulder. Bump, bump, bump across the long garden. Mother stood in the lighted French window.

'It *is* naughty of you, Arthur,' she said, in a tone of voice that belied her words, 'to keep him up so late.'

'It made him happy,' Father said.

Mother carried me up and tucked me into bed. I was too big to be carried, really; so that it was a great treat. I fell asleep thinking of the grey grasses and the grey butterflies clasped so tightly to their stems.

* * *

Pupal expeditions belonged to a different kind of weather. We would choose a dull grey afternoon when not many butterflies were likely to be on the wing. (All the same, we took a net, in case.) We would make for fields where stood large oaks or elms. But first we would pass through a farmyard, and when we came to the old black barn we would stop. Here, attached to the boards, above the dusty nettle-clumps, the chrysalids of the three common Vanessid butterflies, the Red Admiral, the Peacock and the Small Tortoiseshell, would hang, head downwards, from a little silken pad. Fascinatingly small objects of a greyish-purple colour, with humps and excrescences of silver or golden sheen, like burnished metal. Sometimes the nettles below would swarm with the dark, spiny caterpillars of the three butterflies that love to feed upon them. Sometimes a full-grown caterpillar itself would be hanging, motionless and head downwards, from the boards, awaiting its strange metamorphosis. I would collect a few chrysalids and put them in my tin among the protective dried moss, startling, as I detached them, a specimen of the strange, rufous autumnal Herald Moth that was sheltering beneath the overlapping tarred boards. Irritably fluttering its wings it would creep away for safety through a knot-hole into the dark sanctuary of the barn itself. And just by the hole was a yellowish chrysalis, that of a Small White; angular and pointed, with a silken girdle round its waist.

Reluctantly, in response to Father's urgings, I would move away from the barn and prepare myself for the real business of the afternoon. Out in the open fields again we would select a large oak tree, and taking out our narrow-bladed fern trowels would start to dig in the little bays and creeks of earth at the base of the trunk. Sooner or later a shining red-brown chrysalis would turn up, probably that of Aprilina, the Merveille de Jour, a beautiful moth that when it came out, after we were back in London, would look just like a piece of grey-green lichen, or perhaps of Poecilo-campa Populi, the December Moth, that would break its chrysalis in the darkest days of winter. Sometimes I would find to my sorrow that a careless job with the trowel had sliced a chrysalis in half, revealing the pale green liquid that would later have formed itself into a feathery winged imago.

We would move from the oak to a tall elm. Sometimes, among the ordinary chrysalids found at the base of every tree, I would unearth, to my intense joy, the rough dark pupa of the Lime Hawk. A couple of inches long, it would lie there on the blade of my trowel, irritably wriggling its abdominal segments until I tenderly placed it in my tin, carefully packing it among the softest moss. Next spring, the large olive-and-brick-coloured moth would hang one morning, like a folded leaf, from the top of my chrysalis box, an exquisite reminder of the summer holidays before.

Strange and memorable are the digging afternoons, when the grey still weather lapped us round, and the friendly cows would come nosing up to us in an attempt to find out what we were doing on our knees before the great spreading oaks and elms. Strange and memorable the return through the fields and the busy farmyard to Mother, and tea from the willow pattern cups and the silver teapot and sugar-basin; the kettle singing its small low song over the methylated spirit flame, as we gave her an inventory of all the chrysalids we had found.

*   *   *

Though it was not until I was considerably older, ten or eleven, that I was allowed to go sugaring for moths because of the late hour at which it was conducted, it is so much a part of the experiences recorded in this chapter that I must recount it here.

The preparations took place just before dusk. In the pantry, Father would find a large jam-jar, and in it he would mix coarse brown sugar known as Foot's sugar, with rum, and jargonelle, or pear essence. I would stand by and watch; and the dying light filtering through a small north window is forever associated in my mind with the smell of this mixture that rose in rich wafts from the half-filled jar. Pear-drops and rum and sugar—no wonder the moths were attracted by it! When Father's back was turned I would dip my finger in the jar and suck it, and the delicious golden thrill would traverse my gullet and burn in my chest. Once he caught me, and for a moment looked very angry, and then, to my surprise, burst out laughing.

Leaving a fragrant trail behind us in the stone passage, we would sally forth. The dusk was everywhere, the garden lying drowned and mysterious in it. From the flowerbeds flowed wave after wave of scent; the rich warm smell of the red roses mingling with the sharp sweet breath of the tobacco-plants that, with the ending of the day, were opening their pale stars to the long-tongued moths. The white flowers glimmered; the red ones had turned black. We made our way into the kitchen garden. On the trunks of the apple, pear and plum trees, Father painted, at eye level, a foot-long strip of sugar with a small house-painter's brush that he kept for the purpose. The smell of the sugar mingled with the smell of cabbages, onions, earth and the cooling, sun-steeped walls of the old garden. We retraced our steps to the tree-lined drive, and on the trunks of the chestnuts, limes and oaks more sugar was painted, this time by me. The long, neat, oblong patches glistened and dripped and perfumed the air with their message that here was a feast for moths, an alcoholic feast, moreover. In the deepening dusk the patches showed, dark against the grey trunks as we turned into the house, in whose windows lights were now springing, to have our supper and await events.

Although Father, by nature tidy, hated open doors and un-curtained windows, he endured the latter on summer nights for the sake of any moths that, attracted by light, might fly in. So that supper, and coffee afterwards in the study, were usually accompanied by the banging and fluttering of frenzied moths as they dashed themselves against the oil-lamp in a violent attempt at suicide, and frequently Father would spring up, net or box in hand, in an effort to capture some prize. Round the room they would go, the blundering moth and the excited father. On an armchair Father would leap as the moth rose to ceiling height. A deft swoop, the Victorian mantel-ornaments jingling and clash-ing, and the moth would be struggling in the net. Father would box it, and sink into his armchair again, mopping his brow with a sigh of relief. But not for long! In a moment the process would be repeated; and it is surprising, looking back on the scene, how very little ever got broken. Sometimes a bat, attracted by the light, would fly in, and then there was indeed a to-do, with Mother cowering, hands to head, in case it should get in her hair, and Father wildly chasing it with his butterfly net, and everything in the room chiming and rattling in sympathetic alignment with the general mood.

About ten o'clock, Father, with a certain solemn dignity, would slowly rise, saying, 'I think it's time we looked at the sugar-patches.' He would glance inquiringly at me. I would nod and follow him out into the hall. On the table there stood a red-painted triangular candle-lantern. Father would slide the shutter up and light the wick, shutting it safely in again once he was sure the flame had taken hold.

How feeble a gleam did the candle throw into the fearful, pressing darkness! Dim shrubs would loom up suddenly in the rays as we crossed the garden. Little moths would hurl themselves against the glass of the lantern and circle around our heads. On the paths huge black and brown slugs crawled, leaving silver trails of sticky slime that led back to the box-edging from which they had emerged as night fell.

'We might get something tonight,' Father would say as we approached our first tree; 'it's warm and there's not much wind; just enough to carry the smell of the sugar without deterring the moths from flight.' He would stop on the path and hand me the lantern. 'Hold it, John, so that I can have my hands free for the boxes.' We would reach the tree, and I would raise the lantern, shining it suddenly on the sugar-patch. The moment was tense with excitement. Would there be a rarity? Rarity or not, the sight that met one's eyes would be reward enough.

The patch was practically obscured, alive with dozens of excited moths. Ceaselessly they fanned their wings; their eyes glowing ruby balls in the candlelight, so that everywhere were moving, gleaming points of fire. Jostling and struggling for their share of the feast; big moths, old and grey; little, frisky moths; somnolent moths that already (alas!) were too intoxicated to know what they were doing; detached moths, cleaning their antennae with their forelegs, like cats washing; greedy, pushing moths that shoved the small fry right out of their way in their haste to get drunk. And everywhere, turning and twisting, the twin, fiery eyeballs of each moth, fierce pink and red jewels; and the long, slender, hair-like tongues lapping up the nectar as fast as they could go. At this tree there were no rarities; Yellow Underwings, Dark Arches made up the bulk of the guests. And sharing the feast with them were two daddy-long-legs, a thin-legged spider that walked as if on stilts, disdainfully; dozens of earwigs and an old and sophisticated-looking slug that had crawled all the way up the trunk for its share. Even as we watched, two more moths flew in, suddenly appearing, white in the lantern's rays, and settled down to feed. We left the struggling, fluttering mass and passed to the next tree. Here among all the commoners was something we wanted, a specimen of the second brood of Batis, the beautiful Peach Blossom Moth. Skilfully Father boxed it, extricating it somehow from the hosts of moths that jostled and pushed it.

Thus we went from tree to tree, and at each tree it was the same. So that when, at last, I tumbled, tired out, into bed, my mind's eye would show me a single picture; the dark tree-trunk in the yellow candlelight, and the dozens of vibrating wings and shining ruby eyes of the impatient, excited, jostling moths; while to my nose was borne the intoxicating smell of rum and pear essence and brown sugar, and in my ears I could hear the sound of the night-wind soughing in the tops of the trees.

*   *   *

And so we had from eggs, from caterpillars, from chrysalids, or caught on the wing, or at light, or at sugar the beautiful denizens of the cabinet. Father would pin and set them with great care on the long grooved setting-boards, where they must remain until the wings had dried and were rigid, and they could be moved to a store-box, and thence to the cabinet. So that, on a winter's night in London, we could take out the drawers and muse over the high days of summer, when we had collected them.

*   *   *

For three days, while I have been writing this chapter, I have kept my female Eyed Hawk in the hope that I should find a mate for her by the process known as 'assembling'. I have failed, and now I must let her out for good, to find her own mate and her own honey. She is sitting on the curtain, her favourite place. It is dusk; time for her to go; now, while the predatory sparrows are snatching their sleep. I push my forefinger under her head and thorax. Lazily she lifts her lovely chocolate forewings, revealing the rose-pink, blue-eyed hind pair. She crawls along my finger. I open the window. The air of dusk is exciting her. I hold her right outside in the cool twilight. She begins to vibrate her wings with incredible rapidity. Something of this trembling ecstasy is communicated to me; I watch her with a deep thrill of pleasure. Faster and faster the wings vibrate. And suddenly she has launched herself into space, flying strongly against the darkening sky. Up she goes, wheeling and circling, free at last. Smaller and smaller she grows, a dark spot in the distance. She has vanished. I can see her no more. I have lost my little friend; but later in the year I shall find her handsome green children on my apple boughs, and for the sake of their mother I will take them in, protect them from the sting of ichneumon flies, provide them with a pot of good earth when, tired of eating, they wish for the dark pupal rest, and let them fly next summer, as I have let their mother fly. For in these three days she has been a true friend to me; she has made to live strongly in me those vanished days of which Wordsworth so beautifully wrote: 'And summer days, when we were young; Sweet childish days, that were as long/As twenty days are now.'

16

The Air-raids

Alas, that birds and butterflies and moths were not, even in those days, the only winged things! In London, in the autumn of 1916, began the air-raids. I well remember the first daylight one; because, though I didn't understand it, I saw panic on the faces of the grown-ups, and it frightened me. I was at the Class; and for some weeks there had been an epidemic of mumps. Every day the children were dosed with a very curious medicine called Yadil; it had the strangest taste of onions, and it burned you as it went down; I never could decide whether I liked it or disliked it.

On this especial morning Yadil-time had come round, and it was being poured from a huge brown glass bottle by Miss Richardson, when there were a lot of bangs outside. A strange moment of helpless irresolution followed, when everyone looked at each other. Then someone said: 'It's the maroons,' and then the mistresses all began running about hither and thither, in a kind of aimless alarm. Miss Josephine paused in the act of pouring out some more Yadil, holding the bottle aloft and poised, and an unpleasant whiteness spread over her face. We caught the general sense of alarm and began to run wildly about. Miss Richardson put the bottle down, her hands shaking. She tried to make herself heard above the growing uproar. 'Children! Children!' No one paid the slightest attention. The bony white hand of panic was upon the room. There was a rush for the door. In the scrimmage a girl's foot was trodden on and she began to yell and shriek. The uproar increased. So many people were round the door that it wouldn't open. And then, suddenly, a stentorian but calm voice boomed above the noise. 'Children, be quiet! Listen to me!' Silence fell. Everyone turned towards the blackboard where, towering from the dais, stood dear Miss Hilda Morse. Her earrings swung and nodded; her rugged, kindly old face was set in stern authority. 'You will proceed to the lobbies,' she said, her voice like the crack of a whip, 'in an orderly manner. Wait, please,' as someone put their hand on the door knob. 'I shall lead you. You will follow me, class by class, and the mistresses will bring up the rear. Stand still, please, until I have reached the door and am through it.' As she moved across the room I could hear the drone of planes over-head, and bursts of shrapnel fire in the distance. A few minutes later, having arrived safely in the underground cloak-rooms, we were all chattering excitedly. Miss Richardson, determined to prove her devotion to duty, had carried the Yadil bottle down with her, and was unctuously pouring out doses and handing them round.

It was fun to be down here, doing no lessons, in the dark, with the electric light on. Then presently, the all-clear maroons sounded, and after waiting another five minutes we were all trooped up again and lessons were resumed. I was excited and thrilled. Who would have thought that gentle, kindly old Miss Morse who couldn't say boo (with any conviction) to a goose would have saved the situation? While harsh old Miss Richardson was trembling like a leaf? I knew that I should never forget the way Miss Morse had looked as she stood by the blackboard, very noble and fine, as though a light had played round her head; or as Joan of Arc (who we were doing at that time, and who greatly interested me) might have looked, as she led her armies.

*   *   *

The night raids were very different. Too young to understand the danger, I admit that I loved them. In the middle of the night

I could hear Mother in my bedroom, and know that the planes were over. She would lift me from my bed, wrap me, still half asleep, in an eiderdown, and begin the long journey downstairs. Glancing around from the safe shelter of her arms I would watch the black alcove as we passed; though it would scarcely matter if a black figure were standing in it as long as I was in my mother's arms. Overhead, the guns thundered and the house, down whose stairs we were steadily proceeding, rocked and swayed. Behind and in front of us, other figures were walking, wrapped in blankets and dressing-gowns. Father was absent; he was seeing to the boys in the College Dormitory. Down we went, past the drawing-room landing, past the study door, across the hall and down the kitchen stairs that led only to the basement . . . groping our way down the old, worn stone steps, past the pantry and the kitchen that were wrapped in the black silence of night, groping along the dark wall until, suddenly, light shone through a half-opened door and conversation and bursts of laughter could be heard from within.

'Here we are,' Mother would announce, as she pushed the door open, 'quite safe and sound!' I would open my sleepy eyes wide, and sniff with deep appreciation the smell of must and cobwebs, and an all-pervading odour that coloured and deepened the other smells; faint and elusive; something that as yet I only understood and loved instinctively; the frail, lingering fragrance of the spirit and soul of the grape itself. We were in the wine-cellar.

It was a small, square stone room, lit by a naked electric light bulb, bare but for the wooden bins around its walls. On every available inch of floor-space mattresses had been laid. On one of these, Muriel and Harold were already reclining; and a moment later we were joined by Nurse, Cook and the housemaid (by then we had no page-boy). Cook was carrying her parrot and her brass clock, and her hair was tied with little bits of paper. Father had not yet arrived. We settled down on the mattresses and I was unwrapped from my eiderdown. Everyone began to talk. Overhead the noise of the gunfire was increasing. Father came in. The boys had all been shepherded into the undercroft. Father sat down. The noise overhead continued and Father looked restless. A moment later he rose and glancing guiltily at Mother, said, 'I think I'll just have a look outside, dear.'

'Must you?' Mother asked, sighing.

Father went out of the room again. Muriel and Harold

were doing an elaborate jig-saw puzzle on a tray. One of the bits fell down between the mattresses; there was a scrimmage and words were bandied. Mother knitted placidly. I was reading in the *Strand* magazine a most horrible story (which was to haunt me for years afterwards) called 'Inexplicable', about alligators that materialized at night on the stairs of an old haunted house. I can remember now the description of their musky smell. But the house in the story was much too like Number 3. I was glad to be in this fuggy, bright cellar, with the soothing noise going on overhead.

The door opened, and Father came in again. 'They're still at it,' he said. 'Shrapnel falling all over the garden.'

'I do wish you wouldn't go out, dear,' Mother said, nervously.

Father, looking a little ashamed of himself, said nothing. It was funny down here, I thought; why did we have to come? It would be much more fun to stand on the garden steps, like Father, and watch the fireworks in the sky. Still, it was cosy, and excitingly damp; there were beads of water on the wall, near my head. The little room blurred and swam; then righted itself; then swam again. I heard Nurse say something about 'them 'Uns'. Then I must have fallen asleep; for the next thing I knew was that I was sitting in Mother's arms. I looked up, she was smiling down protectively. 'It's all over, darling,' she said; 'the maroons have just gone off. Listen, and you'll hear Mrs Gow blow her trumpet.'

I listened carefully. Far away I heard a thin, clear sustained note. After each raid, the headmaster's wife (who was also my godmother) used to make the rounds of the school, blowing a toy tin trumpet, so that everyone was sure of knowing that the raid was over. It was a comforting sound. I have the trumpet still. It has a piece of red, white and blue ribbon tied round it.

I was disappointed that we had to leave the cellar. Only dull bed now, unless there was another raid later on. My disappointment was mitigated, however, by Mother saying: 'We're all going to the study, darling, to make café-au-lait. We need a hot drink.'

Sleepily, I watched Father making it over a spirit-lamp. The tin had a picture of a suave, bearded Frenchman on it. It was good stuff; but better if you could get hold of the tin when nobody was looking, and eat it. It looked and tasted like (and probably was) coffee-coloured condensed milk. A lovely, rich warming drink, sweet and soothing.

No longer could the good-nights be spun out. I was firmly bundled off to bed. Long before Mother had finished tucking me up I was fast asleep.

*   *   *

In the morning I would run out into the garden to collect the pieces of shrapnel that had fallen in the night. In those days, I was the victim of a collecting mania; and this particular hunt had all the thrill of a butterfly or birds' egg expedition. I would poke about in the grass of the lawn; stealthily walk on the flowerbed when Father wasn't looking, rake among the dead leaves in the little roofless potting-shed, filled with a lust to unearth those queer, jagged bits of ribbed metal. I would polish them till they shone like silver. Great was the day when I found a brass nosecap half embedded in the gravel. I had long thin bits; short fat bits, and one round bullet, like a lead marble. I kept them all in a cigar-box with a pretty picture of tropical dancing-girls on the inner lid; and I polished and arranged them daily. Among the silvery pieces, the nosecap shone like gold, king of the collection.

One afternoon I took them to show to Mrs McNeilly, the old Irish school matron, in her little sitting-room that was so excitingly lit by gas instead of electric light. An old King's Scholar dropped in to tea, resplendent in his lieutenant's uniform and shiny Sam Browne belt. I showed him my collection. To my horror, he was scornful. 'We see much better bits in France,' he said, grinning at me. (He was only about nineteen.) 'I'll send you something worth looking at.' However, he never did; for a fortnight later he was killed in the Battle of the Somme.

After that, my interest in shrapnel subsided slightly; and soon at the Class I had something else to brag about. I had seen a Zeppelin.

*   *   *

It was probably very wrong of Father, but I am always grateful to him. One night, after the air-raid warning had sounded, he took me in his arms, despite Mother's protestations, from the cellar to the top of the garden steps. It was a brilliant night of full moon, very clear and still with searchlights circling the sky. Suddenly, the beams converged, to pick out and hold a long silver cigar that sailed in a kind of rich, fat silence across the sky.

'A Zeppelin!' cried my father. 'Do you see it, John? A Zeppelin! We'd better get under cover!'

At that moment the guns opened up, shattering the still serenity with a deafening roar. We dived down the steps and back into the cellar. Excitedly I told the assembled company what we had seen. Harold was envious, and wanted to go up in the hope of seeing the Zeppelin himself; but Father peremptorily told him to sit down.

Then, from up above, we heard a long, sinking whine that rapidly grew louder. I saw on the faces of the grown-ups a look that was, for some unknown reason, terribly frightening. Louder and louder the noise grew; I knew that something dreadful was going to happen. Then there was a tremendous bang and a thud; and the whole house seemed to rise from its foundations and settle again. Plaster rained down from the ceiling of the cellar upon our heads; a bottle of wine shot out of its bin and, narrowly missing my neck, crashed on the stone floor at Father's feet, its red life-blood trickling away between the cracks of the flag-stones.

A moment dreadful beyond description followed; faces, set and drained, staring at each other in tense horror and anticipation.

Nothing at all happened. I felt the beat return to my heart with a violent upward thrust. Gradually, the terrible set look on the faces relaxed, but no one moved.

Then the silence was suddenly broken by a screaming howl that rose in pitch, a blend of diabolical laughter and utter horror. It came from old Cookie, who had risen to her feet, and was tearing at her hair in its funny paper plaits. Father rose and went to her, but she gave him a push that sent him reeling backwards. Then Mother, shouting: 'Be quiet at once, do you hear?' seized a jug of water and threw its contents violently into Cook's face. The screaming stopped, her expression changed, and sinking back on to a mattress she moaned softly, plucking at her breast.

'Come along,' Mother said gently, 'I'm going to tuck you up on the sofa in the kitchen. It's all over now. There's nothing to worry about. Come along!'

'You had better not leave the cellar, Ada,' said Father sharply.

Mother looked at him.

'I must,' she said. 'She must be got out of here.'

'I'll come with you, then,' he said.

'No,' said Mother firmly, 'you must stay here and look after the others, Arthur. I shan't be many moments.'

She led Cook out of the cellar.

Suddenly everyone started talking at once. Nobody noticed me. I began to cry silently. And then, through the babble of voices, the all-clear sounded, strangely loud and shocking. But no one made any effort to leave the cellar. Everyone stood there, waiting for Mother to return. She came to the door at last, her face hard, white and strained. She stood in the doorway, looking sightlessly at us. And suddenly her face crumpled up and she burst into tears. 'Poor Cookie,' she said; 'poor, poor old Cookie!'

Father took her in his arms; and Muriel carried me up to bed.

*   *   *

In the morning I was told what had happened. One of our own shells had crashed into Little Dean's Yard, about twelve feet from our own front door, burying itself deep under the paving-stones. It had not gone off. (It remained there, in fact, for about four years, unexploded, until it was finally dug out.)

Can I, even now, realize what so nearly happened? I knew a boy at school who was sitting on a beach when a bomb fell and exploded near him. He was forever afterwards deaf and dumb; and several times a day he used to whirl his arms about his head in a kind of shivering fit. When he tried to speak he made a strange noise that was oddly like a dog barking.

17

Yule-tide

The famous Latin Play of Westminster School, of which Father was director, producer and stage manager in one, has been many times described by other writers. And although I shall say something about it in a later chapter, I mention it here because it formed a landmark in the year, coming, as it did, after a great deal of preparation, at the end of the Play (or Autumn) Term. The sense of fulfilment, with its ensuing relaxation, marked off sharply the summer and autumn from the approaching feeling of Christmas. The Play was over once more; the boys had departed, the Yard was silent; the page had been swiftly turned in the night, and the new one lay open and unfilled, as white as the snow that, hourly, one hoped would fall from the heavy grey skies.

The first morning of the Christmas holidays was always a great one. In and over the house there was a feeling of happy expectancy. I would jump out of bed, dress hurriedly, and race downstairs. Everywhere was this new feeling of freedom; a feeling that time was not as important as it had been all through the long term; that a minute or two of lateness would be quickly forgiven. Up the stairs would float the smell of coffee and frying bacon. I would race into the dining-room, nearly late for prayers. Already Father was sitting at the table, fiddling with the spirit-lamp over which was placed a small enamel pan filled with water for the poaching of his eggs. To one side of him lay his heavy silver watch and chain; in front of him a bible and a prayer-book. 'Ring the bell, will you, John?' he said, as I rapidly crossed to my chair. I pressed down the black china knob. Far away, in the kitchen quarters, I heard: 'Ter-ting, ter-ting, ter-ting, ting, ting, ting, ting.' We all sat waiting. Harold, from the other side of the fireplace, gave me a rapid wink. I caught Father looking at me, and pretended not to have seen this irreverent gesture from my brother. The door opened, and the servants filed in. First came old Cookie, by virtue of her age the leader, then Nurse, then the housemaid, and finally (if we had one, which during the war wasn't often) the page-boy, resplendent with smooth hair and shiny buttons. He shut the door carefully and the procession seated itself on a row of chairs. Father opened the Bible and read; a psalm and a passage from the New Testament. There was a pause; and then everyone slid off their chairs, turned round, and knelt. The Collect for the day and some prayers followed. After that, we all said the Lord's Prayer. In the interval between this and the blessing, the water in Father's frying-pan could clearly be heard bubbling and muttering to itself. I used to try to hear the first sound through the uplifted voices of the Lord's Prayer. 'Our Father which art in Heaven (silence), hallowed be Thy name (silence). Thy kingdom come, Thy will be done on earth as it is in Heaven.' There it was: -s -s -s -s, plick, plick, plock, plick-plock. It interested me a great deal in that it nearly always started at the same moment; it said so much for Father's exact measurement of the water, and the stable heating-power of methylated spirit.

After the blessing, the little procession would re-form itself and leave the dining-room as it had entered. We would all begin talking. In a moment the maid would re-enter, bearing a silver entrée dish filled with crisp ringlets of bacon. (I used to wonder why it wasn't spoilt during prayers, when there was no one to look after it. I still do.) Father would stand up and say: 'Bless, O Lord, this food to our use, for Christ's sake, Amen.' Only on very rare occasions did he alter this Grace. One of them I remember well, with amusement. There was some slight delay, and the unfortunate housemaid entered the room a couple of minutes late. As she moved across to the table with the food, Father rose rapidly and, glancing at her, said: 'For what we are *about* to receive may the Lord make us truly thankful, Amen,' and sat down again, waiting patiently for the dish to be set before him.

After the Grace I would tuck into my toast and bacon with a zest and an appetite that were largely born of the knowledge that there were no more lessons until Christmas Day itself had come and gone.

*   *   *

For a few days not very much would be seen of Father. He would spend his time in the study, resting after the strenuous activities of the term. Then one afternoon he would, as I have already related, take me on a shopping expedition; and the following afternoon ask me if I would like to help him get the house ready for Christmas, an invitation I would joyfully accept.

Together we would go to his store-cupboard in the hall. Long and deep, it was crammed with exciting things : tools and electric light bulbs, picture-wire, watering-cans and oil-cans. It was as completely masculine as Mother's cupboard, that adjoined it, was feminine. Mother's was stacked with stone jars full of sugar and rice; with tins of treacle, golden and black, with matches, candles, soap and piles of clean dusters. The smell of Mother's cupboard was rich and sweet, a blend of prunes and soap. Father's cupboard smelt of nails and dubbin and old cigar-boxes and leather; a very secret smell, faint but all-pervading. If you opened both doors and stood back a little, both smells would meet at your nostrils and make a new and wonderful smell. Because of the smells, I remember the handles of the cupboards; hinged metal rings round which one firmly curled one's fingers before turning and pulling.

In Father's cupboard we would find a little pail, an old sponge and a piece of wash-leather. I would be sent down to the kitchen to get the pail filled with warm water. Father would bring the steps, and we would proceed to wash and polish the three great windows of the dining-room, I holding the pail while Father carefully wetted and wrung out the sponge and passed it across the panes. While he did this he would tell me fascinating stories of what he did when he was a little boy; of the country round Hazeleigh and the exciting lepidoptera to be found in it. After the washing came the polishing, and Father would not be satisfied until every speck of dust had been removed and the panes sparkled and shone crystal-clear. How beautiful the bare trees in the garden looked through them now, as though there was no glass there, or even better than that : for the glass was adding its own soft lustre to the scene. A rift in the clouds, and for a moment the sun poured forth, and everything shone and danced brilliantly. And then the sunlight faded from shutter, carpet and table, as though it had been sucked back into where it had come from, and all was grey and wintry again.

'And now,' said Father, 'for the electric light shades. Get some more water, will you, boysie dear, and I'll go and find the Selvyt cloth.'

Down to the basement I would go again, and return to find

Father unscrewing the shade-ring of the first lamp-holder. Passing the ring to me to hold, he would carefully remove the fluted, cloudy, blue-green glass shade, sponge it and polish it with the Selvyt cloth until it reflected like a mirror the light from the window and, replacing it on its batten-holder, he would screw the ring back into place. Then he would do the same with the other two shades (it was a hanging three-branched pendant), and cautiously get down from the table on which he had been kneeling. Now came a favourite part of this unvarying annual ritual.

Normally, because all three bulbs turned on with one switch, only one bulb was kept in the three-branched pendant, it being considered (though not by me) that the dining-room was thus adequately lit. Now we had to select two other bulbs in order that the Christmas dinner-table should bask in unparalleled brilliance. Father went to his cupboard and returned with what was, to me, quite its most exciting inmate : the wooden box full of electric light bulbs (or globes, as Mother would always call them). Carefully we turned them over. There were round bulbs with thick carbon filaments, coiled in three spirals, that gave a thick yellow light; there were pear-shaped bulbs with fragile tungsten filaments, up and down like a long circular hairpin (if such a thing can be imagined) that gave a much whiter light; and there were some very old bulbs, twice the size of any of the others, enormous and circular, like toy balloons, the bottom half of ground glass, the top clear. These, despite their size, gave the worst light of all; and Father always laughed when I suggested that we should use them just for the sheer melodrama of the thing (though that was not how I then put it to myself). In fact, I can't think why he kept them, unless as sentimental keepsakes to remind him of the earlier days of his marriage when electric light was first put in. All these exciting electric light bulbs had sharp points at the bottoms, where the air had been sucked out, instead of it being done on the filament-tube as is now usual. (Moreover, in those days, the half-watt gas-filled bulb had not come on the market, so that electric light was much yellower, softer, and generally more pleasing than it is nowadays.)

Usually, we chose two forty-watt tungsten bulbs; but occasionally a very bright carbon one would win a place. I, who was always for violent and dramatic display in those days, would plead for the sixty-watt, or even two hundred-watt bulbs; but Father would firmly discourage this suggestion saying that (a) we did not want to be blinded for life, and (b) the electric light bill was high enough as it was. So in the end I had to be contented with what I considered his modest and unenterprising choice.

When this matter had been satisfactorily settled, and the bulbs washed and fixed into the holders, Father would look at his watch. 'Nearly tea-time,' he would say; 'not worth starting anything more. What about a look at the other sort of bulbs—the real bulbs —before we wash our hands?'

The bulbs were in the wine-cellar, in fibre-filled bowls that stood along the walls in the empty bins. Every autumn they were left there, in the dark, so that they would grow roots before they grew tops. We would turn on the light and examine them critically. The roots had formed and the yellow hubs were beginning to grow towards the invisible sky. Very pretty they looked against the black fibre; the six pale crocus-points; the four or five daffodil sheaths; the hyacinths in glasses that had struck a snaky tangle of white roots into the water, and whose fat tops were full of promise of blossom to come. Some of them were ready to come up. Father would carefully place a bowl in my hands, with the strict admonition on no account to drop it. He would carry a couple, one tucked under each arm, and we would climb the long stairs again, and place the bowls on the side-table in the dining-room where no sun could reach so that they could slowly be inured to light.

On another table stood the earliest bulbs that had already been hardened off, and that would soon be in bloom. Critically we would examine the green spike of buds on the Roman hyacinths; the tall, humpy-looking bud-sheath of the Paper White Narcissi. One of these had burst, and the buds were spreading out, and showing their white petals. Very soon now the flowers would open. Anxiously I would smell the closed buds, but as yet there was no fragrance.

'I do believe this one'll be out tomorrow, Daddy,' I would say; but Father would shake his head.

'Another couple of days at least,' he would say. 'But there's no hurry, is there? We shall have a wonderful show for Christmas.'

For Christmas, that glorious time that was getting really near now. Father saw my shining eyes. He smiled. 'Thinking about your presents?'

I nodded.

'Would you like a treat?' he asked suddenly.

'O-oh, yes please.'

'Well, you've helped me a lot this afternoon, even if you did spill that water on the carpet and rub it in with your foot when you thought I wasn't looking. Well, then; here's your treat; how about tea in the study with me? With toast and potted meat? Your mother's out, so we shall be by ourselves.' An almost naughty twinkle gleamed in Father's eye. He wrinkled his nose to make his pince-nez fall.

'Oh, how lovely!' I said. 'But what about Nan?'

'That's all right,' said Father. He touched the bell. The housemaid appeared. 'Tell Nurse that Master John will be having tea in the study this afternoon,' he said, 'and ask Cook to send up some crumpets, if she has any. And the iced walnut cake. And the Russian cake.'

'The Russian cake that has *rum* in it, Daddy?' I said, unable to believe my ears.

Father nodded. A completely naughty twinkle gleamed in his eye. He replaced the pince-nez, as if to hide it.

'When the cat's away . . .' he said; 'not that your Mother's a cat; far from it. . . . Run away, and wash your hands now, quickly. Tea'll be here in a few minutes.'

Excitedly I ran up to the bathroom. Christmas had suddenly got a great deal nearer.

*   *   *

Steadily the days drew on. One would enter a room suddenly, and see an unwieldy brown paper parcel shoved hurriedly under a cushion or behind a sofa. I went round to the toy-shop in Marsham Street and bought packets of coloured strips of paper at two a penny, and after tea sat at the nursery table, pasting these strips one into the other to form a long chain of interlinked rings, that as it grew longer billowed and rustled to the floor. Bundles of evergreens arrived at the back door; butchers' and grocers' boys kept up a perpetual knocking; something that looked suspiciously like a young conifer was whisked away to a corner of the cellar by Cook.

At last it was Christmas Eve; my paper-chains were all finished, and I was bundled early off to bed, protesting loudly. Despite my excitement, I quickly fell asleep.

In our house, we did not hang up stockings. It was not one of our family traditions. I never minded, nor felt that I was missing anything. As soon as I was dressed I would run into the nursery, knowing what I was going to see, yet always surprised by it. The whole room would be transformed. Festoons of paper-chains sagged in graceful loops from corner to corner. A long streamer of the flags of all nations which had been kept from time immemorial hung from end to end of the room. (The German and Austrian flags had been snipped off by Father.) In the window and the doorway hung a couple of huge crinkly paper bells, one pink, the other blue. Along the centre of the ceiling were suspended Chinese lanterns of varying sizes, and behind all the pictures were sprigs of holly and other evergreens. After wishing Nurse a happy Christmas and being wished it back, I would sit down to my breakfast, almost stunned by this magnificence. Then would come a long hour, playing by myself with my old toys, and wondering what new ones were in store for me. (I remember one Christmas singing to myself : 'Oh what have you got for dinner, Mrs Bond?' and Nurse stopping me with the remark : 'You ought to be singin'' *'Ark the 'Erald Hangels Sing*, not that stuff,' to my intense indignation.) Then at long last, about ten o'clock, I would be washed, dressed, and combed for Abbey.

If ordinarily I detested Mattins and Ante-Communion, it was nothing to what I felt on Christmas Day. How interminable seemed the Lessons and the Anthem; as for the sermon, delivered in slow mumbling tones by a grey-haired old man who had obviously got past all joy and excitement on Christmas Day, it filled me with a diabolical frenzy of impatience. Only the hymns I couldn't help loving, despite my impatience; and the best, and most beautiful of them : *O Come all Ye Faithful.* This reminded me, at the very pitch of excitement and longing for my presents, that I owed it all to the child who this morning lay once again, newly-born, in his manger-cradle. Most of all did *O Come all Ye Faithful* stab with ecstasy and pain my, to begin with, unreceptive heart.

As the majestic diapasons of the Great Organ rolled out in the last verse, and the voices of choir and congregation were uplifted, without reserve, in a single strain of joyful welcome, the last defences of my hard little heart and soul were swept away; and I, too, was uplifted into a region of ecstasy and bliss too blinding to be long borne.

'Yea, Lord, we greet Thee, Born this happy morning; Jesu, to Thee be glory given; Word of the Father, Now in flesh appearing: O come, let us adore Him, O come, let us adore Him, O come, let us adore Him, Christ the Lord.'

I am deeply grateful now that my parents made me go to Abbey on Christmas morning before I received my presents.

*   *   *

At last Abbey was over: and to the strains from the organ of Bach's Chorale Prelude on 'In Dulci Jubilo' (the one in A major; the key of and to Christmas) we would file out through the nave door into the stone-and-dust-smelling west cloister. There were so many people to greet I would wonder whether we should ever get home. But at last we would emerge from the Dark Cloister into Little Dean's Yard, and opposite us was Number 3. It looked different; new and exciting; you could tell that within it were presents and happy secrets soon to be revealed.

I would join the family assembled in the hall. Then the study door would open; and Father, standing smiling in the doorway, would welcome us in. On the great round mahogany table (that later, a friend of mine was to sell for ten shillings and that I managed to get back, remembering the past and thinking it worth more than half a sovereign), in neat brown paper piles, were arranged the presents. And beside them any late cards that had arrived to swell the collection on the nursery mantelpiece. Oh, how inviting that parcel looked; large, square, with sharp edges. 'For John, with love from Mummy and Daddy.' With trembling fingers I opened it. It was . . . it wasn't . . . it was! Just what I had wanted so badly; a Hobbies Fretwork Set. And this, a Hornby train, from Muriel and Harold—a new book on butterflies from Edith and Francis—something rather childish from one of the aunts. This looked funny, this small one. A knife! With two blades, corkscrew and a thing for getting stones out of horses' hooves, from Nan, Cook and the housemaid. An Ansonia watch in a washleather 'pocket' from Grandfather. In an ecstasy of excitement I undid, with impatient fingers grown suddenly clumsy, brown paper and string. Why was there that silly rule about untying, and never cutting, string? What was the new knife *for*? I cut, when no one was looking.

The room was full of murmurs of : '*Exactly* what I wanted!' 'How on *earth* did you know?' 'I shall use it when I write my letters of thanks.' 'Isn't it *sweet* of him!' 'I should have thought Ethel might have run to more than a *pincushion*!' 'Thank you *ever* so much, my dear!' 'Do you think he ought to be allowed the knife yet?' And so on. Then there were the cards. Robins, snow scenes, Santa Clauses, Infant Saviours came tumbling out of halfpenny envelopes, to be stood up on the table to be admired. Boxes of sweets, of preserved fruits, of rich chocolates, were opened by Father; addressed to the family in general, they reposed in a sort of no-man's-land on a side table until he was ready to undo them.

I heard subdued laughter, and Father's voice raised in mild astonishment. I gathered, from sentences dropped, that one of the King's Scholars had had the incredible temerity to send Father (his housemaster) a rude postcard. I wanted to see it, but was told to play with my toys. Out of the corner of my eye I saw the card being handed round; finally it was placed on the chiffonier with a lot of other things. I managed to have a good look at it while Father was opening a case of walnuts and everyone was watching him. It depicted a man with a jolly, red face, standing sideways, whose stomach was an enormous bulging plum-pudding. Underneath, it said : 'Hoping that you will not be *confined* to bed this Christmas.' I frowned over it, puzzled; I thought it was a very pretty card indeed; why did the grown-ups think it was rude? And the hope it embodied seemed to me most practical and right, since over-eating was so difficult to avoid, indeed one never tried. It was something to do with the plum-pudding bulging, I was sure. And with that I had to be content, as the opening of the walnuts was now complete. I sidled away from the card and returned to my heap of presents. It was now nearly lunchtime, a purposely dull, cold and light meal. All the long afternoon stretched before me, to play with my new presents. The happy party in the study broke up, retiring, with parcel-filled arms, to wash for lunch.

*   *   *

Dinner was at half-past seven. At half-past five, Father entered the dining-room and locked the door. There must be no noise, no scampering in the hall, nothing that could possibly disturb, on pain of grave displeasure. If you listened, naughtily, as I sometimes did, you could hear strange sounds coming from within: clankings, tinklings, rattlings, muttered words, and then silence. It was no good trying to peep through the keyhole; Father had carefully arranged the key so that it entirely blocked the view. About a quarter to seven he would emerge, with ruffled hair, looking wild and strange, but still very dignified, and hurry upstairs to dress for dinner.

At the same time, I too was being dressed in my best. What did I wear? Had I risen to the glory of my first Etons? I have no recollection; it wasn't the clothes that mattered, it was the food! At about twenty past seven the family assembled in the study to await the sound of the gong. The golden light of the study shone on the assembled family: Father, Mother, Muriel, Edith and her husband, Harold and myself. With a thrilling sense of climax the gong suddenly rang in the hall. Father took Edith's arm; Francis, Mother's; Harold, Muriel's; and I, in solitary splendour, brought up the rear.

We entered the dining-room. Being behind everyone else I could not at first see the table. When I did, I gasped. The extra leaf had been fitted, and a snowy cloth of damask covered the enlarged table, its pleated folds hanging stiffly down. It had been laid with superb artistry. In the centre, towering almost to the base of the electric light pendant, rose an enormous grape-and-vine-leaf-patterned epergne, its dishes loaded with tangerines, raisins, blanched almonds, figs and dates. All over the table were scattered, in a kind of star pattern, little silver dishes filled with salted almonds, chocolates, fondants, crystallized fruits, and strange sweets. Other dishes held sugared almonds and burnt almonds, walnuts and liqueur chocolates. Crackers were laid out by every plate and wine glasses and silver shone bravely. To the left of each place a fluted finger-bowl sparkled, filled to exactly the right level, and any intervening spaces on the table were filled by Elvas and Carlsbad plums in their own delicately coloured square boxes. Under the bright electric light the table was a feast of colour and sparkle.

The sideboard, too, had a clean white cloth spread upon it. A huge pineapple reposed there; and dessert dishes filled with black and muscat grapes; and wicker-covered jars of stone-ginger in syrup, and more walnuts and tangerines in silver paper. And over the whole room lay the simple, happy feeling of Christmas, kept traditionally by people who having paid tribute to the Christ-Child were going to seal the transaction by a feast in His honour.

Grace was said and we all sat down. The silver soup tureen was brought in and the soup ladled out by Father. I did not pay much attention to it; soup was dull; I was waiting for the next course. I ate salted almonds with the soup, and curbed my impatience. Father filled the wine glasses. Mine was filled with special non-alcoholic raisin wine. At last the soup plates were empty, the bell was pressed, and the maid entered, bearing the focal point of my whole young being. A magnificent turkey, browned to make the mouth water, steam rising from it, surrounded by tiny sausages and ringlets of crinkly bacon, was set before Father. I can see him still, beginning to carve it, the sharp steel knife gliding through the white-fleshed breast, the flakes, brown-skinned, that fell under the gentle onslaught; the humps of green aromatic stuffing that rewarded the knife's probing point; and the vegetables, the delicate roast potatoes, the succulent sprouts, green outside, yellow within and rose-pink in the centre; and the thin, clear gravy. And the red wine in the shining delicate-stemmed glasses, held to the light; to the nose, to receive the bouquet.

Of my feelings as I ate I can scarcely speak; I knew the fleeting quality of all experience as the gravy-dipped pepper-and-salt-starred bird melted in my mouth. Soon, oh, so soon, too soon, I should know the feeling of having had enough. But not yet, please God, not yet! And the green, pink and yellow sprout was divided into halves under the impact of my eager knife; it consolidated the message of the succulent turkey and the flaking roast potato.

Soon it was over; but there was more to come. The deflowered turkey was removed, and an unlit candle and a bottle of brandy were set before Father. While the maid brought in the plum pudding, Father busied himself lighting the candle; the pudding, huge, round, nearly black, a thickly-berried sprig of holly rising from it, was set before him. The maid left the room.

'Harold, will you turn the lights out?' Father said.

My brother got up and went to the door.

'Ready?'

'Yes.'

And suddenly the room was in darkness, but for the light of the single candle. Very dim and ghostly now looked the glasses and the silver and the circle of eager, watching faces. Everyone stopped talking and focused their attention upon Father. Standing up, he removed the piece of holly, with its silver paper wrapping where it had entered the pudding and laid it on one side. Then he filled a tablespoon with brandy, and held it over the candle-flame. For a breathless few moments nothing happened; then suddenly with a little splutter the brandy caught fire, and a soft blue flame appeared above the spoon, lighting the golden liquid from which it was rising. Deftly, Father poured the burning spirit over the pudding, and the rivulets of blue fire ran and trickled over and down it. With incredible speed he cut slices and handed them round, while Harold turned up the lights; the great game being to see whether you could actually get a piece of flaming pudding into your mouth before it went out. This was very difficult; and though there were many claims I rather doubt whether anyone actually achieved it. Through the dark piece of pudding on my plate something gleamed silver, its edge just poking out. I jabbed it with my fork. Yes, it was; I had got the very first threepenny-bit.

After that came the dessert; tangerines and nuts and almonds and raisins and sweets. Perhaps I loved this most, the smell of the tangerines was so haunting, and so evocative of Christmases past and to come, so different from the smell of the more plebeian oranges. By now, alas, my tummy was like a drum; but I could just manage, I thought, another Elvas plum, another walnut, another salted almond.

And then Father suddenly rose, and a silence fell on the assembled company. He held his wine glass in his hand.

'Let us drink our customary toasts,' he said quietly. He raised his glass. 'To our dear ones, to all we love, who are with us tonight.'

'To all we love!' the murmur ran round; the glasses were raised.

'To all our absent friends, whether near or far.'

'To absent friends.'

There was a slight pause.

'To the memory of those we love, who are no longer with us on this earth.'

'To the memory of the departed.'

(It was always at that moment that the solemnity of Christmas, in the midst of its gaiety, assailed me. It was as though a sigh passed through the room.)

'To the King and Queen and all the Royal Family!'

'To the King and Queen and the Royal Family!'

There was a moment's silence, and then suddenly the Babel of talk burst out again. Father held out a cracker to me; we all picked up crackers, crossed our hands, formed a circle and pulled. There was a concerted bang. In a second, as it seemed, we were all fitting caps to our heads; I blew unendingly on a whistle shaped like a lute; Harold had a thing that clicked when you pressed it; Edith had a firework, one of those that spit tiny sparks from a glowing, wobbly orange blob; Francis had a tinsel locket which he solemnly presented to Mother, who had nothing but a motto in her cracker ('perhaps it fell out,' someone suggested, and everyone searched among the paper flotsam without result); and Muriel became the proud possessor of two white balls, the proper use of which defied the ingenuity of the whole company. Father collected some mottoes, and, his grey locks escaping from beneath a pink dunce's cap with shiny green blobs, stood up to read them out. 'The rose is red, the violet's blue, the tulip's pink and so are you,' he solemnly declaimed. 'Q. What is my favourite tree? A. Yew, dear, of course!' And all the time there were interjections of popping as somebody demonstrated their affection for someone else by holding out a cracker to them.

'Shall we adjourn?' said Father. I took one last lingering look at the littered table as I followed the others into the study. Christmas dinner was over for another year; but I wouldn't be sent to bed quite just yet if I were skilful and managed things well.

In the golden study before a blazing coal fire Father was pouring out brandy and port. Everyone stood around chattering; a box of cigars lay on the table. Father offered one to Francis, and with it a small sharp penknife. After being felt, smelt and cut, the cigars were lit. A tiny drop of port was poured into the bottom of a glass for me, despite Mother's not very serious protests; it tingled all down me, like and not like the moths' sugaring mixture. I wanted some more; but knew better than to ask. There was a beautiful anecdotal feeling in the air. Francis told us about the first cigar he had ever smoked, with some other boys, when he was twelve; Father capped it with his own experiences. Mother pretended to be a little shocked. I saw something very nice; that the grown-ups had descended from their lofty pinnacles, and had become as children, full of fun and happiness. I edged my way to a box of chocolates and tucked in merrily. No one would stop me; and tonight it wouldn't matter if they did.

Mother came across to me. 'Darling, you really *must* go to bed.'

'Oh, just a few minutes longer!'

'Well, just a few then, darling.'

So I stayed for another quarter of an hour, and then I was led off by Mother, too sleepy and too happy to make any further protest. After the talk and laughter in the brightly lit room it was so strange and quiet on the stairs. Moonlight fell through the great square windows and lay in cold stripes on the stair carpet and the banisters. The only sound was that of Mother's footsteps and mine as we climbed towards my bedroom.

I was so sleepy I could hardly undress myself. I stumbled over my prayers and jumped into bed.

'Have you had a happy Christmas, darling?' Mother asked, as she bent over me, smiling, to tuck me up.

'Yes, thank you, Mummy; a *lovely* one!'

She turned out the light and drew aside the curtains. She stood there for a moment, looking out of the window.

'How bright the stars are tonight,' she said, half to herself. 'I can see them, nearly two thousand years ago, shining down on the stable, can't you? Good night, my darling, and sleep very well. I must go back now. Good night, and God bless you.'

She left the room. Snuggling down into the warm bed, I listened very carefully, and heard, a long, long way below, the faint sounds of laughter and voices. Christmas Day was ending. Its memories swam together in a happy blur as I fell asleep.

The Child-self

18

The Dark Angel

On and on went the war; the *Great* War; the War to *end* war.
It became clear that Harold would be involved. I remember so
well a small, strange incident in the summer of 1917. We were
spending our annual holiday that year at Eridge, a little village
on the Kent and Sussex border. One afternoon, Muriel, Harold
and I went for a walk in the woods. We crossed a field and began
to climb a tall tree-clad slope. Half-way up it, standing against a
tree-trunk, was a small middle-aged man. As we approached him,
he held out a leaflet and began to speak.

'Pity the poor German people. End the war now. Pity the poor
Germans who are suffering from the blockade. We are starving
them. Demand that the war shall end.' He held out the leaflet
appealingly. I looked at Muriel and Harold. Their faces were set
like stone. Harold shook his head grimly. Still the man went on.
'I beg of you to take one of these leaflets. Read it please, and see
if I am not speaking fairly. Forget your hate, that is so natural,
and indeed, understandable, and remember your Christianity.
The Germans are human beings like ourselves.'

'I don't want your beastly leaflet,' said Harold.

The man made one final effort. In a voice trembling with
emotion he said quietly : 'I don't like importuning people, but it
is a matter of such importance. Won't you please take one?'
Again he pushed a leaflet forward. Harold took it.

'Oh, thank you,' the man said. His face was irradiated with
pleasure. He smiled timidly, and I darted a surreptitious smile
back at him. Muriel and Harold still looked stonily in front of
them.

'Good afternoon, and thank you,' the man said. No one replied.
We walked on half a dozen yards. Harold and Muriel were
glancing at the leaflet. Then they stopped and turned round. I
turned round, too. The man was still watching us, happy at having
his leaflet accepted. Harold, looking steadily at him, held up the

leaflet, tore it and tore it again into little pieces. They fluttered on to the ground like snow, and Harold stamped them into the mud, with slow, deliberate determination. I saw the man's face turn crimson, and pain come into his eyes. I had never before seen a person humiliated, and I watched with fascinated horror, and a sick feeling in my stomach.

'That,' said my brother slowly to Muriel, 'will, I am afraid, scarcely begin to show him what I feel about conchies.' My sister nodded agreement.

I didn't know what to do. I walked with burning cheeks and downcast eyes beside them; I knew what it was to be utterly ashamed of my own flesh and blood. I tried to remember all that I had been taught about courtesy and gentleness; and I could in no way reconcile it with my brother's action. After a time my brother and sister noticed my silence and asked me what was the matter. But I wouldn't answer. Dumbly I trotted round after them, all the time thinking of the human being they had so callously hurt; haunted unutterably by the look I had seen on his face.

Now, in later years, I understand, and do not blame my sister and my brother. War breeds bitterness as does, and can, nothing else. Both had lost friends on the battlefield, both were young and ardent. It says a lot about war that it should have the power thus to undermine the essential sweetness and gentleness of human beings. Yet the pain inflicted was terrible; an exhibition of the very spirit that makes war possible, and is distilled by the sheer fact of war in such quantity as to remain like clouds of poison gas until such time as it is again needed.

That afternoon I learned many things. I learned that human feelings matter more than the catchwords of nations; that it is quite unforgivable to humiliate anyone. I learned that there is no hope for the world until the attempt to love replaces the attempt to hate; an attempt that, politically speaking, has never yet been made. Since that afternoon I have held the fixed and unswerving belief that there can be no justification for war. 'Man's inhumanity to man' became burningly real to me; a truth, not an aphorism.

I must have suffered deeply that day. For I remember the look of the grey beech trunk against which the man stood, and that the leaves were beginning to turn yellow, and that there were heavy grey clouds in the sky, and the way the path wound through the trees. These details are imprinted with clarity upon the strange part of me that records and harbours such things. And all these details are suffused with pain; a pain that grows into something like a shout, when I remember the bowed head, the slowly crimsoning cheeks and the expression in the eyes of the man whose leaflet was torn up and ground into the mud.

What is Fate? Was it also an important moment in my brother's life? Who knows? Had he kept the leaflet might he be alive now? Such speculations are too painful to pursue. The concerted pressure of long tradition and a period in the world's history that was great, but rigid to the point of bitterness, would surely have been too much for him, for any boy of his class and upbringing. The fact that when I was growing up that period had already, betrayed by its bitterness, cracked into a thousand pieces, may be responsible in turn for the fact that the only rebel in our family, the only one who claimed the right to think for himself, was me. It grieves me bitterly to realize that my brother, had he cared a little less for the nation's honour, and a little more for himself, would have been alive today.

My mother once told me that Harold died (and how glad one is for his sake) in the firm belief that that *was* the war to end war. He was a person of the utmost integrity and sincerity in his beliefs. So, in my opinion, was the man with the leaflets.

* * *

A month later Harold started his military training at Oxford. (I remember him tearing about London in the Christmas holidays in a taxi he was learning to drive.) In the following January he got a commission in the Rifle Brigade, was stationed for a time at Sheppey, and towards the end of April was sent out to the Western front as a Second Lieutenant. On 22 May he was wounded by a bomb, taken to the base, and after a few days was shipped to England and brought to the Empire Hospital in Vincent Square, only a stone's-throw from Little Dean's Yard.

My memories of this terrible fortnight in our lives are painfully clear. I happened to be standing in the hall when the dreaded buff envelope arrived. I was talking to Father. He opened the door himself. I saw his face drained of all colour as he took the envelope and turned it round and round without opening it. I knew—the knowledge flowed from him to me—that this was bad news.

'Run along upstairs,' he said.

Slowly and reluctantly I went. I heard him call my mother. The house was very dreary and empty, and each landing seemed a long way above the last. Later, while I was having tea, Mother came to me and told me that Harold was wounded. Even as she re-assured me, I knew, and I knew that Father and Mother both knew, that there was no hope; that the unfolding of fate was awful in its slow inexorability. In all our conscious minds there may indeed have been hope; but that other part knew with dread-ful certainty what this telegram portended.

By now I was nearly nine years old and went to a real prepara-tory school at Sloane Square. This was my first term, and I liked it. I was in the third form, two from the top, which was presided over by a very kind woman, a Miss Pearce, whom I liked and who liked me. But now, every morning, I set out with a heavy heart, shying away from what the day might bring. On 4 June, the eve of my birthday, I was taken to see Harold. The incredible had happened; despite the severity of his wound he was regaining strength; there was every reason to expect that he would live. I remember vividly that as we entered the hospital, a nurse was saying good-bye to a recovered soldier. I dreamed of the day when she would say good-bye to my brother.

Harold was lying in bed in a small ward, by himself. I scarcely know what I had expected, but I was surprised and pleased to see that, apart from being a little pale, he looked exactly as he always did. His dark hair, a little longer than usual, fell across his brow and touched his cheek. He smiled, and talked to me for ten minutes or so, and then I was taken away. At the door I was almost overwhelmed by an impulse to go back and say or do something, but I did not know what. Earlier, I would have kicked and screamed; now, the pride of a well-mannered schoolboy stepped in, holding me in the merciless grip of 'correctness'; and I re-pressed the impulse, contenting myself with a strange long last look at Harold. I never again saw my brother. Three times in my life have I been overwhelmed by that particular strange and indefinable impulse; each time, as though it was predetermined, I have equally strangely resisted it. The fear of being foolish, of being sentimental, of being disapproved of, has won. And in each case, I have never seen the person concerned alive again; and have later realized that I wished to make to them the true farewell. I left Harold that afternoon happy at having seen him, unhappy because it would be some little time before I saw him again.

The next day was my ninth birthday. All seemed as usual, on the surface. I was allowed, as always, to choose my birthday lunch, and I chose, as always, roast chicken, meringues filled with cream, and strawberries. Father and Mother gave me a luminous wristwatch; Harold, a chemistry outfit. I have no recollection of any other presents, though there must have been some. Everyone tried to make my birthday happy and normal. Harold was getting better; everybody said so. Yet my birthday was not happy; the frightened inner knowledge and pain persisted and would not go away. As the truth drew nearer in time, I knew it with increasing certainty. Despite my new watch, and the fact that I was now a schoolboy who must never, never show emotion, I cried myself to sleep on the night of my birthday, in the bedroom that was Harold's and mine.

Yet nothing happened the following day; everyone was again reasonably cheerful; Harold *was* getting better. The day after that, Friday, 7 June, I set off for school with the dark knowledge grown inside me to its fullest proportions. If this day passed without event, all would be well. Otherwise. . . . And so I scarcely dared breathe on my decorous way to school. In some strange way, I wished not to attract the attention of the Gods, or the devils. I tried to make myself as inconspicuous to myself (as well as to others) as possible. If we could get through this day, all holding our breaths, the tension would relax; and, the gale dropping, we should find ourselves once more in a calm sea.

The morning wore on. I was reprimanded by Miss Pearce for inattention, and I tried to attend, in order not to attract notice of any kind. I went home to lunch. Neither Father nor Mother were there; it had happened. I swallowed down the food somehow. Then Nan came to me and told me that they had gone to the hospital, and that I was not going to school in the afternoon; we would go for a walk instead.

That dreadful walk I shall remember all my life. We walked and walked for miles and miles, aimlessly, as it seemed to me. We came to St Peter's, Eaton Square; that thin, aloof superior tower stared at me and I stared at it. We hated one another. The round clock-face, that usually I loved, looked like a black drum in a sandy desert. We had walked so far that we had nearly reached my school. I did not want to be seen and laughed at by any of the boys for being with a nurse, and I persuaded Nan to take a different direction. Almost mockingly and slyly I kept asking her what was the matter. She would tell me nothing, having obviously been given orders to that effect. But it did not make the least difference what she told me; for now I knew in my conscious mind; and what I knew stood up in tall, thin, fiery letters against a dark background; letters that tumbled about, lost their rightful position, formed and reformed to spell again and again one unchanging message. 'Harold is dying.'

That was the longest walk that I have yet had to take. When at last we got back to Number 3 we were met by Mrs McNeilly, the school matron, who whispered something to Nan. My sharp ears caught the words, 'he died this afternoon'. Both women were crying. Instead of going up to the nursery, I was taken up the back stairs, through College Dormitory, to Mrs McNeilly's to tea. By now, I was so miserable and so frightened that I scarcely knew what was happening to me. I longed to say straight out : 'I know what it is—Harold is dead', but I dared not, since I was supposed (ye Gods !) not to know. So I sat, miserably gulping tea and cakes, and longing for the world to get right again, and knowing that it wouldn't, for a very long time—if ever.

At last we left Mrs McNeilly's, and Nurse told me to go to Mother's room. I knocked timidly on the door, and heard her call faintly : 'Is that you, John ? Come in, darling.'

With beating heart I turned the knob of the door and entered the room. Mother was lying on the bed, and she had drawn blinds and curtains so that, although outside it was a brilliant June evening, in the room it was quite dark. Yet it was not a frightening or oppressive darkness. From it came Mother's voice : 'Come and lie on the bed beside me, darling. There's something I have to tell you.'

I lay there in her arms. Quietly she told me, and with faith, of Harold's passing. And gradually the fear ebbed and receded; the fear of the black unknown, the oldest and most primitive of man's fears; and for a while there was the colourless stunned blank, calm and almost peaceful. And as we lay there, my mother and I, on the bed in the darkened room, the pain that cannot be kept at bay began to throb in waves through me, coming and going and returning again; the pain of new death that has in it surprise, shock, defiance and sheer disbelief, and that seems to stab a point that is at once in chest, throat and head. This I knew for the first time; and I buried my head in dreadful tearless anguish in my mother's breast. The pain ebbed and flowed between us; I knew that my mother had lost the son she had borne, and that nothing could bring him back to us. I knew, also, the magnificence and unshakeability of her faith in God. And gradually a great calm followed the pain, not like the false stunned calm of the earlier moments; a calm of which I would not write, even if I could. For a long time I lay there with Mother, quite still in the darkened room; while outside in the hot golden limes the sparrows chirped and twittered, and the brilliant evening moved imperceptibly towards its tranquil close.

*   *   *

The following day, Harold's body was taken to St Faith's Chapel, in the Abbey, where it rested until the funeral service at Heston. I remember the flag-draped coffin that contained, I knew, the earthly remains of my brother, and with what strange awe it filled me. Could he be in it? No, not Harold, who had so loved movement and gaiety, surely? And yet, yes! My brain struggled with something it could not and cannot grasp : what death is.

Of the funeral I remember curiously little, but for one thing; the sound of the bugle that blew the Last Post over the fresh grave. I hear that still as I heard it then; the greatest music that man has yet learned to make; that for one fleeting moment joins this life to the afterlife. Thus was the shattered body of my brother Harold committed to the earth, which bore it; and his soul to God, who gave it. My brother Harold, whom I never really knew; whose eyes, the sad and haunted Livingston eyes, speak to me across the years from a piece of light-sensitized paper. On the day of his funeral he was exactly nineteen and a half years old.

*   *   *

Harold's death was a blow from which my father never really recovered. It aged him prematurely, and quietly embittered his life. My mother, whose resignation to the acts of God was deeper than my father's, recovered slowly. Father could speak of it to no one; he carried it deep in his heart. I admire him for his lack of resignation as much as I admire my mother for her gift of it. I knew that for a long time life would epitomize pain to both of them. I tried to be tactful; but, being nine years old, I rarely succeeded. There was a terrible morning when, at breakfast, I mentioned a letter that someone had written which quoted from *Pilgrim's Progress*: 'And the trumpets sounded for him on the other side.' To my horror, Mother burst into tears; and Father angrily ordered me from the room.

And there was the occasion when, having obtained some real luminous paint, and being intensely eager to use it, I painted a cross on a sheet of paper, that would shine in the dark, and presented it to Mother, 'so that she could remember Harold at all times, even in the night'. What Mother thought of this strange action on my part, I scarcely know; but she dutifully hung the luminous cross on her bedroom wall, opposite the bed, where it used to scare me into fits, if I ever went into Mother's room in the dark, having forgotten about it. It had a pale mauve glow that was all too phosphorescently reminiscent of my conception of the worst type of ghost; reminiscent too, as I now see, of a certain morbidity in my action in making it at all.

*   *   *

My brother was an individual human being; he had a beautiful body, a gentle spirit, and a divine soul. No one in the world—no country, no ideology, no patriot, had the right to ask him to die for his king and country at the age of nineteen, when he might have lived for them. And the fact that he was willing to die for his country is an irrelevance.

In the 1939–45 war I was a conscientious objector. My mother understood both points of view, Harold's and mine (but not the point of view of those who cheaply condemn either). I like to think of what, in later years, she told me about my brother's passing. 'At the moment of his death he smiled, a smile of pure recognition. He had seen someone on the other side whom he knew and loved; and who was waiting there especially, to welcome him.' There lies in this simple statement a faith that has power to mitigate what each one of us dreads : the awful passage between the two worlds; the moment when we will have to relinquish our humanity and prepare, in nakedness of spirit and soul, to meet our God.

19

The Approach of the Dove

The summer term passed slowly on its course, weighted with the knowledge of Harold's death. At last we went away, to a village called Latton, in Essex (is it still a village?) and slowly, so slowly, the cloud began to lift. Yet it was aways there; and perhaps it was only for me that this holiday was a happy one. The need for tact on my part remained; sometimes I was not equal to it. I have a vivid memory of a summer evening at Latton, when we had found some Poplar Hawk caterpillars, Father and I; and we were standing facing one another on opposite banks of a ditch bordered by willows. The sun was beginning to go down. On a sudden impulse that I was unable to control, I said : 'I wish Harold was here now, Daddy!' Directly I had said that I was filled with shame, and awaited Father's as it seemed to me most justified anger. But he turned his head away, and said in a choking voice : 'John, don't, don't talk like that, please,' and I looked into the sluggish water of the ditch, and can remember the pattern the trailing weeds made on the slow-moving current; and when at last I lifted my head the sun had dropped behind a large elm clump, spreading a dusty halo of golden light around the trees, and the fields were sleepy with evening. And Father said briskly : 'Come along; we must get home now to Mother,' and the dreadful pain in his heart communicated itself to me all the way back; and I wished—oh, how I wished—that I had not said that silly thing.

Someone else had died too, at Latton, which complicated things; the vicar's wife. I used to wander into the yellow drawing-room that had been hers. She had died two months before, and it was still very much hers. Since her death, the vicar had not used the room, and the dark yellow blinds were always kept drawn down. Fringed with lace, deepened in colour by the sun, they filtered to the room only a rich strong golden light. On the mantelpiece under a glass shade stood a French clock enamelled in blue and gold, with tiny scenes painted on the dial, and at each side of it vases to match. The sun, through the closed windows and the drawn blinds, drew from the room a smell; eloquent, pervasive; a Sunday drawing-room smell, hot and yellow and musky. Outside, birds flew in the garden, butterflies flitted and hovered, the leaves trembled in the breeze and bumble-bees boomed, furry and fat, through the summer air; but here, in this silent room, it was still hot and dusty—and aware. There was a toy in the form of a book. Each picture was cut out of cardboard strips; each had a sort of lever. When this lever was pulled the man with the butterfly-net caught the yellow butterfly; the fisherman landed his salmon; the wheels of the railway train ran round; the statesman lifted his top hat. These were the only movements in a room that was breath-held, waiting, expectant; as though someone had either just left it, or was about to come in. I would sometimes wander in there alone, and sit on the dusty sofa and listen. But the only sound that disturbed—no, it didn't disturb, it emphasized—the silence, was the very faint metallic ticking of the French clock under its glass shade; and the sound of its thin, high-pitched silvery bell at each half-hour. For a moment the dust seemed to dance and shiver and hiss as the fragile bell-strokes smote it, and then it would settle down again as the sound faded into the background of the past, and the golden motes would swirl and eddy in the dim sunbeams and the stillness again became absolute.

And was Mrs Oliver looking over one's shoulder as one played with the strange book–toy, or not? Anyway, it was her room, and one really had no right to be in it, no right at all. Better go out now, on tip-toe, and scrounge a hot rock cake from the kitchen, and try to net one of the innumerable Red Admirals that fluttered round the Michaelmas Daisy clumps in the herbaceous border.

So I would leave the yellow drawing-room; and almost forget it, but not quite. For as I stood, waiting upon the feasting Red Admirals, I would dart surreptitious glances at the drawn blinds viewed from the other side, the outside. And wonder who or what was in the room now; now that I was in the garden.

*   *   *

Latton Vicarage stood in its own park, and though it was only twenty-two miles from London, it was an old-fashioned place. There was a pony and trap and an old coachman to drive it. Every afternoon the trap stood outside the front door to take Father and Mother visiting, or for a drive. Often I went too. I remember the delicious smell of the rug that covered our knees, and sometimes had horse's hairs on it. The climbing into the trap by the bright iron 'pedal'; and the good sound of hooves clip-clopping at a smart pace along the leafy Essex lanes. Old things, and old days, gone for ever. The flick of the whip; the pricked ears; and the sudden rude load of dung, steaming in front of some aristocratic mansion. How deeply I enjoyed it when the pony lifted his harness-encircled tail, and the great yellow lumps began to roll smoothly out, falling with a soft splatter on the gravel drive; and the old coachman's half-humorous, half-deprecating acceptance of the pony's bad manners.

Old Linsell, the coachman, initiated me into the lore of the countryside. He had a wealth of stories, some polite and some otherwise, that mostly began : 'I remember when I was a lad but *that* high. . . .' He lived with a grey-haired old wife in a little cottage by the stables. I remember going into his kitchen one day, to find him observing, hands on knees, an extraordinary-looking object beneath the flagstones of the floor which he had dug up and removed, to get at it. It was like a huge ball of grey paper.

'Found un at last!' he said, straightening himself slowly, and grinning at me.

'What is it?' I asked.

'Whoy, it be a waasp's nest. Biggest I ever see. Them plaguey old waasps been about for weeks. The missus was fair frit out of 'er loife. ('Go on with yer, Fred!' interjected Mrs Linsell.) So I dug up floor. I 'ears 'em buzzin', and I sez to meself—that's where they be, under them flagstones they be, orkard little beggars. But I got 'em out, see? Now I got to put them 'eavy stones back, and you could 'elp me, if you loiked.'

So I helped Linsell replace the flags, and then I examined the wasps' nest. I didn't like it, though its workmanship was wonderful; it was grey, like ash, and there were dead wasps in every cell of it. It was as large as a Victorian soup-plate, and I have never seen such a big one since. We tried to burn it later on the garden rubbish dump; but it would not burn, even; only an ugly blackish charred mass resulted.

I have always hated wasps and their nests. They seem to me to be ugly, vicious and sinister insects that have about them a nameless horror. I shall always remember that summer at Latton because I was haunted and pursued by them as never before; and to crown my fear Father brought home a live hornet which he had found on the Harlow road. I felt sick when I saw this great angry-looking tawny insect frantically pawing the glass of the butterfly box in which it was imprisoned, and continually whipping out its terrifying sting. The phrase: 'O Death, where is thy sting?' that I had heard lately, became connected in my mind with this hornet; and I looked on the thing with loathsome fear. Even when it was itself dead in Father's killing-bottle, I could hardly bear to look at it. And when he offered to give it to me for my collection, I surprised him by the intensity with which I refused it. So it was cast into the fire, which I hope purified its horrid soul; but its mental image remained for many a day to strike terror into my mind whenever I saw anything on the wing that even remotely resembled it.

One of my experiences with wasps is worth recounting. It happened on a Saturday morning. Mother had gone to do the altar flowers, ready for the Sunday services, in Latton Church, which stood about a quarter of a mile from the vicarage at the end of the park. When she had been gone about half an hour I set out to meet her. I didn't get very far, for a hedge offered a good hunting-ground for caterpillars, and there I stayed, examining the leaves. I was wearing the usual schoolboy flannel shorts and woollen stockings. Suddenly, without any warning, I felt the most terrible red-hot pain half-way down my left leg. Frightenedly, I touched the spot. Immediately, I felt the pain again, a little lower. Then, as I stood transfixed with terror, it came again and again, all round my calf.

I screamed and began to run. And as I ran, so did the pain break out everywhere around the lower part of my leg. Shouting 'Mother! Mother!' I ran wildly about, first one way and then

the other, mad with pain and fright. The next thing I knew was
that I was in Mother's arms. I couldn't say a coherent word, but
I pointed to my leg. Mother quickly rolled down the stocking;
there was another agonizing stab that made me yell again, and
a half-dead wasp fell to the ground. Mother put her foot on it. My
leg was already swelling. I managed somehow to limp home, feeling shivery and very shaken, and the usual remedies were applied.

Later I said to Mother: 'How did you manage to get there?
You were doing the flowers, weren't you?'

'I heard you call me,' Mother said.

'But weren't you in the church doing the flowers?'

'Yes.'

'Then you couldn't have heard me call. I only called you just
before you came; and the church is a long way off.'

'I heard you call seven or eight minutes before I got to you,'
Mother said. 'I heard you call "Mother! Mother!"—and I knew
you were in trouble from the sound of your voice.'

'I was by the hedge all the time,' I said slowly; 'I was looking
for caterpillars until just before you came. I never called or made
a sound. You couldn't have heard me.'

'I did,' Mother said; 'and I put down the flowers and came as
fast as ever I could. It took me quite five minutes.'

'Did my voice sound loud?' I asked puzzledly, knowing that
the church was completely out of earshot of the hedge.

'Yes, it did. Very loud.'

'How did you know where to find me?'

It was Mother's turn to look puzzled. 'I really don't know,' she
said. 'I knew you needed me badly; and so I knew where to find
you.'

With that explanation I had to be content. My leg was stung
in ten places and it was days before I could walk properly. What
would have happened had Mother not turned up, I don't know;
but I do know, and have known since that morning, that what we
call time can, if urgent occasion demands it, be as elastic, in either
direction, as it is normally rigid and unyielding.

* * *

Shortly before we were due to leave Latton, I told old Linsell
how much I wanted to keep some rabbits. To my surprise, he said:

'I can get you some, then. I know a burrow where there's young ones, and if I get you a two-three you could take 'em back with you, and keep 'em as pets, loike.'

I looked at him in ecstatic admiration.

'My father would never let me,' I said.

'Well, then, we must make 'e let you,' said old Linsell. He bent towards me, rather unnecessarily, as there was no one around, and asthmatically whispered a plan. I nodded agreement all the time, looking at him even more admiringly.

And so it came about that when the trap arrived to drive us to Harlow station a cardboard box was stowed away beside the driver. As the baggage was unloaded at the station, so too was the mysterious box. Father immediately saw it, as I had guessed he would. I never knew a man so difficult to keep things from.

'What is that?' he asked, adjusting his pince-nez, to see it better. 'Is it yours, dear?' he added, to Mother.

'No,' Mother said.

There was a short pause.

'They be the baby rabbits for Mas'r John,' said Linsell, touching his hat. 'There's three of 'em.' My father turned on me. 'Did you ask Mr Linsell for them?' he said. 'You're a very naughty boy, John. We can't take them. They'd die in London. Linsell must take them back. Yes, it's no good protesting; they are going back. Where could you keep them anyway?'

I thought the rabbits were lost to me for ever. But Linsell said: 'They were a kind o' parting present to Mas'r John, sir, from me. I'm very sorry, sir, should I 'ave stepped beyond me rights, loike. But you wouldn't deny an old man that pleasure, sir, now would you? It'll be something for him to remember old Linsell by.' There was a fractional pause; then he added: 'Train's comin' in, sir. They don't stop that long in 'Arlow station, loike; if you take me meaning, sir.'

'Good gracious!' Father exclaimed. 'Well, well, it's very kind of you, Linsell; kind, very kind. We must hurry.'

We caught the train easily and so did the rabbits. And as a matter of fact, Father was wrong. They flourished exceedingly in London. A year later, I let out at least a dozen at Heston, when we went to visit Harold's grave. I couldn't get a hutch big enough for them all.

*   *   *

The autumn went by uneventfully—a sad autumn, for the blow of Harold's death could not quickly pass. One Monday morning at half-term, I went to the Army and Navy Stores with Nan. We were about a hundred yards from the stores when the maroons went off. There were cries of : 'It's an air-raid; they're here again,' from some passers-by, and a stampede ensued. Everybody ran aimlessly about; and I saw panic stamped on certain faces. Panic —the vilest of all mass emotions. A man was knocked down and trodden on; I saw something red and white and still as the people surged relentlessly on. Somehow, we gained the shelter of the auxiliary stores. Then a murmur began to go round : 'It's peace ! It's peace ! Thank God !'

Yes, it was the eleventh hour of the eleventh day of the eleventh month in the year of Our Lord, one thousand nine hundred and eighteen. The eleventh hour. Yes. It was certainly that. We went home down a Victoria Street stampeding as madly now it was known to be peace as when it was feared to be an air-raid. Though I was only nine, I thought quite consciously : 'If Harold had been born in 1899 instead of in 1898, he wouldn't have died.'

There followed the second English scourge of the Black Death; that Spanish influenza that ravaged Europe and took more lives than the Western front, or indeed all the battlefronts; the avenger that stalked the unhappy victims of the politicians, and followed with its pale bloodshed in the wake of the red bloodshed.

I had it, but mildly, and while I was having it, Muriel came home one day from her warwork. 'They say I've got 'flu,' she announced lightly. Would she die too? It was in the lap of the gods. But she didn't die, although she had acute double pneumonia, and we could get no oxygen. I remember one afternoon, when Muriel was thought to be dying, tramping the back streets of Westminster with Father in a vain attempt to procure a cylinder. At the last moment, oxygen was procured, and somehow, God knows how, Muriel passed the crisis. Slowly she came back to the land of the living. All her hair fell out, that beautiful red-gold hair that was her pride. But she lived—to wear for months a little cap, until by the end of a year the hair had returned.

Six weeks after the crisis I myself did my best to kill her. Wishing to cheer her up I offered to let off one of my home-made fireworks in her bedroom. She said I could, if I would promise that there would be no fumes, and that the firework contained no sulphur. I was so keen to cheer her that I promised, and lit the firework. Sulphur being its basis, the room was immediately filled with choking fumes. Poor Muriel began to cough. Mother came, and was furiously angry with me, a rare event for her. My sister was seriously ill again for several days; but as Fate appears to have decided that she should live, she once more recovered. I was so frightened that I never again let off a firework within miles of Muriel.

*   *   *

One winter's afternoon, a few months later, I was coming back from school. It was a blue-grey afternoon, misty and still. I left St James's Park Station at about twenty to five and began slowly to walk home along Tothill Street, looking in the shop windows, thinking of nothing in particular, idly swinging my satchel of books. I stopped to look into the sweet-shop. And as I stood there, staring, an incredible thing happened. The air was suddenly full of sound; an old sound; an almost forgotten sound; it trembled with the long, melancholy sweet fall of bells. Big Ben had chimed the quarter. I stood there transfixed; the blood drained from my face; my little world in turmoil about me. I had not heard that sound for nearly five years; and it brought back in a wave of tenderest nostalgia, the days of my earliest childhood. I listened, enraptured, as its echoes died away, shivering into silence on the darkening, half-empty street. In some strange way I knew that, though I was only nine years old, I was also of no age at all, because of this extraordinary power that beauty had over me. Beauty of sound, of sight, of feeling, of memory. I was an old man come home at last; I was a small boy, knowing what the sudden chance sound of those bells would mean to me in exiled adult life. I turned and saw that the two visible dials of the great clock-tower were lit also for the first time since the war, glowing rosily upon the rapidly falling night. At that, my heart was wildly uplifted in the purest ecstasy. My feet felt no pavement as I walked and danced, flinging my satchel about. I was supposed to be in by five; but I was not going to be. When I had turned into Dean's Yard, I halted, before going into Little Dean's Yard, by the railings of Green. There I waited, silent in the silent yard. The gas-lamps shone on the bare branches of the elms and on the grass. Far away the traffic hummed and softly roared its distant sea-noise; a paper-boy went whistling round the other side of the Yard. The scarlet pillar-box and the old commissionaire's hut stood, motionless in the soft gaslight; waiting, waiting.

And then it came. With matchless precision and purest beauty the four quarters were chimed upon that silent, expectant yard and the child who stood there waiting. It seemed that the fulfil-ment of all his desire, all his longing, had come. A long-held pause; and then the five solemn strokes, slowly, one after the other, of the great hour-bell rocked and broke in vibrating waves of sound, leaving behind them long trembling pools of dying sonority that slowly drained away into utter silence.

I stood with my arms round the railings, while the storm of tears broke. I stood there, abandoned to and by the world, weep-ing my heart out—for what? I didn't know. For something; for something. It seemed, perhaps, that the bad dream of the war was really over; that we could start again; and that, and that. . . . But there my thoughts failed.

After a little while the tears stopped. Licking my handkerchief and rubbing my eyes so that no one would see I had been crying, I turned slowly into Little Dean's Yard. Mother was in the hall as I entered.

'You *are* late, darling!' she said. 'What happened?'

'I listened to Big Ben,' I muttered, shortly. Mother glanced at me sharply. Our eyes met, and were held for a timeless second in complete mutual understanding. Then I turned and ran upstairs to my tea.

20

The Friend

School, to a boy of my particular kind of imagination, was a tire-some intrusion into the long vista of daydreams and percipience of which his day consisted; so that I do not propose to spend much time upon it. In any case, it has been done hundreds of times before : the sensitive misfit. Though I don't think I was a misfit, for I was in no way unhappy at school. I sensed, however, and resented, the knowledge that people would if they could try to force me to their way of looking at things; try to make me more practical and tough, more superficial and less truly myself. I was early aware of this danger, and resisted it with all my might. So that, with one exception, I made no deep friendships. I also suffered rather from a sense of inferiority; I felt that I was ugly, that my nose was too large, and that no one understood me. I was, indeed, at a truly horrible period of my life. Because really, of course, I was also vain; I felt that I was extremely good-looking, and that my rather Roman nose gave me distinction. All the same, I never expected to be liked; and it gave me a great deal of surprise and pleasure when one day an undoubtedly very handsome and very popular boy asked me to his home for a Saturday tea. I went, feeling much honoured and flattered; and it was thus that I made the first great friendship of my life, and one that has never altered in feeling, though I have not seen my friend in the flesh since I was twelve. He was an extremely reserved boy, proud and arro-gant, and did not, I discovered, make friends easily. In fact, despite his popularity, I alone was admitted into the world of his inner life in the three years that I knew him. I suspect that this was largely because no one else had an inner life worth speaking of. I found in him a most satisfying response to my love of beauty. Till then I had thought always of myself as being quite alone in possessing this strange, girlish and not quite decent quality. The fact that this older and much cleverer person than myself loved pictures, music and beautiful things; and even took dancing lessons (a confidence given to me under the seal of strictest secrecy) every Friday evening, filled me with delight and gave me inner self-assurance. Nor could anyone call him 'soft', for he was a good athlete, and shone both at football and cricket, which, alas, I did not. (I shone only at finding cricket balls in the boundary grass that had been given up for lost. I shone not at all at football, for the ball was too large to be lost.)

We became inseparables, in the strange way of small boys. Every Saturday one of us visited the other's home for tea, which was followed usually by rowdy games, such as 'he' and 'touch-last'; games that Michael Redgrave invariably won. I have never forgotten the streams of mocking laughter that came to me across Little Dean's Yard, as, the evening over, Michael ran gaily on his homeward way, having made me 'he'; a position that I would have to retain right over the week-end until we met at school again on Monday; a position of great indignity that, in my excited state, I felt was more than I could bear all that time. I would feel a surge of amiable frustration, of blended hate and love that would make me want to kill or kiss or kiss and kill Michael; in which order I could never decide. Nor did I ever do either of them. But he knew exactly how to tease me to flash-point, and then leave me. Just as he knew in the strangest way how to extend a warming and tender comfort if I had been hurt, physically or spiritually. I knew that Michael was a being of a rare kind, because he understood what others did not; what I had yet to learn, was just how rare such beings are. His greatest gift was that of casting the whole of himself, without stint or hesitation, into what he was doing; especially in defence of a friend, a conviction or a principle.

*   *   *

There was a wild and terrible ecstasy in those games of 'touch-last'. Soon after tea they would start. We would switch off the staircase lights, and race about the dark landings and up and down the four flights of stairs. All the smells in the house and all the ghosts would pour out to join us. 'Touch-last' was so compelling that one had to enter, in order to retain one's honour, the very bad, the very black places. Time and time again I have found myself in the dreaded alcove half-way down the nursery stairs; found myself there with a horrible shock of realization; and stood listen-

ing with slowly rising hair to the sounds—of shuffling, of breathing, of nothingness; not knowing where Michael was, wondering
what to do, whether to stay there or run—into what? Oh, it was
a fine, a dangerous, a macabre game in that house of ghosts. On
and on for hours it went, up and down, round and round; past
dimly lit landings; past the housemaid carrying a hot-water can;
past the sound of the piano in the drawing-room; of voices in the
study. And the frantic final scramble down the long flights of stairs
to the front door, swerving to avoid by inches Father who was
statelily ascending to his dressing-room to dress for dinner, and
who showed his profound disapproval by continuing statelily to
ascend; and the awful final battle at the front door; touch and
touch and touch again, and jab and thrust and side-skip and
touch, and the loud slamming of the door and the mocking
laughter, and the turning-round to face—a silent and empty hall,
and the long curving flights of stairs going up and up to the top
of the house; and—and—before the nursery the alcove to be
passed. And by the time one realized it the last remnants of fire
had died in body and spirit, the excitement turned to prickly fear,
and nothing ahead but bed. When I saw the alcove from below,
my bowels would turn to water, and sullenly muttering a prayer,
I would shove, force, push my body past it, my body that was
prickling with goose-flesh from head to foot, and resolve that never,
never again would I play 'touch-last' with Michael Redgrave at
night in our house. And never did I keep that resolve. As the last
of the tea-things were cleared away, the mad intoxication would
seize us, relentless, glorious, all-compelling; and once again 'touch-
last' as played at 3, Little Dean's Yard, would hold ecstatic sway
over caution, advisability and fear.

*   *   *

This was the naughtiest period of my childhood; and, ably aided
and abetted by Michael, I did many reprehensible things. For
example, having been given a tiny 4-volt electric fan, meant to be
used with a dry battery, Michael and I connected it, in blissful
ignorance, across our 230-volt mains. The setting we chose for this
little drama was, of all places, Mother's bedroom. Having placed
the fan on Mother's dressing table, on top of a fine lace-edged
cloth, we plugged it into a wall socket and turned the switch on.

There was a blinding flash, a streaming of molten metal, a hurtling through the air of certain internal portions of the fan, and then—silence. Or almost, for the flames that were burning up Mother's cloth made a slight hissing, especially when, panic-stricken, we poured the contents of her water-jug over them.

This interesting event was the culmination of a long series of electrical experiments. The culmination because Father, for the first and last time, threatened to cane me. I never could understand why he minded my blowing the main fuse at least twice a week, though I do understand now that it must have been difficult for him to explain things to a grumbling electrician without letting himself in for at least a silent rebuke about keeping children in order. And besides, the family often had to sit for hours in darkness after one of my 'experiments' for, the main fuse box being locked and sealed by the electricity company, it was not possible to mend it, and an electrician could not always, even in those days, be obtained at a second's notice. I must admit that Father was always willing to mend a secondary fuse himself; but such small game was beneath my notice; in honour bound, it had to be the main fuse; or, at any rate, it always was.

And so, banished from my own house, electrically speaking, the following week I started on Michael's. I broke the glass of an old electric light bulb, and fixed a stout strip of wire between the terminals. (In an earlier experiment I had done the same thing with a thin piece of wire, and it had, when placed in a lampholder, cascaded gracefully to the ground in a series of shining, red-hot blobs.) I took this contraption to school and gave it to Michael, telling him to put it in a lampholder and turn the switch on, when he would see a beautiful firework.

'Are you sure?' Michael asked, looking at it gingerly.

'Quite sure,' I said eagerly.

'It won't blow the fuse, will it? There'd be an awful row if it did.'

'Of course it won't,' I said. 'No. I can guarantee this. You will really enjoy it, I know you will. It will be a specially good one, because the wire's so thick.'

'All right,' said Michael. 'I'll trust you, absolutely. I'll tell you all about it when you come to tea tomorrow. I'll do it when I get home.'

That was a Friday evening. The following day when I knocked

on Michael's front door it was opened by his stepfather, who grimly beckoned me into a little room I had never been in before. Of Michael there was no sign.

'I want to talk to you, young man,' said Colonel Anderson. 'Are you trying to exterminate us, or what?'

'Why?' I asked, very frightened.

'Well, you gave Michael some contraption last night, and it fused every light in the house. We were plunged into utter darkness for what seemed hours and hours. It was horrible, I assure you.'

'I'm very sorry, sir,' I gasped.

'You are, are you? Well, what I have to say to you is, don't do it again. Don't do it again, do you see?'

'I won't, indeed I won't,' I said.

'Very well. Now you can run and find Michael. He's upstairs.' The Colonel smiled charmingly at me, and dismissed me with a wave of the hand.

I found a very subdued Michael upstairs; subdued, but infuriated.

'You are a rotter,' he said at once. 'Giving me that beastly thing. You might have blown us all up. There was an awful row about it.'

'Why?' I asked. 'What happened?'

'What happened?' said Michael indignantly; 'what happened? Nothing at all. It wasn't a firework like you said. I put it in the lampholder and turned on the switch and it just stayed there. It was a rotten swizzle. Then suddenly all the lights went out, and we had to get an electrician to mend them; and he said : "Whoever done that must 'ave a screw loose," and of course he thought it was me. And so did everybody else. Beastly rotten swiz it was. It would have been worth it,' he added, with the old gleam in his eyes, 'if it had *done* anything.'

'I'm very sorry. I really thought it would go off like a firework.'

'Well, it didn't,' said Michael crossly.

After a time, he forgave me. But it was the end of my career as an electrical experimenter.

*   *   *

If Michael and I had rather more than the usual animation and vitality of small boys, we had also rather more than the usual amount of tranquil enjoyments. Sometimes, throughout a wet afternoon, we would solidly read, side by side, each with a different book. If it was fine, we would go for long walks, often to Green Park where it was quiet, almost like the country, an illusion that was aided by a bedraggled flock of sheep that used to graze there. We would find the last and loneliest seat in the Park, where no human was to be seen, and talk for hours of what we would do and be, when we were grown-up. Michael wanted to be an actor; I, whose ideas were always less formulated than his, knew little more than that I wanted to be myself. I had no idea what I was; but I think that Michael did know what he was. That, perhaps, was the difference; that Michael knew consciously a good deal about himself and about me, whereas I understood but little about either of us, except in a deep subconscious way. It was a difference of upbringing; for whereas Michael was taught to be self-expressive, I was taught to be self-suppressive. Yet there stirred strongly in me the unquenchable spark. Even then Michael played the piano beautifully; outwardly, I felt that this accomplishment of his was unmanly; something 'not done' by boys; but inwardly and secretly I worshipped him for it. I knew, when I heard Michael play, that music could say what was not expressible in terms of words; it could voice and consolidate the very heart of our friendship; it could speak of the sea, the hills, the sun and the moon— I mean of what they really are, not of their outward appearance— it could speak only of itself and of the soul of man, according to the kind of music it was.

It must seem strange that a boy so sensitive to beauty of all kinds as myself should, even for a moment, entertain any doubt as to the rightness and manliness of music and the arts. Yet it must be remembered that boys live entirely by a series of signposts that stand, solid sentinels, along the unknown path of life. On the surface, at any rate. And since Westminster, like all public schools, stood for the safe, the British, road of good manners, good breeding, and lack of enthusiasm, I could not but steer my course by what I knew. It was just 'not done' to get excited about music, poetry or painting; and though I got extremely excited about such things, I tried to conceal that excitement almost to the point of blinding myself to its very existence. Yet I failed; and was thrilled that I failed.

I remember one afternoon when Michael played the piano at a little party; he played a piece that I think was probably *La Cathédrale Engloutie*. It completely enraptured me; it bore me to a very distant land indeed; I looked at Michael and I saw him as he really was; I loved him for it, and I loved the sincere absorption that his attitude and playing conveyed. I never forgot that moment; and my heart and soul never allowed me again lightly to condemn as 'unmanly' the composition or performance of music, the painting or the looking-at of pictures, or the writing or reading of poetry (or even of prose). It was probably my first conscious acceptance of beauty as a thing meant for me; an air that I must breathe, or perish. Hitherto my experiences, though conscious in a sense, had been on another plane; they had never broken through into, and fused with, the meaning and the purpose of life. I was for a time puzzled, and in a state of turmoil. I remember vividly Michael asking me afterwards if I had enjoyed his playing; and not knowing what to reply, because the task of wrestling with words was too great for me. I expect that I said tamely (and lamely) that, 'yes, I had,' and left it at that.

It was at such moments that I realized my debt to Michael, however dimly; and it gives me the deepest pleasure to acknowledge it, in adult life, in this book. For I feel that the divine fire, the pure stream, does not come to a boy usually through the medium of a friend of his own age, and that I was exceptionally lucky therefore to find it. For the fact is, to a young boy the beliefs and opinions of a contemporary count in a way that those of his elders do not. I had always sensed and resented my complete aloneness in the company of any contemporaries; now I had found my counterpart, like and unlike, and to have done so made me very happy.

21

The Mortal and the Immortal

I have often wondered why certain quite insignificant happenings remain imprinted upon the memory, whilst other events, that seem at the time so important, fade into the limbo of unremembered things. I find it difficult to arrive at any conclusion. The fact remains : certain apparently pointless impressions live as long as we do, as freshly and as brightly as the moment of their happening.

I am thinking of a certain morning, early in the September of 1919. It was a bright, still, sunny morning, cool, with a hint of heat to come; it was a Sunday. For some reason it seems best to write of it in the present tense.

I am standing, then, beside a tall hedge bordering the lawn of Didmarton Rectory, in Gloucestershire. As it is Sunday, I am wearing my Eton suit; the collar as usual is scratching the nape of my neck. It is about ten o'clock, and apart from the hum of flies, it is very quiet. Soon, I shall be going to church. There is this small breathing-space of freedom in the sun before I am enveloped by the cool, damp-smelling stone building. I am standing there all alone, thinking, when suddenly a Speckled Wood butterfly comes fluttering along the hedge, and settles on a raspberry cane that has somehow rooted itself there. It is a newly emerged male, and it sits in the sun, lazily opening and shutting its wings. Then, suddenly, it is quite still, displaying itself before me, flat against a raspberry leaf. And the strangest feeling comes over me, a kind of giving at the knees, a creeping of mystery through my body. The butterfly *is* everything; it *is* Sunday, it *is* September, it *is* the still, aware morning; and I am watching it. Thus, for a few moments, everything remains poised. Then with a sudden upward flutter, the butterfly is gone, over the hedge; and the spell is broken. A window is flung up in the house, a voice calls me, everything starts to move, and I begin to make my way indoors. All is ordinary again; and I am ordinary, too.

Now, what happened? It was not a moment of great beauty;

the Speckled Wood is rather a dull butterfly, brown with a few creamy spots, and the hedge too was dull. Nothing was outstanding. Yet, I have never forgotten that moment, a moment filled with the greatest mystery and awe. A butterfly lives for three weeks. Yet that newly emerged Speckled Wood, with the furry sheen still on its wings and body, cannot die until I die. A mystery; and I bow before it.

*   *   *

Of all the summer holiday places during the whole of my childhood, Didmarton lived most. It provided the richest background for spiritual adventure that I had yet found, apart from Westminster. In what lay the perpetual secret excitement that was to be discovered there? I don't know, and when I again visited it in 1937, eighteen years later, it took me a long time to recapture that excitement, because, I suppose, the child's perceptions are so much sharper than those of the adult. Yet exist it did; and coloured the whole of the seven weeks we spent there. Something secret, heavenly and pagan burned unendingly in the grey Cotswold stone, in the tall woods, in the glowing fields, in the blue wild geranium that haunts that land. A land that retains something of the feudal outlook at its best :

> The clock upon the Hall struck twelve,
> And down across the field of corn
> The mellow chimes of noon were borne.

Those three lines, that were written by a country villager, half yield up the secret of Didmarton. Its very name is magic. Say it aloud. 'Didmarton. Did-marton.' Yes, and what does it mean? Not in terms of derivations; but in terms of strangeness and magic.

At the end of the last century the Old Church had been considered too small for its purpose, and a totally hideous sham-Gothic building had been erected on the other side of the Rectory. It was (not unnaturally) known as the New Church; its single feature of interest being that it had a bell near the ground, hanging in a sort of alcove, that one could give a resounding whack to with a walking-stick as one passed.

The Old Church was a small, frail single-storeyed building, built probably of lath and plaster, with a tiny turret at one end. It was of great interest architecturally and in 1937 had been, with some difficulty, preserved. In 1919, it was covered with a rich glossy mantle of ivy that made it look almost comically the midnight-haunted church of old steel engravings. It seemed only to need a bat and an owl or two to complete the picture. Yet it was a church of sunlight. In this strange little building, love and fear seemed to have united to make something else; a rich, curious atmosphere, not frightening, but to be deeply respected. It was settling comfortably into a warm decay (why will man forever try to prevent old buildings from doing that?) and death was very near one, in and around it. I do not mean actual death; but a knowledge and understanding of death and the dead. Its air swarmed and teemed with ghosts; it was a place in which I loved to wander, unafraid, but knowing that I was surrounded. The wonderful thing about it was that it was never used, and so the charged atmosphere was disturbed by no one but myself and Mother and the old gardener who daily wound the clock. It was full of peace because it was left in peace; a brooding, classic, time-honoured peace. And the same applies to its little churchyard, that abutted on the rectory lawn and was entered through a small wicket gate. Long grass and knapweed and meadowsweet waved and were fragrant in the sun, grown, untouched by man, to the height of the grey old table-top tombs that were splashed and spotted with brilliant orange lichen. The sun seemed to burn with special hot stillness.

On one golden morning, before the dew was off the tall grasses, I wandered happily into this beautiful place on a visit to the church. Sauntering along, I noticed a hole in one of the square tombs, where a piece of stone had crumbled away. It was just large enough to take my bare arm. I rummaged and fished about with my hand. There was something loose. I pulled; it gave; I triumphantly brought it forth. I was a bone, white and fleshless. I held it in my hand, looking at it. It looked ordinary, like a bone for a dog. This, then, was what happened to man. Or to his body, anyway. One day, this would happen to Father, to Mother; one day, ever so far off, to me. I couldn't avoid it. I stood for a long time, quite still, with the bone in my hand, before I put it back. I don't know what I really felt. But because of the bone, I saw the little square enclosure of tombs in their flowery grass; I saw the sunlight glinting silently on the prismatic dew-drops; I heard the deep, steady hum of the summer insects, and smelt the creamy heads of meadowsweet, and drank in the deep purple knapweed flowers. And felt dissolved and possessed by the sun. This was being alive; in my hand was what (in part, at least) being dead was. I was ten years old. But time was moving. In the eternal quality of the old churchyard was the answer to my mortality. I was pleased that time went so slowly. Why, here I am, and we are at Didmarton, and I am only ten, and it will be quite all right, because look what ages it is to dinner-time even. It will be sixty years before—anything happens. And see how still the flowers and grass and tombs are; they are fixed. . . .

I put my hand with the bone in it back into the tomb. Inside the darkness that I couldn't see my hand uncurled its fingers, and the bone fell with a little rattle among its fellows. I pulled out my arm that had been into a tomb. And still the dew-drops shone in a mist of rainbow colours, and the meadowsweet yielded its fragrance to the warm air. The morning sang for the joy of being; and I sang too, with a sudden thankful happiness. But in the depths of my heart was a tiny sadness for the dead, and the slightest of misgivings. Why, otherwise, on an impulse only half understood, did I run back to the Rectory for my box camera? I stood by the tomb again, camera in hand, and took a snapshot of the Old Church standing among its tombs. I have it before me as I write.

I look at the hand that holds the pencil with a certain wonder. Extraordinary to realize that it is the same hand that pulled a bone from a tomb many years ago on a hot summer morning. Father, Mother, Nan, Cook—are all dead now. Steadily, imperceptibly, the years pass; and as they pass they gather in their harvest. The cruel blessed scythe reaps man and meadowsweet with exquisite indiscrimination. A faded snapshot only remains to torment the visual eye with what once was; the inner eye remembers, and bows before the utter mystery of mortality and immortality. For I can feel that cool white bone in my palm, and the sun on my bare arms; and smell the meadowsweet and grasses still. They *are*; and we are back at the ending of the Speckled Wood incident. (The ending in scratches on paper, I mean; for there is no ending to the reality.) This chapter, in fact, since it is about Didmarton cannot be other than a theme and variations. For Didmarton was, to my mind, concerned exclusively with mortality and immortality, in their more or less undiluted essences. Again and again during that holiday the veil was for fleeting moments drawn aside.

*   *   *

One evening, towards sunset, I was standing idly, butterfly-net in hand, by a low grey stone wall at the bottom of the garden. On the top of this wall grew a clump of red valerian in full bloom. The sun was still warm on the rich flowers. Suddenly, something that looked like a shadow appeared above them, a still but vibrating shadow, a little patch of dimness. I knew at once what it was —a Hummingbird Hawk Moth, though I had never seen one before. For a moment I watched the extraordinary insect as it hovered motionless, its hair-like tongue probing deep into the blossom. Then, with lightning rapidity, it had shifted and was over another part of the valerian clump. Still I watched it, with that curious inability to seize the moment lest I should fail to seize it. I *mustn't* miss this treasure. So I stood there, undecided, watching the moth and feeling myself watched by eyes not human; by the eyes of the garden. At last I struck with my net. I must have caught it, for it had not flown away, of that I was sure. Excitedly I felt in my pocket for a box. I held the net up against the light, so that I should be able to see the dark outline of my prize. But there was nothing there; the net was empty. I couldn't believe it; I looked inside the net, I turned it upside down and shook it. Trembling with disappointment, I stood by the valerian clump in the forlorn hope that the moth would come back. After a time I cried, with the old cry, because I had failed to capture beauty; because it wasn't enough to see it, I wanted it for my own. They were tears of selfish disappointment; yet they were a preparation for what was to come; for tears soften and open the mind, making it receptive to impressions as soon as they are spent. It is as though they wash the slate clean and one sees the world entirely afresh.

The tears stopped. It was now clear that the wary Hummingbird Hawk was not going to return. The sun was beginning to set, and the valerian was in shadow. Disconsolately I made my way up the garden. Against the hedge where I had seen the Speckled Wood there was an old seat. I sat down on it. And what happened then seems impossible to describe. For it was nothing—and everything. As I sat there I became slowly aware that the evening was one of rare beauty. I could see across the lawn to an old barn which was so thickly covered with the creeper called Ampelopsis Veitchii that no stone was visible, only the beautiful green inverted triangle, behind which rose the little bell-turret of the Old Church. The whole scene faced due west, so that it was brilliant with the level rays of the sinking sun. Above the golden weather-vane of the turret swallows were wheeling and flashing, their white breasts creamy in the light. The leaves of the creeper shone with the brightest, tenderest green-gold, and a climbing rose on the barn overlaid this colour with softly glowing pink clusters. The fine-weather sky trailed a few feathery linked clouds that as I watched were tinged with a softer and more glowing pink than that of the roses. Not a breath of wind stirred; only the swallows dipped and flashed, wheeled and tumbled above the old gilt weathercock.

Slowly the colours deepened, and still I sat on, entranced, unconscious of my body, with all the hampering restrictions it implied. For the first time, with the whole of my consciousness, I saw beauty. And I became aware then of the tremendous creative forces that moved through me like a great wind, and could tear and shake my being. I knew that I saw, felt and was what few people feel, see or are; and in a strong, quiet, uplifted ecstasy I gave myself unreservedly to the forces that have moulded, and always will mould, my life. For a long time I sat on, until the light had faded from creeper and roses, from barn and turret; until the sky, ever deepening, was a clear blue-green, and the silver points of stars were pricking out amongst the wisps of smoky cloud; until the night scents of the garden began to creep with heart-breaking intensity to my nose, and a little breeze ruffled the grasses and sighed in the dark, uplifted branches of the great cedar at the end of the lawn. In the rich, warm afterglow of a pure and innocent summer's evening I made my way into the lighted house. Bats had replaced the swallows, white moths purred softly past me as I crossed the lawn. I was limp, drained of vitality, filled with a happiness such as I had never known; I had given myself with whole-hearted dedication to this beautiful world in which we have our being; that reveals in such moments so clearly that it is but a foretaste of the landscape beyond the high, forbidding gates of our mortality.

And still, as I write, it *is*; that evening at Didmarton so long ago, when I knew my purpose in life, and why I had been born. No boy of ten could bear that knowledge for long; and sleep drew the veil across it with merciful hands. Yet I went about for days filled with ecstatic happiness. Something had happened to me that I had forgotten, but that was now there, deep inside me, and would always remain.

*   *   *

The parish of Didmarton embraces also the outlying hamlets of Sopworth and of Oldbury-on-the-Hill. I have little recollection of Sopworth, but I am never likely to forget Oldbury, for it possessed the same qualities, in a different way, as Didmarton itself. There was no village; only the church stood, high and lonely, on a round green hill. It was a large church, with a tall, dark, square tower, and it dominated in a gentle way the landscape for some miles around it. Because it was so far from habitation, very few services were held in it. It was a dark and lonely church; so large, with so small a living congregation.

One evening, another beautiful evening of full summer, Mother and I decided to walk over to it. We had got two-thirds of the way when we came to a round duck-pond whose clear bright surface mirrored the evening sky. At the edge of the pond, ducks were waddling and diving for food in the mud. Near them, driving a couple of geese with a little switch, was a woman. She was tall, gaunt and middle-aged, and wore an apron. There was a strong nobility about her aquiline face, and her grey hair was screwed tightly into a bun.

She stopped, and stood staring into the water as we came up to her. There was something vaguely disquieting in her attitude. I knew that Mother sensed it at once, for she left the path and walking over to the woman wished her good evening. The woman replied 'Good evening, Ma'am,' in a toneless voice.

There was a silence, and then, somehow, Mother and this woman got talking. Impatiently I shifted about, wanting to get on. I heard pain in the woman's voice. 'I've 'ad a 'ard life, ma'am.

Nine I've borne, and 'E's seen fit to take 'em all from me. And now me youngest, me youngest'—the voice was choked with tears —'I came out 'ere and I 'ad a mind to be done with it all; yes, finished and done with it all. For it don't seem right, ma'am; it don't seem fair. . . .' She broke off and, pointing to the church on the hill, outlined against the saffron sky, cried : 'They're up there, ma'am; all of 'em; laying up there in their little graves. And I got nothing, nothing at all. . . .'

The woman had spoken loudly, in a kind of fighting call. Mother's voice was very low; I could not hear what she said. For a long time I caught the murmur of that voice, so sweet, so gentle, so full of comfort, as no one knew better than I. And the sun grew lower, beginning to sink behind the church in a broad sea of flame, so that the tower stood, solid against the gold, its battlements cutting the sky in strong patterned formation; and the pond at our feet was a pool of still brightness.

I heard the woman say : 'God bless you, ma'am, and thank you. You've given me the courage to go on again.'

She pressed Mother's hand and, calling the geese, turned on her homeward path. Mother said : 'It's too late to go to the church now, darling. But we'll go another time.' She took my arm, and together we stood looking at the soft golden light of the setting sun behind the dark tower that stood so firmly but so friendly upon its green hill. The level gold rays stained each grass blade in the field; the pond was a plate of beaten gold. And suddenly I saw that this was not an earthly landscape at all; these were the fields and hills of Paradise itself. For one long, pure unforgettable moment I knew that, as I stood with my arm in Mother's.

As I write, my feet are crushing that grass, the ducks are splashing and dipping, and the strange, noble, distraught woman is expressing her pain; and my mother, staring across the valley at the church, is drawing from the deep wells of her faith the comfort that only she can give. And over all is poured with divine bounteousness the rich, calm sunset light of Paradise, its low streaming rays making holy all that they touch.

*   *   *

And now let me reverse the machinery of this chapter and muse upon two memories that, far from being ever-present in almost tangible form, have assumed the half-forgotten, vivid quality of a dream.

The first intimation was upon a Sunday afternoon. Crossing a field, I spied a strange and beautiful flower all by itself, springing from the grass. It had no leaves; the pale, naked stem supported a chalice of the frailest mauve which contained in its depths a few golden anthers. Though I had never seen it before, my botanical knowledge at once told me what it was : the Meadow Saffron, Autumn Crocus, or *Colchicum*. Singing the wordless song of which I was so fond, I happily looked around for others. There were none.

The next morning, a heavenly, light, cool sunny morning, I went for a walk past the Autumn Crocus. It was still there. I stopped again to admire it, and became drunk upon its beauty. I wandered on, anywhere, in a daydream, quite aimlessly. I came to a gate that led into a meadow. Idly, as I climbed the gate, I looked over it. And there I saw an unbroken sea of mauve that stretched to the farthest hedge; a sea that glinted and shone in the morning sunlight; that was composed of thousands of autumn crocuses in bloom, whose chalices, crowdedly separate in the foreground, merged into solid colour in the middle and far distance. And as I looked, it seems to me that in some way I lost consciousness. For I am never certain of what happened. Sometimes I think that I tore off my clothes and rolled naked among the crocuses until my whole body was stained with the purple juice of the petals of this most pagan flower; sometimes I believe that I merely stood there at the edge of the field, idiotically trembling and irresolute. Nor have I any idea of how much of what we call time passed. I know that ultimately I found my way home to lunch and was tongue-tied and couldn't say where I had been, because the frightened, secret exhilaration sealed my speech. For many, many years I never told anyone of this strange and elemental experience; it was, as I later realized, the nearest I ever came to seeing the earth-gods and to hearing the syrinx of Pan.

Eighteen years later, I tried to find the crocus-field. But, though I remembered, or thought I remembered, the way with complete clarity, I found nothing, not even the gate. And sometimes I wonder now whether indeed it was a real field, and whether that single, signpost crocus was no more than a figment of a fertile and eager imagination. And even as I wonder, something in me extends, trembling, towards the blinding, overpowering ecstasy of that pale sea, pagan as the human body itself, lying virginal and unraped in the cool sunlight of the morning.

*   *   *

An old lady lived in Didmarton; a strange old lady, tall, and gaunt as a horse. Of impeccable ancestry and high breeding she combined great learning with great eccentricity. I adored her, for she had the childlike mind that never talks down to children. Her name was Miss White, and we all grew to love her; even Father, who was rarely affectionately flippant, nicknamed her The Large White, in playful reference to her gigantic stature.

I often used to go for walks with her, and one evening we set out on a long ramble to find a house in the woods of which a friend of hers was housekeeper and caretaker. On the way there I heard a lot about this house from Miss White, and what she told me greatly fired my imagination. Without saying so, she conveyed to me that the house was haunted, especially a room that was lined with fifty-two great mirrors, one for each week of the year, so that as you entered you saw yourself fifty-two times in the act of entering. And, once inside, whatever you did was repeated fifty-two times. I did not altogether like this, but I was filled with excitement at the prospect of seeing it. As Miss White talked, the house assumed a fabled mythical quality in my mind. Would we ever reach it, this strange large house in the middle of the woods?

On and on we walked, through the fragrant, dusty evening lanes; I trotting beside Miss White, whose peculiar draperies fluttered voluminously as she strode, and eagerly taking in all she had to say. Her talk veered from the house to foreign countries, and seafaring men, and shores where blue-green seas washed, forgotten, upon golden sands, in the hot sun by day, and under brilliant stars at night. And then she told me of a wonderful collection of sea-shells that her brother had made, and how when you held them to your ear you heard in each shell the different, individual roar of the sea from which it had been collected. I listened, entranced. And somehow the shells became connected shadowily with the house of the mirrors that we were going to see. What would it— what could it—be like?

We had, for a long time now, been walking through the woods, and suddenly we entered a long, broad, grassy ride. And at the end of it, framed in trees, stood the house. Tall, old and grey, its windows looked out over acres of unbroken woodland, and each window was a blind square of scarlet fire, for the low sun, travelling over the tree-tops, shone directly upon the great western façade. A dozen blazing eyes stared with an indescribable fierce sadness at us; it was as though the rooms behind the windows were being consumed by infernal flames. So this—*this* was the house of the mirrors! There was something monstrous, substantial yet unreal, about it.

Miss White went on talking as we approached.

'It is a long time since I have seen *dear* Lily Skinner. I hope that we shall find her well. It is a *big* house, isn't it, dear, to be all alone in? For the family are rarely here, you see. But she does not mind much, though of course, the *loneliness*—' she broke off, drawing a feather boa closer round her ample neck as though she was a little cold. Then she resumed in brisk tones. 'We must get her to show you the room with all the mirrors. I know she will love to.'

The house now seemed to be towering above us, mighty, malignant, as though it would like to fall upon us and crush us to death. We passed along a dark, tangled little path and arrived at a side door. Miss White pulled the long iron bell-handle. Far away, somewhere in the depths of the house, we heard it tinkle. But no one came to open the door. Again Miss White rang the bell. There was no answer.

'Oh dear!' Miss White frowned and tapped her enormous foot impatiently. 'Lily must be out, or away. Fancy! after that long walk of ours. How disappointing! And now you won't see the room with the mirrors. But I can show you its windows. Come round the corner, dear! There!'

She pointed along the western façade. 'There it is! Just think of it, dear; all those mirrors by themselves in the empty room—that great room—reflecting nothing. But stained now with the sunset, my dear; stained with the sunset . . .' her voice trailed off with startling suddenness. She looked at me almost appealingly. 'I think we had better turn back, dear, don't you? There is nothing else to be done, is there? And soon it will be dark.'

So once more we entered the long, broad, grassy ride, leaving the great brooding house behind us, and with every step we took my breath came more freely and my heart lightened. At the end of the ride we turned and looked back. The sun had left the windows, and the house stood, heavy, glowering, sullen, among its trees, far from anywhere, something born of dream that touched upon nightmare.

We did not talk much as we walked back to Didmarton in the falling dusk. As we entered the village it was nearly dark. I could only just see Miss White, a huge, looming, friendly figure beside me. The hour and the mood tended toward intimacy.

'You know, Miss White,' I said happily, 'I don't mind not seeing the room with all the mirrors.'

'I think perhaps you are right, dear,' she said slowly; 'it is a very beautiful room, but . . .'

There was a silence.

'The windows looked like angry eyes,' I ventured.

'What a funny old-fashioned little thing you are,' she said, '*so* sensitive.'

I made no reply. I felt sleepy. Already the whole thing was fading. I could not even feel sure that I had ever seen the house. She left me at the Rectory gate. And as she prepared to turn away, she said a very strange thing.

'You are a very little boy,' she said, 'only ten years old; and I am a very old lady, over seventy. People laugh at me and say I am *odd*, and wear funny clothes. Perhaps I am. Perhaps I do. But you have what I have followed all my life, and have not perhaps made the best use of. Remember old Miss White sometimes when you are grown up. Remember how she took you to see the house of the mirrors. Perhaps when you think of this evening it will remind you of the funny old lady who understood you. Goodnight, my dear, *and keep your gift*. Don't let them take it away from you!'

And she was gone. I turned into the Rectory gate, feeling exhilarated. Miss White was cracked, but you couldn't help loving her. In the darkness, I heard the little bell of the Old Church striking nine. I ran up the steps to the front door, and the lighted house swallowed me up. The door closed behind me, and Didmarton Rectory stood once more, islanded in the sea of night.

Miss White, because of her deep humility, was wrong. For that strange evening does not remind me of Miss White; Miss White reminds me of the evening. The old house is but a far-off memory; Miss White is very real indeed. For, after all, the house of the mirrors was only a house, haunted maybe, and dominated by the elemental earth-gods of the vast forest in one of whose clearings it stood; but without a soul, like those gods themselves, and subject therefore to higher authority. So that it has the quality of dream, of fantasy, as had the crocus-field in another way. The unreality of utter reality, but not reality lifted to God.

But the gay, adventurous, childlike soul of old Miss White *is*. She is with me as I write; she is one of that invisible but ever-present company of loved persons who have passed from the mortal to the immortal; who watch me with tenderness, with understanding forgiveness for my mortal blindness, as I put down the last words of a chapter that for me has been from beginning to end the purest labour of love.

22

The Child-self

That wonderful holiday at Didmarton marked for me the end of a period. The first stage of childhood was over, having reached its perfect blossoming; I entered now upon the second stage. Though I never forgot, nor lost sight of in my heart, the experiences that had been mine, for a long time no more such adventures occurred. Especially is that true of the sunset-experience in the garden of Didmarton Rectory; it was not until mid-adolescence that I was again visited by the same degree of conscious knowledge of what I was, and the purpose of my existence.

I arrived now at what was in many ways the dullest part of my whole life. I became the perfect little schoolboy; squabbling, scuffling, fighting, spoonerizing everything that was said, stuffing my belly with popcorns and peanuts, ragging masters and bullying smaller boys. Yet, as I have said, I never denied what I had been, nor turned my back on the possibility of a recurrence; and the steady Michael was always at my side to keep my spiritual life, however faintly, alive. The change must be mainly ascribed to school, for by now I was working fairly intensively in the hope of a scholarship later on, and so had little time for imaginative excursions. Also, I was taught entirely by masters, and so missed for the greater part of the day that feminine influence that is of such inestimable benefit at any period of a man's life. Men and boys thrown constantly together get rowdy, childish, bigoted, coarse-grained and tough. Anyone who has ever seen inside the workings of (a) a School for the Sons of Gents; (b) The Army, will know how sadly true this is. The only thing that is slightly more horrible than the sight of men thrown exclusively into the company of their own sex is that of women ditto. And so, as well as tending to become an unpleasant little hooligan who tried to outbelch other little hooligans during break, I became—what was much worse—a bore. Routine, imposed from without, dominated my life. The walk to St James's Park Station, the journey on the underground train with its yellow wickerwork seats, the walk from Sloane Square to school; the interminable boredom of a misspent day learning lessons; and then the evening reversal of the journey, followed by a hurried tea and hours of prep made up my day. I think hard, and I can only recollect two incidents that slightly enlivened the tedium of a very grey year and a half. One was at school on a hot summer's day, when a man strolled along the pavement outside playing a bagpipes, which caused one boy to wet his trousers, to the excitement of pupils and master alike. The other was on the way home from school one winter's evening when, avoiding my usual sweet-shop, I penetrated the recesses of a very gloomy-looking one, whose large window contained only a box of thin, flat, flyblown chocolate which, for some unearthly reason, had caught my eye and tickled my fancy in the morning.

As I entered, out of some dark hiding-hole, came a fat, bald, yellow-faced man with twirled spiky moustaches that looked sharp enough to run into you, should you get in their way.

'Good evening, my little man,' he crooned, staring at me and rubbing his pale hands together.

'I want that chocolate, please,' I said, my courage beginning to fail.

'But certainly,' he said, 'I will get it for you.' And he reached into the window and drew the box out. I quickly paid him and prepared to depart. But before I could do so, he bent low over me, his moustaches almost touching my school cap.

'Do you not like liquorice allsorts, my little man?' he whispered; 'they are so good for you, you know; very, ver-y good for you. They cure—*constipation*.' As he said the last word he leered right into my face. Into the word he put every conceivable and inconceivable meaning. I saw his yellow face close to mine, his whole expression one of evil intent and, firmly hanging on to my chocolate, I ran for my life, feeling his hot, fetid breath on my nice clean neck. After that experience I gave his shop a very wide berth indeed, shuddering a little sometimes when I saw him standing behind the glass-panelled door, idly looking out, like a yellow spider in search of an enticeable victim. I stuck severely to my own tried and trusty little shop in Tothill Street, and to those machines on St James's Park and Sloane Square stations that, made fertile by a penny, travailed until they gave birth to strangely delicious, nostalgic-tasting bars of Reeves Chocolate Cream, which wasn't like any other chocolate I had ever tasted. It tasted of the Underground, I thought; like the magazines smelt on the bookstalls; like the clanking stairs up which one raced, the riser of each step adorned with enamelled advertisements for Iron Jelloids and Jeyes Fluid, so that a panorama of good advice and warnings flashed by as one climbed. It tasted frowsty but not of this earth, that magic chocolate in its little white, green-lettered box stamped at the bottom 'The Automatic Company, 14 Appold Street, W.1.'

*   *   *

Surely the most extraordinary thing about the mind of man is the way it stores impressions? During the months that I have been writing this book, great things and things of the utmost triviality have been dug up by memory. The smells of the hall, of the Blue Room, of the study, have assailed me; the exact picture of a dull little table near the back stairs that held the folding IN and OUT notice printed in tarnished gold against a rubbed and faded black background; the fuse-box above it. And even more trivial things: in the nursery the two electric lights, the shade-ring of one made of bright brass (albeit, spotted slightly by decay), and the other, a dull oxidized metal. Then there are the things hard to describe that one yet would like to describe, such as the pattern made by a kind of square iron railing on the roof of College that said something in its own language, and the rusty old cowl on the roof of Grant's that said something else. What did they say? I don't know, in words. What did the tiny blue by-passes say that were alight all day in the gas-lamps of the Cloisters? And the bell-pull of Rigaud's, that had rubbed a semi-circular slot in the soft brick beside which it hung? And the little thing like a peacock's crest on the top of Big Ben? And the handle of Father's store-cupboard? And the three-forked lightning conductor on the Abbey? There was an old tin, dark with age, that had once held something called 'Frame Food', for the words were in raised letters on the lid; and later someone had scratched the word 'Tea' in very large spidery letters, thus: T Frame E Food A. This lived in the cupboard outside the nursery; and I have only to think of it to smell the sweet blended scents of tea and sugar and butter and cake that were kept in the cupboard. It has become far more than just a tin through the years; it is a tin of character, of personality, of active emanation; I can hear the particular noise it made when hit, and can remember how the top right-hand corner of the lid had to be coerced into position.

It is thus that a child lives. By the object and by its familiar. And the sad thing nowadays is the nature of the familiar attached to most objects; a mass-produced, hatefully dull familiar. For the familiar follows a descending scale, from that of the object made with craftsmanship and love out of some real substance like wood, to that of the unreal and deathly plastic community object which daily replaces the interesting and true thing. The child of today, it seems to me, has a poor time of it. For he has to make do largely with the impoverished mean familiar of a mean object; to give his mechanical-minded love (and all boys are in part mechanically-minded) to the ghastly, blood-stained sadistic familiar of tank or aeroplane, instead of to the gentle steam-train, the Puffing Billy, or the spring-wound clockwork driving-unit. And soon, I suppose, to the mechanics of the atom bomb.

I have left so much out of this book. I have left out the two bells that rang every afternoon for Abbey Evensong at half past two as I was getting ready for the afternoon walk; a monotonous, unending ding-dong, ding-dong, that was like falling coloured rain. I have left out the poster called the Marmalade Lady that frightened me so much that I turned white when I saw it, and once lay down on Lambeth Bridge during a walk with Edith, and wouldn't get up, because I saw in the distance a Marmalade Lady. I have left out the clocks that I dreamed of when I was very small, called Bim-Bom clocks, that had black weights and faces made of black velvet that crept suffocatingly near to my own face. I have left out my horror of spectacles and bellows, and how I used to pray to God every night to deliver me from them. I have left out my white mice, in particular the one that climbed all the way down the Virginia Creeper and was found in the garden a week later, a nearly black mouse. And my cat, Peter Karoo, and how it used to sit on the stairs near the alcove, in the dark, with its tail outspread, and shriek horribly when I trod on it by mistake. And the firework I made that burnt Nurse's hand; and my hobbies, which included photography—developing films in the cellar by the light of a candle stuck in a red hock bottle. And the books of boyhood: *The Scarlet Pimpernel*, *King Solomon's Mines*, and the Sherlock Holmes stories. So much, so very much, has been left out. Yet I hope that I may have made the reader hear, see, smell and love that far-off age of innocence in the early years of this century, before the devil that has the world in fee assumes his full stature. He was crouching then; ever since, he has been straightening himself out, slowly, slowly, until he is towering in evil, grey majesty above us all. Nor has he yet reached his full height, though faith and hope pray that he has done so. And we must pray that the twin buds of faith and hope will not 'go blind' and wither before they open flower, like the silly snowdrops I grew in fibre this winter. Poor snowdrops; even they seem to be held in the grey, amorphous grip of the now ever-present devil, Frustration. I do not altogether like living in the past; but it has been a joy and relief to do so, in this war-weary, nerve-ridden, underfed, mean-souled, frustrated little period that we know as the present—the Age of Progress.

I hope that I have made the reader hear the bells falling into the quietness of Little Dean's Yard against the hushed murmur of distant London streets, as I heard them; have made him feel the leisurely spaciousness of our life and our household; have excitedly quickened his soul by the recounting of the simple, unshaken and unshakeable holy faith of my mother and father, a faith that, demonstrable scientifically as worthless and complacent, lives still in their three children, and in the memories of good works that smell as sweet now as then.

* * *

We left John Theodore Livingston Raynor eating Reeves Chocolate Cream on the Underground. Eating and eating and eating it; and eating pink and white coconut ice and raspberry noyeau and peardrops and Theatre Mixture and sugared almonds and peppermint creams and almond rock and toffees. And swallowing great undigested lumps of Latin, Greek, French and History (biased), Geography, Science and Mathematics; and that which in schools is called 'English'. Learning long 'poems'; 'To Flores in the Azores Sir Richard Grenville came' (or went, I forget which); 'Not a drum was heard, not a funeral note, as his corse to the ramparts we hurried' (or is it 'carried'?); and 'If', which I thought then and think now, to be, with its whining, petulant self-righteousness, the vulgarest 'poem' in the language; those piteous shams of poetry, that never once struck the slightest spark in my heart and were merely pumpings of patriotic propaganda; learning all these, and swallowing them wholesale, but not, thank God, digesting them. What made me emerge, alive, in the end? Even my friendship with Michael waned, and I took up with a boy, a fat grey-faced prig, whose conversation was solely about marks, and games, and money, and doing-of-other-boys-down; who never spoke of music or real poetry, of pictures or of beautiful things.

Slowly, slowly school was getting me down; killing my own unique vision, putting the vile mass-produced aims in its place. To be good at games, to be tough, to be slick-witted, this was much better and more desirable than being me. On my reports such remarks as: 'Is gaining self-confidence', 'Is learning to hold his own', were frequent. What a farce! For whatever I was learning to do, I was not learning or being taught, to hold my own, but other people's own. I can scarcely end this chapter better than by quoting from Charles Morgan. 'To go to school is often to exchange the truth of angels and devils for the everlasting lies of reason.'

And so, let us draw a veil over my eleven-year-old self, and have done with him. Let us shift the scene to an afternoon in August 1921, two months after my twelfth birthday.

23

The Curtain Falls

This time, Conington, a village in Huntingdonshire, was the scene of our summer holiday. Father had been away for two or three days, a very unusual proceeding; 'on business', Mother told me. He returned after lunch one day, and he and Mother retired rather mysteriously to the study for the rest of the afternoon. We all had tea together, and at the end of it Father carefully replaced his cup on its saucer, pulled out his pouch, filled his pipe and lit it, sat back, hands clasped behind his head, and looked at me thoughtfully. 'How would you like,' Father said, leaning forward and keeping his gaze fixed upon me, 'to live in the *country*, John?'

For a moment I was not sure whether he was teasing me.

'Did you mean it, Daddy?' I asked, trying to control my excitement, in case it wasn't true.

'I do,' said my father. 'I have been offered, and have accepted, the living of Steventon, in Berkshire. I am retiring from Westminster at the end of this term. I've been at it for thirty-six years, and I should have been retiring at sixty in any case, only three years ahead. Various circumstances have made me decide not to wait until then. . . .' And Father proceeded, rather volubly for him, to enumerate these circumstances in a manner as sardonic as only he could make it. 'And so,' he concluded, 'we are going to live in the country. Think of it, John—butterflies and birds and flowers all the year instead of just in August. You'll love that, won't you?'

'Oh, I shall!' I cried, hardly able to breathe for rapture. 'When are we going?'

'At the end of the year. It's near the downs and it's near the river—which river?' he shot at me suddenly. 'Come, come, I told you it's in Berkshire.'

'The Thames?' I hazarded.

'Yes,' said Father, smiling; 'our old friend, the Thames, so we shall still be linked with Westminster.'

He opened his pocket-book and extracted some postcards of a peculiar purple hue. 'Here's the church, and the main street, and the inside of the church. I couldn't get one of the Vicarage, but it doesn't matter. You'll soon be seeing it, for we're all going down for the day before term starts.'

I gazed at the postcards in unclouded joy. I thought they were the most beautiful I had ever seen. I got up and flung my arms round Father's neck and kissed him in my excitement. Then, seeing Mother sitting there smiling, I had to kiss her too.

* * *

The summer of 1921 was phenomenal, in that no rain fell for seven or eight weeks, so that it was upon a brilliant, blazingly hot day that we arrived at Steventon station and walked up the long village street with its cool, shady elm-lined causeway, to the Vicarage. In the bare dusty rooms empty of all furniture we sat cross-legged on the floor and ate our sandwiches and drank our lemonade. After that, I pottered round the garden alone, while Father and Mother took measurements. I had brought my camera, so I took some photographs of the long, low, comfortable-looking, red brick house. It had been empty for six months, so that the garden was gloriously overgrown. The huge lawn was like a field, its foot-high growth spotted with red and white clover and yellow hawkweed flowers. I lay down in it, hands behind head, utterly content, watching a few white clouds sailing the depthless, translucent blue of midday. Then, feeling a little sleepy, I began to explore the kitchen garden. There was a long sun-steeped brick wall that ended in a little white greenhouse, and against the wall grew a vine with bunches of grapes, tiny and almost colourless. I picked one and stripped the little grapes. They were delicious, cool and sweet. I showed them to Father, who had joined me; and he told me that the phenomenal summer had ripened them, and that we would probably never have any more again. (He was right;

they never ripened again all the time we were there.) We picked them, to take back to London.

Beside the kitchen garden was a huge field that extended to the churchyard boundary. Hardly daring to ask, I said to Father: 'Is that ours?'

'Yes,' he said. 'And all that bit beyond.'

And just as the country stretched away into the hazy distance, boundlessly, so did my happiness.

We went into the grey old church. Mother knelt down to pray for a few moments, as she always did upon entering any church, and Father and I walked round on tiptoe so as not to disturb her. Then she joined us, and we again went round, over clanking grating and soft carpet, looking at the bosses and wall monuments. The sun poured through the south and west windows, filling the building with late summer calm and brilliance.

Soon it was time to go, and we returned to the Vicarage to pack up our things. Mother had the grapes in her bag; I carried a great bunch of silvery-pink Japanese Anemones; Father had cut an enormous nosegay of everything that was flowering, half-choked by weeds, in the garden. His pockets bulged with plums, apples and pears; and so did mine.

So we returned for a little time (but how long a time it seemed to me) to London.

*   *   *

That was a strange autumn for me. Under the hard crust of the schoolboy, the old sensitivity was trying to assert itself. And now something else was happening to me; I stood upon the threshold of puberty. Sometimes in my body now there was a thick suffocating golden thrill, terrifying in its power. One afternoon, just before I returned to school, I went for the old walk, alone; the walk from Lambeth to Westminster Bridge along the little secret pathway below road-level; and that walk burns my mind still, for during it I knew clearly, for the first time, the overwhelming passionate desires of the body. I walked and walked, my whole being filled with ungainsayable lust, for hours as it seemed, returning at last to tea with trembling hands and flushed and guilty face. I felt that everybody must know about my private thoughts; and still I could not quell the torment of unappeasable sensuality. And looking back, I realize that I have never since been visited by quite such an overpowering, irresistible whirlwind of physical desire. Perhaps it was because it was the first time; for I was only twelve and a quarter.

But that afternoon of unpleasant (or pleasant?) memory was, I am glad to say, an exception. On other afternoons before term began I went to the Army and Navy Stores with Father to buy gardening tools and oil-lamps and other things that were needed for country living. It was fun going from department to department choosing what we wanted; Father, top-hatted and benign, rejecting this, accepting that, and always ready to lend a willing ear to suggestion. Then suddenly those afternoons were finished; and Father went back to his school and I to mine.

Michael had now gone to Clifton. And one afternoon occurred a small incident that showed me how unsound was the community spirit to which I had tried to pin my faith. I was in the top form by this time, the headmaster's form. About a week before, being in a jovial mood, he had said : 'If I ever overrun the last lesson of the afternoon, I want any boy who notices it immediately to tell me, for I don't like to think of keeping you boys from your teas.'

He had smiled kindly, and we said we would tell him. On this particular afternoon the period was English. The headmaster was reading to us, a fairly interesting story. I looked at my watch and saw that it was just after half-past four, when school was due to end. I waited five minutes, and then I put up my hand. He had asked us to tell him, so I knew that it was my duty to do so.

He saw my hand and stopped reading.

'Well?' he said, rather irritably.

'Please sir, it's after five-and-twenty to five.'

He stared at me. I flushed.

'Please sir, you asked us to tell you the other day if you overran the time, so I thought . . .'

'Aha, I see,' he said, rubbing his dry hands together. 'Raynor, boys, does not like my reading. He wishes for his tea. Do *you* like my reading?'

'Oh, yes, sir!' chorused a dozen voices.

'Well, I shall not finish the story now,' he said. 'Raynor wants to go home.'

The rest of the form turned round and glared at me, muttering: 'Sneak! Swine! Rotter!'

'But, sir,' I began, 'I only . . .'

'Be quiet!' said the headmaster. 'You may go, boys. And if any of you wish to know the time, ask Raynor. He is so punctilious—and punctual.' He warmed to his theme. 'I wish we were *all* like that, don't you, boys? But, alas, sometimes we get so *interested* that we do not remember to look at our watches. It is then that we must turn to Raynor; he will always be able to tell us, I imagine.'

He closed his book with a snap, and banged down the lid of his desk. I slunk out, surrounded by a hooting mob, in the foreground of which was my fat, grey priggish 'friend'. It was then that I poignantly missed Michael, who would not only have supported me, but would have viewed the incident with that glorious detachment of which he was capable.

For weeks I was not allowed to forget my *faux pas*. The headmaster would take out his watch and say: 'Tell me, Raynor, is it 4.29½ yet, please? Living as you do under the shadow of Big Ben you cannot fail to know.' I would mutter that it was. 'Thank you, thank you,' he would say, pretending to correct his watch. 'It is fortunate that you are always here to tell us.'

But he never once overran his time again.

*   *   *

The fine weather broke. The dark evenings and the winds of autumn came. Still I did my prep in the old nursery; still the house watched over us in quiet power. But there was a difference; there was a feeling of suspense in the air. Slowly but inevitably the change was approaching. One looked at the nursery, the drawing-room, the study, with a curious feeling, hard to define; not of sadness, exactly; perhaps as though to stamp their images forever on the soul's wax tablet. And one knew that though time seemed to be going so slowly, in another way it was going so fast. The winds that rocked the great plane tree, the quiet bright stars reflected in the river by Westminster Bridge, the golden tobacco-scented study, the shadowy staircases, all seemed to give of their best, to be distilled down to their last and brightest essence. Now at nights that far-off sullen roar of traffic seemed to render up the very heart of its magic; its sound was as the sound of the hushed seas that break upon the shores of Avalon; and the faint glare reflected in the night sky from the submerged lights of the distant city held the heart in poignant uplifted wonder. Not for long now, these things; soon they were to be replaced by equally wonderful things; but different. And, ah, the bells; those magic haunted bells into whose note were already creeping the tones of farewell.

I was, of necessity, much alone, and I was glad, dwelling now in the inmost heart of life; slowly tasting, as something foreign, those things that I had always unquestioningly accepted as the permanent background to my life. All day I was at school; and in the evenings Mother was busy packing, Father engrossed by the production of the Play, his last Play. Often, when my prep was done, I roamed around the house, or walked by myself to the river and watched the twinkling lights on the slow-moving barges, the moon-silvered water flowing silently below the Houses of Parliament, flowing to the sea; watched the rosy faces of Big Ben and the trams and the buses on the bridge. And returned to the echoing silence of Little Dean's Yard that seemed tangible after the noise and rush of the streets; returned to sit in the nursery firelight by myself till supper-time; only half-consciously absorbing into the core of my being the essential quality of the house in which I had lived the twelve years of my life. The essential quality of Westminster.

And sometimes I would wander through the cloisters, unafraid now—utterly unafraid because we were going—and into the Abbey. The great dark building would envelop me in its own fragrant warmth; I would sit in a pew by myself, and sometimes there would be a little light in the organ-loft, and the threads of sound would steal out and grow upon the darkness into a majestic tree of music whose roots were deep in the earth and whose branches broke through the fan-vaulted roof until they touched the ceiling of heaven. And I would steal home through the chilly, gaslit cloisters uplifted, prepared; keeping vigil for that final revelation that, as the days steadily passed, could not, I knew, be now far off.

*   *   *

The term at my school ended and I said good-bye to masters and boys without breaking my heart. A few days remained to the end of term at Westminster. I helped Father with necessary preparations for the play. I noticed that he was unusually silent during these days, and I wondered why. I helped rig up the electric light over the fanlight of our front door, to guide the audience across Little Dean's Yard to their destination; and when the first and second nights arrived I switched it on each evening at dusk.

I, myself, was going to the third, and last night. I always viewed the Play with mixed feelings. I loved it in itself; though, since it was in Latin, I never understood a great deal of it. The real terror it held for me is so banal that I scarcely like to confess it. The truth is that, once in one's seat, it was impossible to get out to go to the lavatory without causing terrific commotion and upheaval; which meant that because I worried about it, my bladder would begin calling attention to itself directly I was in my place, long before the curtain went up. The rest of the evening was spent in writhing agony. But this year I had confessed my difficulty to Mother; she gave me some lemon-water, and it was all right.

Behold me, then, dressed in Etons, with fair hair well brushed, rosy-faced and blue-eyed, looking (I hoped) and feeling very handsome and important, as I stood at the back of our hall, watching the stream of distinguished and famous persons filing in at our front door, ascending the back stairs and pouring through the great black door of College, that tonight stood wide to welcome them. There was always about the third night an air of great glamour; the perfumes, the dresses, and the sparkling jewels of the women and the tails and decorations of the men brought always with them a feeling of great, if transient, ritual. But this time something else was added to that feeling, something I didn't understand. There was in the air a restless, noble excitement that seemed to make my bones turn and turn about in my body. I suffered it; I felt it with every sense. Everywhere it was stirring. and now it was time for me to join the throng and find my place. A hurried last dash to the lavatory and back, and I was in the great smokily-dark, dimly-lit dormitory of Christopher Wren. Everywhere was the subdued buzz of conversation as people settled into their seats. At the end of the long building was the stage; a red curtain with golden tassels hung before it; blind, vacant. Finding my place, I looked up at the high walls covered with the names of former King's Scholars. Why, tonight, did those names look so grave? I turned round, searching the glittering audience for a face I knew, but could see no one.

Then, as the audience subsided into a hush of silence, Father, from the Master's Pit, rang his handbell for the Play to begin. Why did the sound tonight make me tremble; and why did it sound like a knell? I didn't, as yet, understand.

The Prologue, with its Latin tribute to Father, passed; and the Famulus, with its intricate traditional presentation, began; a presentation that had been carried all through the playless years of the war in the mind of one man only, my father. I thought of this, and there was a great pride for him in my heart. I watched the scenes of the Play pass before me in a dream; I watched the beautiful background that I loved so much and knew so well, with its details of amphitheatre, Acropolis, hills and cypress trees. I became lost in a long reverie that was half dream, half reality, so that I scarcely noticed the witty Epilogue that always looked so strange in modern dress against the back-scene of ancient Athens.

From the thunder of applause rose what I had never heard before : a great unappeasable call for Father. At last he stood there on the front of the stage before them, small and whitefaced, the man who had, from 1886 to 1921, produced, in this great dormitory of Wren's, the traditional round of Plays with unflagging love and devotion.

I found that I was trembling violently. I was beginning to understand. I was near the front, and I could see Father's face clearly, and it looked not ordinary. In the seat behind me, someone whispered to a friend : 'Poor old Raynor; I'm afraid he's taking it very hard.' I turned round and glared; I couldn't bear to face what the speaker meant.

There was a pause, as Father stood there, waiting for all sound to die down. But it wouldn't; on and on the clapping went, until with a sudden gesture of his hand, the gesture of a master to his beloved pupils, Father silenced it.

Then he began to speak. So small was his voice in that great building; yet so clear, with that perfection of English and diction of which he, more than any man I have ever known, possessed the secret. I don't know what he said, except that he spoke the age-old timeless truths. By now there was a wild thumping of my heart; I wished this scene, and the great pain and ecstasy in it, to end.

I heard Father begin a fresh sentence.

'It is when I think of the great love and affection that I have been given through the long years; the great love and affection, and ... and ...'

For the first time in my life, I heard my father's voice fail. I looked quickly straight at his face, and quickly away again. My father stood there, in tears. In that moment, the last veil was torn from my eyes, and I saw, face to face, what with deep instinctive knowledge I had for so long known was coming.

The moment passed. Father resumed his speech, finished it. A great ovation of applause broke round the dormitory, filling it with sound, 'as of a mighty rushing wind'.

But I hardly noticed it. I was thinking of the years, falling like leaves, so slowly, so quietly, until this one arrived. I was thinking of the day when Father, a young man of just twenty-two, first came to Little Dean's Yard, to take up his lifework. I was thinking of his falling in love with Mother, and of their wedding in Henry VII's chapel, and the four children they had had. And the years, the human years, passing; and the immortal work, forged with love and honour, that would forever remain, held in the very stones long after it had been forgotten by man. Those stones trodden by Father for nearly forty years. Those stones eloquent always of the immortal dead, of all those who, like my father and my mother, had given the service of a lifetime to Westminster; had sacrificed their years upon the eternal altar of duty and love, of love and duty, a sacrifice whose sweet savour rises forever to God.

I knew now what, for many weeks, the bells had been trying to tell me. It was a message of the utmost simplicity; so simple that it had passed me by. And suddenly I saw that this was what they had always told me, from the first day, that, held in Mother's arms at the landing window, they had spoken to me until now. Love and Honour, they sang; Honour and Love: Duty and Faith; Faith and Duty. As I made my way out of the dormitory with the up-lifted, excited crowd of people I heard them calling once more across the Yard, and, with tear-filled eyes and humility of heart, I bowed my head in understanding and acceptance of their message.